CW01465984

PARIS
1924

A GUIDE

for Stanley, from his great-uncle, the author, who hears that you too enjoy writing.

[signature]

2023

Copyright © 2022 Nicholas Whitlam

All rights reserved. The author asserts their moral rights in this work throughout the world without waiver. No part of this book may be reproduced, or stored in a retrieval system, or transmitted in any form or by any means, electronic, mechanical, photocopying, recording, or otherwise, without express written permission of the publisher. For information about permission to reproduce selections from this book, write to editions@booktopia.com.au.

ISBN 9781761280191 (print)

Published in Australia and New Zealand by:

Brio Books, an imprint of Booktopia Group Ltd
Unit E1, 3-29 Birnie Avenue, Lidcombe, NSW 2141, Australia
briobooks.com.au

Inside cover illustration by David Rowe

Printed and bound in Australia by SOS Print + Media Group

Proudly Printed In Australia

booktopia.com.au

NICHOLAS WHITLAM

PARIS 1924

A GUIDE

brio BOOKS

WARD, LOOK, & CO.'S PLAN OF THE CITY OF PARIS

This book is dedicated to the memory of
Margaret Elaine Whitlam
(1919-2012)
who, in a long and happy life,
brought up four large and boisterous children,
gave unstinting support to her much-loved husband,
contributed to causes far and wide,
was an inspiration to many, and
– like almost everyone –
loved Paris

Contents

PREFACE

When I graduated from Harvard in 1967, I had a summer to kill before graduate school. It was the Summer of Love and California beckoned, but I went to Europe. I was twenty-one.

Back in Australia my father had recently been elected Leader of the Opposition and, accompanied by my mother, he wanted to introduce himself to political leaders in Europe. I tagged along. His various hosts had worked out that he was likely to become Prime Minister and the hospitality was upgraded accordingly. When he returned to Australia after his scheduled tour of a few weeks, my mother stayed on; together we completed a Grand Tour with an itinerary not unlike English eighteenth century milords, albeit customised to meet our quite modest budget.

In Paris we stayed at the Hotel d'Isly at 29 rue Jacob, on the corner of the rue Bonaparte and right in the middle of the action on the Left Bank. (It is now tricked up as the somewhat vulgar La Villa.) I was in my element. It was the start of a love affair with Paris.

We knew not of Natalie Barney, who – at ninety – was still hosting her famous salon just two minutes down the street at 20 rue Jacob (see Dramatis Personae). But one couldn't miss the cafes such as Deux Magots, two hundred metres up the rue Bonaparte on the boulevard St Germain, and it was an easy walk to Montparnasse and La Coupole. We ordered prix fixe meals at bistros – the nearby Roger La Grenouille at 28 rue des Grand Augustins and Chez Paul, 15 place Dauphine on the

Ile de la Cité are still there, although perhaps a bit more upmarket these days – and we found the food market on rue de Seine, also still there. We ate omelettes, good salad and cheese, drank draft beer and multiple citron pressés – it was July, and very hot – and we tucked into those hard boiled eggs that were there for a snack at every zinc bar. We "did" the museums. We took the Métro everywhere and walked and walked. The topography and the landmarks all fell into place. And I came to like the distinctive musky smell of the city, then as now well-flushed by diligent street-cleaners. My mother was forty-eight. That time together in Paris, and the embroidered reminiscences of those days, provided a special bond between the two of us for the rest of her life.

I joined Morgan Guaranty (now JP Morgan) and by the early 70s was sent to London. My very civilised boss, a thirty-something énarque, was based in Paris and this meant I regularly visited the city. The Paris office was (as it still is) at 14 place Vendôme, directly across the square from the Ritz. Our banking competitors joshed that the hotel was our staff canteen. While Morgan always did "first-class business in a first-class way", and we did indeed take clients to the Ritz for a drink or a meal, it was thought too posh for a junior officer to stay there. I settled for the nearby Inter-Continental (originally, and in 1924, the Continental), now The Westin Paris-Vendome, or, by preference, the smaller chic Lotti, now "Castiglione", the smartest wing of the Hotel Costes. Such were the compromises expected of a young banker.

Within a couple of years I had the opportunity to sell the Ritz to a new owner. (It was technically an English company, subject to London take-over rules, and most of the shares were in bearer form! The only person who knew the identities of the beneficial owners was Bernard Penché, the Ritz's General Manager. It's a long story for another time.) This meant that I had to spend several days in that opulent auberge putting together an information memorandum. I shared the burden with an English rose, my lovely wife of less than a year. We dined in both Ritz restaurants, sampled the room service, checked out the bars and generally bathed in luxury. Judy was a recent alumna of the Savoy press office in London and was at this time PR for Vidal Sassoon; the Ritz passed all her tests. We stayed there again, a decade later, when my then role as head of a large Australian bank almost justified the expense. This will partly explain why I make much of the Ritz's story in the following pages.

A few years after that second luxurious stay at the Ritz, when my father was Australia's Ambassador to UNESCO – it rather suited the new leaders to have yesterday's hero offshore – we took our two elder children to visit my parents in Paris. Alice, our eldest child, preferred the real thing at Giverny to Monet's paintings in the Jeu de Paume. We took the two children to the Pompidou Centre where a comedian was performing in the square, and he asked for a child to come up and assist him. Our five year-old son Edward was chosen. He stole the show. When the comedian was keen to get rid of him, Edward would not take the hint; his parents were both proud and embarrassed, and the audience was vastly amused. Just as Paris was taken by him, so Edward was taken by it: perhaps fifteen years later, after undertaking his own backpacker Grand Tour, his most vivid memory and greatest praise was for the sheer professionalism of the waiters, young and old alike, who are the backbone of most Paris restaurants and bars. Our youngest child, Peter, who is handicapped, has sadly never seen the City of Lights.

For the two years immediately before our permanent return to Australia, I worked for the great French bank Paribas. (It was always a thrill to rattle off its proper full name – Banque de Paris et des Pay-Bas.) I was based in Hong Kong but was in Paris often, once working there for several weeks. Whereas Morgan Guaranty's house style was something of a cross between the US marine corps and a Long Island country club, Paribas' ambience was – naturally enough – explicitly French, indeed Parisien. My colleagues, all men, were graduates of the grandes écoles. The atmosphere was intellectual. There were ranks, of course – directeur, sous-directeur and so on – but they mattered little; at planning meetings everyone was expected to argue his case and even new boys were heard out. They spoke excellent English. They wore tailored suits and, yes, they smoked gitanes. All of my colleagues lived *in* Paris; no one commuted. There was no compartmentalising of their lives. It was a continuous dance that moved seamlessly through the day and night. My colleagues arrived promptly at the office in good time each morning, always scrubbed up and well-presented. We took coffee breaks, standing at the zinc, in the morning and afternoon. It was there that I learned to challenge any bartender who purported to misunderstand an order; they invariably understood, but were quick to identify a foreigner. Everyone worked late, perhaps to eight in the evening, before going straight out to a bar and dinner with clients or meeting up with friends, a spouse or girlfriend. There is a reason all those photos of smart bars seem to be filled with chic French professionals; it is because they are. At Paribas the great restaurants and entertainments of the city were used as marketing tools for its business. I was delighted to be part of it all and quite unaware that I was already doing research for this book.

My interest in the Olympics was first piqued by those of Melbourne in 1956. I celebrated my eleventh birthday at the swimming, poolside, and hoped that one day I'd swim at an Olympic Games. (Although I did swim for Harvard and represent NSW too, that Olympic ambition proved to be beyond my grade.) So when the International Olympic Committee awarded Paris the right to host the 2024 Olympics, the centenary of the 1924 Paris Games, I started to do some research on Paris in 1924. Moviegoers will know something of the Games from the excellent *Chariots of Fire*. But what was the city itself like in 1924? What was it like to live there? Or visit?

Many would have the Roaring Twenties and Les Années Folles, the "Crazy Years", as being coeval. The Jazz Age is sometimes seen to be congruent with them too. Of course I knew that Paris was one of the hubs of the Roaring Twenties and that the city's jazz scene was an important part of that, but as I dug deeper I found that the city really did not get into full swing until 1925 – that Paris in 1924 established the platform from which the city could flourish and glow in the succeeding five years. This makes 1924 special.

I found a country much recovered from the trauma of the Great War and the "Spanish" flu pandemic, full of confidence in itself, with a new spirit of optimism, and on the way to establishing an accommodation with defeated Germany. Life was good for the bourgeoisie, not least in France's capital city. The conservative government that had held power through the Great War and in the immediate post-War years was replaced with a more progressive lot. Vestiges of Proust's world remained, of course, but the atmosphere in 1924 was decidedly modern. There was an ambivalence towards sexual non-conformity; black people were part of the scene, and negritude was celebrated. The city had become the centre of Western culture – of literature, painting and sculpture, dance and music. Everyone who was anyone in the arts lived in Paris or visited it.

My search for the essence of Paris in 1924 has only re-enforced my affection for the city. My goal was to understand the Paris of that year as much as I could. This developed into what is, in effect, a guide for a middle-class person, such as myself, who might have visited it one hundred years ago. The result, *Paris 1924: A Guide*, is both that guide and also a paean to almost everyone's favourite city.

Where would one eat? Where would one sleep? What were the entertainments? What has changed? What has stayed the same? I found that what was once a nightclub is now an ophthalmologist. (I'm not much of a nightclubber, but I think I would have been one in 1924.) What was once a restaurant might now be a frock shop. Buildings that housed high-class brothels – this was an academic exercise – have been transformed into fashionable blocks of flats and respectable hotels. Hotels and restaurants have fallen in and out of favour, and some of the leading establishments have disappeared altogether. Theatres, cinemas, and nightclubs too. And some landmarks remain totally unchanged; they shouldn't change, or don't need to.

The COVID-19 lockdown gave me the opportunity to complete desk-bound research and put together this book. I wrote it on spec, without a publisher. That way I could write about what I thought was interesting or important. Many friends and acquaintances reviewed early drafts and provided useful suggestions regarding areas to explore, and corrections; their modest reward has been a drink and a meal or two and my deep gratitude. Let me thank them again here for their help and support. The unattributed opinions here are mine alone, however, as are any surviving errors.

The young woman who was with me at the Ritz in 1974 blossomed into a housewife super-star, a great cook and a much-admired gardener. She nurtured three cherished children with great success and, in the fifty years we have been together, has stood by me through thick and thin. Judy is the love of my life. And, to poach a happily apt line, we'll always have Paris.

Nicholas Whitlam
Scarborough, NSW
December 2021

A SATURDAY

It was a Saturday in 1924: Saturday, the twenty-third of February. In the early hours of the morning a young black American had arrived at the Gare du Nord; he had jumped ship in Amsterdam and taken the overnight train. He didn't speak a word of French, but he knew he was in one of the great cities of the world. That's why he'd come to Paris.

Langston Hughes became a celebrated poet, but on this cold winter day he was just a callow twenty-three year old in a foreign city.

"I checked my bags at the parcel stand, and had some coffee and rolls at the station."[1]

Railway stations are always busy and noisy, not least in the morning. Our young traveller would have been surrounded by the puffing and hissing of trains, by the whiff of steam. People would have been going about their business, some quietly, most hurrying. Station attendants would be blowing whistles and crying out directions. Our young man would have started to take in the sweet smell of roasting chestnuts, of coffee and chocolate and croissants and brioches. He would have seen fruit barrows and small stores selling comestibles for train trips about to be taken and food for the day ahead. Porters no doubt hurried about, and you could always get a shoeshine. As ever, touts and layabouts would have populated the concourse.

Today, one hundred years on, there is no steam or hiss from the electric trains – but travellers do find themselves in the busiest train station in Europe with much of the attendant chaos and anxiety. The soaring metal and glass halls of the 1860s still house what is an increasingly hectic precinct best known to foreigners as the terminus for the Eurostar. For Parisians, however, it is more important as a hub for the Paris Métro. And it is all to be completely refurbished for the 2024 Olympics.

Left luggage lockers have replaced the human contact of yesteryear. Coffee is almost certainly of better quality than that consumed by Langston Hughes that morning in 1924. With the internationalisation of tastes, a full English breakfast is now available. French traditions are not lost though, because, if required, a heart-starting *fine* (eau-de-vie) is always at hand. There would have been a whiff of garlic and tobacco back then; less so now. Had Hughes delayed his visit by a year or so he could have tried the excellent Terminus Nord brasserie across the road: it opened in 1925, and has recently had its art nouveau and art deco features restored to their original splendour.

> *"I went outside the station and saw a bus marked Opéra. I knew the opera was at the center of Paris, so I got on the bus and rode down there, determined to do a little sightseeing before I looked for work, or maybe starved to death."*

Just as it did for Langston Hughes one hundred years ago, bus number 45 will get you to the Opéra in about ten minutes.

> *"When I got to the Opéra, a fine wet snow was falling. People were pouring out of the Métro on their way to work. To the right and left of me stretched the Grands Boulevards."*

Ever since Haussmann engaged Charles Garnier to design and build his new opera house in the mid nineteenth century it has been a centre of the city's action. The Métro station, right in front of the opera house in the Place de l'Opéra, is today as busy as ever. In 1924, American Express was just across the road at 7 rue Scribe.

Most people worked on Saturdays; office workers might finish at lunch time. So Hughes would have been witnessing a typical busy morning for this part of Paris. He was in the entertainment district. The cinemas would soon open, as would the restaurants. Cafés would have been open for hours, fruit barrows would already be busy selling their wares, and roasting chestnuts would be warming the cold mid-winter air. News-stands always carried a bright array of the many daily papers and the local magazines. Vehicular traffic was thinner than today, of course, and horses were less common than they had been pre-War; indeed, the fancy horse-drawn fiacres had recently been banned from the city's streets in order to make way for more cars. The hum and grind of the automobile were gradually replacing the grunt and whinnying of the horse, and petrol fumes were replacing the aroma of horse droppings and horse sweat.

"I looked across the street and saw the Café de la Paix. Ahead the Vendôme."

The Café de la Paix has dominated the corner at 5 place de l'Opéra since the 1860s. Proust's character Robert de Saint-Loup would dine in this classic restaurant with the Duc d'Uzès and the Prince d'Orléans. It oozes style and expense, and we know from Langston Hughes' account that he only "saw" the restaurant; that is, he didn't go inside. It was an up-market establishment, and social rules were different then: in the week before Hughes walked past, two American women had been chastised for smoking outside under the awning; they were obliged to move inside.[2]

As he went around the corner into the rue de la Paix, our young visitor saw ahead the Vendôme column and he must have noticed Cartier's flagship store to his right. All black and gold, it has been in the same place, 13 rue de la Paix, since 1899. And he would have seen Place Vendôme filled with expensive parked cars: Hispano-Suizas, Cadillacs and Rolls Royces. It was always so in the 1920s; today, except for the privileged few authorised by the Ritz doorman, all cars – however fancy – are parked in a public garage under the Vendôme square.

Place de l'Opéra by Luigi Kasimir, 1924

Langston Hughes knew of the Ritz and even hoped to be employed there. Place Vendôme is arguably the finest square in Paris, but its demographics had changed in these first decades of the 20th century; what was once an 18th century "hôtel" housing a grand family was now more likely to be a bank or a high-class jeweller: Boucheron has been at number 26 since 1893, and Van Cleef & Arpels at number 22 since 1906. In 1924, the doors of number 14 opened into the Morgan Bank, as they had since 1916 – and have ever since; in 1924 it was known as Morgan Harjes, and it is now JP Morgan. And still on that same side of the square, opposite the Ritz, Charvet – shirtmaker to kings, plutocrats and boulevardiers – had been at number 8 for three years, since 1921; it is now at number 28, opposite Bulgari.

The Haussmann buildings that front the rue de la Paix and the road's continuation beyond place Vendôme, rue de Castiglione, look essentially the same today as when Langston Hughes walked past them in 1924. As he approached the rue de Rivoli and the Tuileries Gardens, he would have seen the hotel Meurice to his left and the Lotti and Continental to his right. The formal gardens of the Tuileries were in front of him; they would have lost their leaves for the winter.

"I walked down the rue de la Paix, turned, and on until I came out at the Concorde. I recognized the Champs Elysées, and the great Arc de Triomphe in the distance through the snow."

Hughes had turned right. Had he turned left down the rue de Rivoli it would have taken him but five minutes to come upon the grand "gold" equestrian statue of Jeanne d'Arc in the Place des Pyramides. It had been erected in 1874, after France's ignominious defeat in the Franco-Prussian War, when the story of the Maid of France was once again being called upon to restore national pride. Within a few decades the far-right had appropriated her as a political symbol. On this day, however, the young poet turned right at the Tuileries (this was not an expression of his own political preference) and walked up the rue de Rivoli, where he came to the place de la Concorde and took note of the Champs Elysées and, in the distance, the Arc de Triomphe.

The same vista is available today, essentially unchanged. Place de la Concorde still has that tall amber obelisk in the middle (where the guillotine once stood during the French Revolution) and its two grand fountains; and, as you look up the Champs Elysées, the Crillon and the Automobile Club are still there to your right. If it is a clear day, you will see lArche de la Défense in the far distance, beyond the Arc de Triomphe – but that is the only major change in that famous panorama since Langston Hughes's 1924 walkabout.

> "...I took to the river, hoping to see bookstalls and Notre Dame. But I ended up in the Louvre instead, looking at Venus."

Hughes would have entered the Louvre via the pokey old entrance near the Seine. (IM Pei's brilliant Pyramide was not created as the new main entrance until 1989.)

> "When I came out of the Louvre...I came across an American Negro in a doorman's uniform. He directed me to Montmartre. I walked. I passed Notre Dame de Lorette, then on up the hill."

To get to Montmartre, or the hill of Montmartre, the Butte, he would have passed through a triangle of excitement and glamour south of the boulevard de Clichy. It was then known as part of Montmartre, although today, debased with sex shops, we would call it Pigalle. It's where the Montmartre nightclubs of the 1920s and 30s were largely housed, and where Langston Hughes would soon be employed; Le Grand Duc, Zelli's and the like would have been shut for the afternoon.

> "I got to Montmartre about four o'clock...[where] I went into a little café..."

We don't know which café he frequented. Perhaps the Moulin de la Galette. Perhaps Café Liseux, which is near where he stayed for the night. He met up with some black musicians at the café. In their minds a black American in Paris can only have had one calling – "what instrument do you play?" they asked – so perhaps the café was their hangout at the time, Chez Boudon. Whatever, by then Langston Hughes had tasted his first *café crème*.

The next day he started looking for work, trying the American Library at 10 rue de l'Elysées, the US Embassy and American Express. To do so he walked through the smartest parts of the Right Bank. He would have become acquainted with the handsome buildings along the rue du Faubourg Saint-Honoré. Whether he knew that they accommodated the high and the mighty – the President of the Republic, the British and American embassies, the exclusive Cercle de l'Union Interalliée and so on – he must have been impressed with the grace and style of the area. And he would surely have noticed the smart restaurants and retailers, like Hermès; they too were along his route.

So far Langston Hughes had only seen part of the Right Bank. He'd had his first French dinner – *boeuf au gros sel* – and he had discovered *eau-de-vie*. Perhaps he'd picked up the distinctive scent of the city's drains too.

"I began to like Paris a little, and to take it personally."[3]

It happens to everyone.

DRAMATIS PERSONAE

Marcel Proust died on Sunday, 18 November 1922. He was fifty-one. His funeral took place at noon the following Wednesday. It was the largest funeral in living memory:

> *"Dukes, princes, ambassadors, members of the Jockey and the Union, in buttoned boots, in monocles, with brilliantined hair (even the bald ones), patrons of the Turf... the leading Parisian homosexuals... and all the writers who mattered, or were going to matter in the future."*[4]

The old church of Saint-Pierre-de-Chaillot in the chic sixteenth arrondissement was brim-full of what looked like the cast of characters from Proust's huge famous novel – and some were. At Proust's request, sacred music was limited to the essentials of a requiem mass and, perhaps ironically, the highlight was a sublime rendition of Ravel's "Pavane for a dead princess".

Among the huge crowd outside the church, standing anonymously, was a newcomer to Paris, James Joyce, Proust's counterpart as the greatest contemporary novelist in the English language. Everyone, it seems, knew where and when the funeral would take place. As the crowds on the rue de Chaillot and avenue Marceau jostled for the best view, Proust's coffin was transferred to an ebony-coloured hearse; it was flanked by a glittering military escort and pulled by handsome black horses. Perhaps one thousand people followed the cortège, which moved slowly from the church down avenue Marceau and avenue George V, then along the Champs Elysées – city traffic had been stopped for the procession – and eventually up the gentle slope to the Père Lachaise cemetery. There, high up in the famous ossuary, after working its way through the scattered tombs, Valentin Louis George Eugène Marcel Proust, arguably the most famous Frenchman of his time, was finally laid to rest in the family crypt. Such were the crowds, it had taken hours for the cortège to reach its destination. The last mourners left the cemetery at dusk.

The funeral had been "a tremendous affair."[5] Perhaps only the French could celebrate the life of an artist so fully and enthusiastically.

He was an odd fellow. Born in 1871, in the months immediately after the settlement of the Franco-Prussian War, Marcel Proust was the elder of two boys. Their father was a very successful and distinguished physician. Proust père was a cultural Catholic and the boys were brought up in that faith; their mother was the daughter of a rich Jewish stockbroker. The family of four (and their servants) lived in a fine apartment on boulevard Malesherbes in the fashionable 8th arrondissement.

In contrast to his brother, Robert, Marcel Proust was a frail and sickly child, asthma being diagnosed at age nine. The asthma stayed with him throughout his life. He attended the prestigious Lycée Condorcet, in walking distance from the family apartment. There he met the children of the upper bourgeoisie and the aristocracy who would become the focus of his literary masterpiece.

Marcel Proust doted on his mother, and the affection was reciprocated. This delicate child grew to be about 165 cm (5' 5"), with a slight build. Despite his medium height, he was always described as having a "presence". He had pale skin, brown hair, parted slightly off centre, dark eyebrows with dark and deep eyes ("like Japanese lacquer"[6]). As a young man he took to wearing a somewhat effete and wispy moustache; later in life the moustache filled out a little and drooped and curled in the fashion of the day.

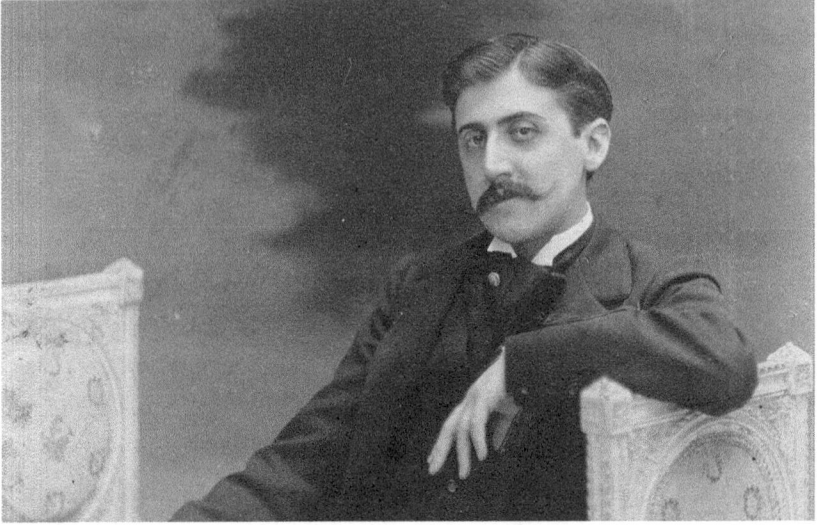

Valentin Louis Georges Eugène Marcel Proust

Young Marcel served briefly in the army – hence the military escort at his funeral – but his interests lay in the arts, particularly in writing and literature. In the 1890s he wrote prose poems and novellas for the many literary journals that flourished in Paris at the time; he translated John Ruskin – it was a joint effort with others, including his very literate mother – and he wrote a novel, short stories and essays that in many cases were not published until well after his death.

He moved with a louche crowd of privileged effete young men, and ingratiated himself with Belle Époque aristocrats and grandees. (Yet, in contrast with much of the *gratin* that he monitored, Proust was a committed Dreyfusard.) Well into his forties, up to the First World War, many who knew him or of him would have considered Marcel Proust something of a social-climber; he was thought of as a snob and a dilletante – albeit someone who added lustre and amusement to Paris's salons and social events. He was incredibly inquisitive, intrusively so; he observed everything. He interrogated dukes and duchesses, waiters and bellboys. But he was charming and entertaining. And he never publicly acknowledged his homosexuality.

Proust inherited wealth and did not have to engage in paid

employment. When his parents died, he moved into a family-owned apartment at 102 boulevard Haussmann – in the centre of his world, the 8th arrondisement of Paris. It was here in this apartment, from 1908, that he started on his magnum opus – *À la recherche du temps perdu* – now, in English, usually referred to as *In Search of Lost Time*. The huge novel comprises seven volumes, the first published in 1913 and the last not until 1927, five years after his death. It is a tour de force. Ostensibly a minute examination of the foibles of the Parisian haute bourgeoisie and aristocracy – and it is that – it revolutionised story-telling. The inner thoughts of his characters are found, developed and recorded. Involuntary memories are generated by the smells and sounds of everyday activities, the taste of food and so on. He analysed his characters' emotions, specu-lated on their motivations and delicately probed into their lives. In doing so, his voluptuous sentences could run on and on, gently punctuated, and always perfectly formed. And, in search of lost time, for Proust and his readers, *time* becomes and became its own moving force.

Proust has been translated into almost every language and his prose has a unique portability from the original French. Graham Greene pronounced him the greatest novelist of the twentieth century, an opinion shared by many.

James Joyce might not have been happy with Greene's assessment of Proust. These two literary giants met but once, in May 1922, at a large supper party for forty or fifty organised after the première of the Ballets Russes's *Le Renard*. Diaghilev was the guest of honour and the hosts, a generous and knowledgeable English couple, wanted to entertain and show off four further special acquaintants of theirs who lived in Paris at the time: Proust, Joyce, Picasso and Stravinsky. Proust's health was in severe decline and he rarely stepped out from his eyrie as he struggled to finish his great book. (Apart from his long-standing debilitating asthma, he "…suffered from insomnia, indigestions, backaches, headaches, fatigue, dizziness and a crushing ennui."[7])

Joyce arrived late and drunk, and a dapper Proust – in a fine black fur coat and white kid gloves – arrived even later, well after midnight. There are a number of competing reports as to the exact conversation that took place between the two, although not to its nature. It was unproductive. Proust mentioned the names of some prominent people who he thought Joyce might know or wish to meet. Joyce did not know or want to know them. They denied reading each other's works, which was untrue. In due course they settled on comparing their respective medical ailments, which in Proust's case would prove terminal in just six months.

James Augustine Aloysius Joyce had come to Paris in 1920. He would live there for the next twenty years. "There is an atmosphere of spiritual effort here", he wrote to a friend. "No other city is quite like it. It is a racecourse tension. I wake up early, often at five o'clock, and start writing at once."[8] Joyce's presence in Paris and his notoriety and work influenced English-language literature from this point on, not least that of his fellow expatriates Hemingway and Beckett. Hemingway and then Beckett became boon drinking companions of Joyce, who was the toast of the Anglophone literary circle.

An amusing and witty conversationalist, Joyce had a gentle Irish voice with a pronounced Irish flavour: "book" rhymed with "fluke"; his masterpiece, *Ulysses*, was "Oolissays". He stood at 180 cm (5'10"), which was considered tall at the time, and he was gaunt and thin. His clothes were sombre and conspicuous – tweed suits were his preferred dress – and he usually wore a jaunty wide-brimmed hat as he ostentatiously strode about the city in old white tennis shoes. Gertrude Stein said that he smelled like a museum. He walked and walked around Paris, that was his recreation. He was usually accompanied – because, suffering from glaucoma, his eyesight was appalling. He had dark brown hair, slicked back, wore a wide straight moustache on a long square-jawed Irish face, sometimes with a small goatee beard, and spectacles, of course. In adult life he developed a serious drinking problem. White wine was his decided preference; his somewhat exotic favourite was Fendant de

Sion, a fruity chasselas from the Valais which, these days, is more often taken as an aperitif.

Joyce was a modernist. He experimented with language and literary styles, drew upon classical analogies, and employed the modernist techniques of interior monologue and stream of consciousness. He was also an intellectual and, as such, he delighted in showing off his knowledge and erudition. Joyce's themes ran from philosophy to religion – he was at times both for and against the Catholic church, usually against – to sex, which he explored with relish and vulgarity.

A brilliant student, one of many children of a middle-class couple in reduced circumstances, he had left his native Ireland soon after graduating from university. By 1904 he was in the port city of Trieste where he eked out an existence teaching English for more than a decade before moving to Zurich, whence Ezra Pound persuaded him to try Paris. Pound, a fine poet and insightful critic, had been promoting Joyce's writing for some years.

By 1924 Joyce was forty-two. His great work, *Ulysses*, had taken eight years to write and had been finally published in full in 1922. "[It] burst over the Left Bank like an explosion in print whose words and phrases fell on us like a gift of tongues," wrote Janet Flanner. Publication had not been easy. Early chapters had appeared in New York and, in 1921, had been banned there. Nor would it be easy to keep the book published; in many jurisdictions it was banned for decades. To some it was pornography, to others literature. *Ulysses'* notoriety only encouraged interest in the work from scholars, writers, avid readers and prurient seekers of smut.

Sylvia Beach and James Joyce, 1922

At the heart of the *Ulysses* story is the story of those who made it happen. There is Joyce himself, of course, but there were also three remarkable women: Sylvia Beach, Harriet Shaw Weaver, and the mother of his children (and, ultimately, his wife) Nora Barnacle.

Nora had gone with Joyce to Trieste in 1904 as his girlfriend. At the time, she was just twenty and he twenty-two. Two years earlier they had gone out together on their first date in their native Dublin – on 16 June 1904 – the day Joyce punctiliously records in the eighteen chapters or episodes of *Ulysses*. The highpoint of their outing was a hand job administered by Nora and featured in the book. In Trieste, Nora and Joyce had moved on to traditional copulation and their two children, a boy and a girl, were born there. And Nora stuck with Joyce for the rest of his life.

Sylvia Beach, who had lived in Paris when her father was a clergyman for the American community, came back to Paris during the Great War and stayed on. By 1919, she was in her early thirties and became a bookseller and publisher, opening a Left Bank lending library, Shakespeare & Co. Joyce had completed *Ulysses* but was having difficulty finding a publisher. Pound introduced Joyce to Beach, who bravely wanted to publish it – and soon the project was on its way. Nothing could have come this far, however, without the financial assistance of an extremely wealthy and radical Englishwoman, Harriet Shaw Weaver. From about 1914 she had kept the Joyce family solvent.

James Joyce was always in straightened circumstances. On receipt of a subvention from Miss Weaver – she visited Paris 1924 – he would become a spendthrift. He would dine at the best restaurants, an early favourite being Les Trianons near the Gare Montparnasse[9]; it was the expatriate writers' venue of choice for special occasions – such as Robert McAlmon's May 1924 dinner for William Carlos Williams, which James and Nora attended with a host of celebrities. Later Joyce would favour the fashionable and very expensive Fouquet's on the Champs Elysées. The Joyce family moved around at Left Bank addresses according to their (usually impecunious) circumstances and subject to the generosity of acquaintances who often lent them accommodation. In 1924, for most of the year, on receipt of gobs of money from Harriet Weaver, they splashed out on a suite in the decidedly up-market Victoria Palace Hôtel in the sixth arrondissement.

Misia Sert was a quite extraordinary woman. With the passage of time her star may have faded among our dramatis personae, but in 1924, "Misa", as she was known to everyone, was the queen of Parisian cultural life. She had been queen-bee since well before the War.

Misia Godebska by Pierre Bonnard, *1908*

Misia was married to the very successful Catalan muralist José-Maria Sert. They had lived together since 1908 but only married in 1920. Sert was Misia's third husband. Born in 1872, in St Petersburg – the circumstances of her birth are itself a story – she came from a distinguished artistic family and grew up in Brussels and Paris. Technically she was Polish, something she highlighted when it was helpful. A coquettish and vital young woman, she was a pianist of concert standard. At twenty-one she married her cousin, Thadée Natanson, who soon established one of the most celebrated literary magazines of the day, *La Revue Blanche*. In the 1890s and through the turn of the century, the Natansons were at the centre of Paris's cultural activities. Each of Renoir, Toulouse-Lautrec, Vuillard and Bonnard, no less, painted Misia, some several times. The Natansons golden circle – in Paris and at their country estate – included Proust, Monet, Gide, Mallarmé and Debussy.

Misia had an engaging charm. She was well put together, pretty in a conventional way, with much-celebrated breasts. Her hair was worn in a chestnut brioche, as immortalised in all those paintings. Misia had "allure", often carried a half smile and she was outspoken and something of a tease. All manner of artists found her attractive.

By 1905, Alfred Edwards, a very rich newspaper proprietor who had been a backer of Natanson's magazine, had fallen for Misia. In a bizarre transaction, Edwards offered to bail Natanson out of his debts if he would cede Misia to him! At thirty-three, Misia became Mme Edwards and a public figure. Then, after a couple of years, along came José-Maria Sert; Misia took up with him. Yet Edwards, who himself moved on to further conquests, continued to provide Misia with a substantial private income.

In 1924 she was fifty-two (or forty-two according to her amended passport) and the centre of attention.

Sergei Diaghilev had come from a cultured and privileged family. Born in 1872, he was educated in St Petersburg, first studying law, then singing and music at the Conservatoire. His family lived beyond their means and was bankrupted, but Diaghilev was able to use his artistic and family connections to obtain administrative positions in the Russian Imperial Theatres.

Diaghilev became an impresario. It was as if the word was invented for him. He was flamboyant and inventive. In the early 1900s, he brought art shows, music and an opera troupe to Paris – and he was successful. Diaghilev was "...an artist whose art-form was to combine the art forms..."[10] He never measured success in financial terms and, despite being flush from time to time, he was more often than not out of pocket. Everything he did was for art.

Sergei Diaghilev was a bear of a man with a big head, big black eyes, and black hair that featured a distinctive white badger's stripe, which caused him to be nicknamed "the Chinchilla". "His linen was immaculate, but his evening clothes sometimes showed signs of wear... He had a suave address, not unlike the bedside manner of a fashionable physician. His voice had a soft, caressing tone, infinitely seductive... He always dressed his hair with a brilliantine perfumed with almond blossom."[11] He was demanding of his charges in their professional lives and supportive, in most cases, in their private lives. He was homosexual, however, and was a sexual predator of the type that would not be tolerated today: each of the men who became his lead dancers were expected to sleep with him.

Misia had met Diaghilev briefly when she was with Natanson, but it wasn't until he brought the Ballets Russes to Paris in 1909 that the friendship blossomed. The impresario would watch performances of his newly celebrated ballets from Misia's box, thereby mutually enhancing each other's standing in the cultural community. It had been a long voyage for these two: extraordinarily, Diaghilev and Misia had been born just one day apart, both in Russia and, once they established their friendship in Paris in their late thirties, and for as long as Diaghilev lived, their lives were constantly intertwined.

The Serts now added the expatriate Russian milieu of Diaghilev, Stravinsky and Bakst to the Paris entourage Misia had acquired with Natanson. Ballet, which hitherto played second fiddle to the legitimate theatre and opera, had become fashionable. Diaghilev's unique synthesis of dance, music, design and painting – plus Nijinsky and the exotic Russian troupe – was an irresistible partouse for the beau monde. Misia became the leading supporter of the new "Russian" ballet and all it stood for. She had lost access to the grand apartment she had shared with Edwards at 244 rue de Rivoli, but continued her artistic salon in a new apartment, at 29 quai Voltaire on the Left Bank, which soon became her usual Ali Baba's cave of fans and furnishings, sculptures and the like. (Proust, who was a balletomane, is said to have based two separate characters on Misia in his magnum opus.)

Misia spotted Stravinsky's music for *The Rite of Spring* and promoted the score to Diaghilev; she was a sponsor of that ballet and the previous year's iconoclastic *Afternoon of a Faun*, when Nijinsky's auto-erotic climax (sic) outraged many in the audience. By 1913, Jean Cocteau, who had ingratiated himself into Misia's circle, joined the long list of distinguished artists who preserved Misia's image for posterity.

From 1916, Misia was first an opponent and ultimately the catalyst for the convergence of a landmark creation: the Ballet Russes *Parade*. It brought together four giants of the arts – Erik Satie, Cocteau, Picasso and Diaghilev – and it is special in several respects. It was Satie's first orchestral score; it was Picasso's first stage décor; and the poet Cocteau created a story without words. Finally, Diaghilev, the glue in all this, brought in his new favourite, Leonard Massine, to put together the inventive choreography.

Parade was a seminal ballet creation. It was avant-garde in every way and it embraced several of the artistic genres that were developing a cutting edge in Paris – music, costume, and painting. (The strangest thing is that Diaghilev did not use the human voice or develop its presentation in his ballets. Voice is of course central to opera, the oeuvre in which Diaghilev first found success. He had studied singing as a young man, yet it is effectively absent from all Ballets Russes works.)

Erik Satie's music was at the heart of *Parade*.

Erik Satie was influenced by Debussy, and Satie certainly influenced Ravel. In the years immediately prior to the First World War, Debussy and Ravel started to promote the middle-aged Satie's strange music. His limpid and clean *Gymnopédies* which are now so well-known, were first composed decades before, when Satie was a mere pianist in the Montmartre boîte *Le Chat Noir* back in 1888-1891, a gig he found "degrading". He had stuck with his oeuvre over the next twenty years, pioneering minimalism and repetitive, hypnotic music, rejecting the established preferences for strong harmony and structure. In modern times John Cage, Philip Glass and John Adams have all found inspiration in Satie.

Erik Satie by Picasso, 1920

This bespectacled, balding and bearded man was forty-nine in 1915 when Misia heard one of his tunes that she thought should interest Diaghilev. It did not. But when Satie and Cocteau came up with the idea of *Parade*, Diaghilev saw that it could work.

Satie had been living in a tiny bedsit in the southern working-class suburb of Arcueil since 1898, when his money had run out. He was a talented session musician, but he would not compromise his artistic principles for paid work. He was a very strange bird. His pince-nez, almost always askew, and his goatee beard gave him an austere look. He wore the same suit – a grey velvet number – for ten years; he apparently had seven copies. Even in his private life Satie was strange: his one recorded romantic attachment was with the painter Suzanne Valadon, in his mid-twenties; it didn't last, and he seems to have never tried again.

Satie worked closely with Cocteau developing *Parade*. They worked in the Right Bank apartment at 10 rue d'Anjou that Cocteau shared with his mother, Satie having invariably walked the eight kilometres to the apartment from his Arcueil bedsit. The plot of *Parade* was simple, if new, in that it embraced everyday life: two hucksters try to induce the passing crowd into their theatre by showing off a parade of circus artists who could entertain them further within. Satie's music was outrageous and spare. Drawing upon his established repertoire of repetition and meditative elements, he added the sounds of the street and the city: sirens, typewriters, even pistols.

Everyone moved to Rome for rehearsals in 1916. Diaghilev and his troupe were largely holed up there during the War, practising routines but out of work. Italy had recently joined the War but travel between Paris and Rome was relatively easy. Picasso took over a large studio on via Margutta, where he worked on the sets and costumes. And it was here, in Rome, that the macho and decidedly heterosexual Picasso and the effete, slight, Cocteau first formed a life-long, if unlikely, friendship. Picasso dressed the policemen and thieves, the flapper, the acrobats, the Chinese fire-eater and the rest of the cast in "cubist" outfits often made of cardboard and papier-mâché; the costumes were not at all practical for dancing, but they did look extraordinary. And he created a famous

Italianate theatre curtain, festooned with a cornucopia of characters – a bullfighter with guitar, circus folk eating a meal before a performance, a ballerina on horseback, a Venetian boatman, the lot. (Diaghilev would use it for years.). The curtain opened to city skyscrapers and the modern world.

The ballet was a sensation. At the première on 18 May 1917 – an afternoon at the Théâtre du Châtelet because of the wartime blackouts – traditionalists hated it, and hissed and booed. The avant-garde loved it, whooped it up and applauded – and they prevailed. In his program notes Guillaume Apollinaire, who would die from his war wounds the following year, used the term "sur-realism" for the first time; it soon became the catchword for a movement.

Serge Diaghilev by Christopher Wood, 1926

After the success of *Parade*, Satie would become the inspiration and mentor for Les Six – six emerging French composers, of whom the most important were Francis Poulenc and Darius Milhaud. Speaking for Les Six, Milhaud enthused: "…the purity of his art, his horror of all concessions, his contempt for money, and his ruthless attitude toward the critics were a marvellous example for us all."[12] Erik Satie was at last recognised for the important figure we now acknowledge. It would be another seven years, however, before Picasso and Satie worked again together. As we shall see, that year – 1924 – would prove to be a grand one for Satie. It was also to be his last: this self-contained, proud and solitary man died from cirrhosis of the liver on 1 July 1925.

Natalie Clifford Barney, known widely as *l'Amazone*, was the queen bee of an extensive lesbian circle. Born in Ohio, she was independently wealthy; a forbear had made a fortune building railway cars. Bilingual, Barney was a fine poet and novelist, and had lived in Paris since the turn of the century. She was a pacifist, a belief she had bravely pursued during the Great War, and an outspoken advocate and recorder of sapphic love.

Natalie Clifford Barney by Romaine Brooks, 1920

A fair-haired beauty as a young woman, Natalie Barney was always self-assured and well-presented. By 1924, she was approaching fifty. Not a believer in monogamy, she continued to manage multiple relationships. Most notorious was a three-way affair with American painter Romaine Brooks and French writer Lily de Gramont, the Duchess of Clemont-Tonnerre, a ménage à trois which extended over decades. Over the years her lovers included, but were not limited to, the courtesan Liane de Pougy, Colette, socialite Dolly Wilde (Oscar's niece), writer Lucie Delarue-Mardrus, and poet Renée Vivien. In what she proclaimed to be "the sapphic centre of the world", Natalie Barney's other lesbian friends included booksellers Sylvia Beach and Adrienne Monnier, the painter Marie Laurencin (who batted for both sides), Edna St Vincent Millay (ditto), Gertrude Stein and Alice B Toklas, British poet Radclyffe Hall, heiress Winifred Ellerman (Mrs Robert McAlman), poet Hilda Doolittle, writer Djuna Barnes, arts patron Winnaretta Singer (aka la princesse Edmond de Polignac or "Tante Winnie"), writer and artist Mina Loy, artist Thelma Wood, and journalists Janet Flanner and Solita Solano.

In 1909, Natalie Barney took out a lease on a unique property at 20 rue Jacob. Over the coming decades, it became a special meeting place for modernist writers, musicians and artists of all types. Through a simple garage door on rue Jacob one came upon a rectangular cobbled courtyard with a two-story building to the left; ahead, behind a huge tree, was a small detached pavilion, also of two stories but with climbing ivy, and trees somewhere beyond. This was Natalie Barney's "pavillon".

Upstairs was Miss Barney's bathroom and an enormous dressing room, a blue bedroom and a small balcony that overlooked the wild garden. Downstairs, hidden away, there was a kitchen, servants' quarters and a WC. One entered the pavilion via its vestibule and soon came upon a drawing room and a dining room. These rooms were lined in red damask and packed with sofas and chairs, portraits, photographs, tapestries and mirrors, and there was a grand piano. Gas lighting came on at dusk and gave added interest to the exotic setting. There was no telephone; Miss Barney preferred to communicate by letter.

Floor-to-ceiling glass French doors opened onto the garden. It was a haven, a miniature forest with tall slim trees, random unkempt paths, wild herbaceous borders, and an occasional wicker chair and table. And, around the corner, behind a smaller garden, stood an exquisite Doric temple, a former Masonic lodge, dedicated by Miss Barney to friendship. She had the salutation *A l'Amitié* inscribed on its pediment and fitted the innards out with a sofa and chairs, somewhat like a guesthouse. Entertainments for all-female audiences took place here, as did other secret women's business.

Temple of Friendship, 20 rue Jacob
by Georges-Henri Manesse, 1909

Every Friday, from about 4:30 to 8:00, for two months or so, from May to the first days of July and again in autumn, Natalie Barney would host a salon at 20 rue Jacob. She became the great *saloniste* of the time. There could be fifty guests and, once a month, upwards of one hundred and fifty.[13] All the lesbians were invited, of course, but Miss Barney did not discriminate on that count: Guillaume Apollinaire, Ezra Pound and Dorothy Shakespear, Sherwood Anderson, Wanda Landowska, Paul Valéry, William Carlos Williams, Peggy Guggenheim, André Gide, Darius Milhaud, TS Eliot, Jean Cocteau, Louis Aragon, Olga Rudge, George Antheil, Isadora Duncan, René Crevel and Scott Fitzgerald were all welcomed. Almost anyone from the Anglophone arts who was interesting and in town was invited, and also the local artsy aristocrats. (Hemingway never attended the salon; Joyce perhaps once or twice. Proust made a private visit to the pavilion, just once, during his last days; it was late at night, as was his want, and the only time the two met. And there is no truth to the story that Mata Hari danced naked for Natalie Barney's guests here; those performances took place, years before this time, for ladies-only audiences at her former residence in Neuilly.)

Barney's housekeeper, Berthe Cleyrergue, would put on a delicious light spread where the dining room table featured her first-class cucumber sandwiches and chocolate cake, tea, glasses of frozen strawberries and (largely for the Americans) liquors of all varieties. The salon and dining room were decorated with flowers, typically white lilies and tuberose. Charles, the butler, would take charge of logistics. And Natalie Barney would make an entrance in one of her long-sleeved white tea gowns by Vionnet, after which poetry readings or musical interludes would punctuate the evening.

Pablo Picasso first came to Paris from Barcelona in 1900. By 1905 he was back in Paris semi-permanently and, with the advent of cubism, he and Georges Braque became well known. Gertrude Stein and her brother were early followers. Short and stocky, always brown, with black slicked hair, Picasso was yet to look like the priapic caricature that he became.

By 1917, in his mid-thirties, he was ready to get married. His first choice backed out. Then, while in Rome developing *Parade*, he set his heart on one of Diaghilev's young dancers, Olga Khokhlova. A Russian colonel's daughter, she had classic Slavic looks and the slim build of a ballerina. Unlike some of her cohort, however, she stuck to her upbringing and wouldn't come across; nice girls didn't in those days. They married the next year, in July 1918, with Misia as a witness. Misia and Picasso's relationship was superficially on the best terms. In a 1918 portrait never published in her time, he worked up a most unflattering cubist number of the round-faced Misia, giving her a small mean mouth and an exaggerated jaw. Yet, on the birth of his son Paul, Misia was named as a godmother.

Pablo Picasso and Olga Khokhlova, 1918

Olga aspired to high society and the beau monde. She never lived at Picasso's old villa and studio in unfashionable Montrouge – she stayed in the chic Hotel Lutetia until they married – and, when it came up, she jumped at the opportunity to take an apartment on the Right Bank. Picasso's agent had found a place at 23 rue de Boétie, next to his own lavish showroom and dealership. Max Jacob, Picasso's first friend in Paris, his old Montmartre roommate when they were both dirt poor young men, dubbed this period in Picasso's life *l'époque des duchesses*: from the end of the War, Picasso (and Olga) were being duchessed. Their friends from the Left Bank were appalled by their move across the river. By 1923 the Picassos had a chauffeur-driven saloon. In due course, however, their apartment described the couple's diverging interests: one floor, the fourth, was decorated by Olga in a conventional bourgeois fashion; that's where they received and entertained visitors. They had a cook, a butler and a maid. The fifth floor served as Picasso's studio and private love nest – a set of rooms with unfinished paintings, a bed, and all the chaos an artist's studio usually entails.[14]

Misia had been at the centre of artistic circles since the 1890s and a new face started to appear in the War years, a face with a name that would in due course be world-famous: Chanel. Gabrielle Bonheur Chanel, born in 1883 in the humblest of circumstances, learnt to sew when she was sent to a provincial Catholic orphanage. She acquired the sobriquet "Coco" while singing part time (although apparently not very well) in Vichy and Moulins and, as a pert little thing with a good body and bobbed black hair, she soon became attached to a rich young man. By her mid-twenties, with the support of well-connected lovers, she had become a fashionable milliner. In 1910, the love of her life, the English aristocrat Arthur "Boy" Capel, set her up at 21 rue Cambon. Success was quick and soon she also had full blown dress shops in the resorts of Deauville and Biarritz.

Coco attended the première of *Parade* with Misia and Diaghilev. In the coming years she would herself design the costumes for several Ballets Russes productions. By 1918 she had bought 23 rue Cambon to establish her fashion house; the *House of Chanel* now owns a slew of buildings on that street that provides the back entrance to the Ritz Hotel. The "little black dress" had long been her signature, as had been the use of comfortable materials like jersey and tricot; indeed, apart from everything having to look elegant, her fundamental theme was the creation of comfortable and sensible clothing. Chanel proved to be a great businesswoman. She never married but had a most active love life. Stravinsky was a lover, as were the poet Reverdy and (later) the illustrator/designer Paul Iribe; Russian Grand Duke Dimitri Pavlovich too.

And for ten years, from 1924, she was the mistress of the richest man in England, "Bendor" Grosvenor, the Duke of Westminster; they expressed a mutual dislike for Jews and homosexuals. Misia became Coco's best friend (and fellow cocaine addict). Coco was a great pal of Picasso and (notwithstanding her homophobia) the artistic polymath, Jean Cocteau.

Coco Chanel with "Bendor" Grosvenor
at the Chester races, 1924

Cocteau was a gay as a daisy. (Coco made an exception for him, and Diaghilev.) He was also, in many ways and for decades, the most talented and ubiquitous artist in France: "…a living concentration of art and intellect, of taste and daring."[15] Cocteau first established himself as a poet, but he also wrote novels and plays; he wrote music, he was a fine graphic artist, a sculptor and an art critic; and he wrote, produced and directed films. By 1924 he was thirty-five.

He came from a privileged background, much the youngest of three siblings. His father committed suicide when the boy was just nine and Cocteau grew very close and dependent upon his mother. Hopeless at school, except at games and drawing – he attended the Lycée Condorcet – Cocteau developed a precocious ability to write. In his late teens he was adopted by high society, and the young Cocteau thrived on their attention. He was always very needy. At twenty-one, after a brief breakout, he moved back with his mother into a very grand apartment on the top floor of 10 rue d'Anjou, near the Madeleine; they would live there together, on and off, for the next ten years, ably supported by Mme Cocteau's attentive staff. With the advent of the Ballets Russes, Cocteau sought and won recognition by Diaghilev and the avant-garde. Misia sponsored him. He was rejected from active military service on the grounds of ill-health at the start of the War, but he signed up to Misia's bizarre ad hoc ambulance team and then Etienne de Beaumont's more professional lot.

A short man, he was slightly built, with an agile gait. At times he looked somewhat bird-like. Somehow – despite ungainly black hair, crooked teeth, a hawkish nose (aquiline is the polite term), a gaunt angular face and sad eyes – he came across as handsome. By the 1920s, everyone knew or knew of Cocteau: "Cocteau was the symbol of 1920s France, echoing the innovation and the liveliness of the decade."[16] Most people admired his artistic virtuosity; some were jealous of him, some were genuinely unimpressed. Romaine Brooks called him "a jumped up social climber". By every measure, Cocteau was a man of notoriety and controversy.

Raymond Radiguet was not sixteen when he introduced himself to Cocteau. It was 1919, and Cocteau was a well-established star of the city's cultural and artistic milieu; he was then twenty-nine. Cocteau was infatuated with the boy who, within the next four years, would become a literary phenomenon.

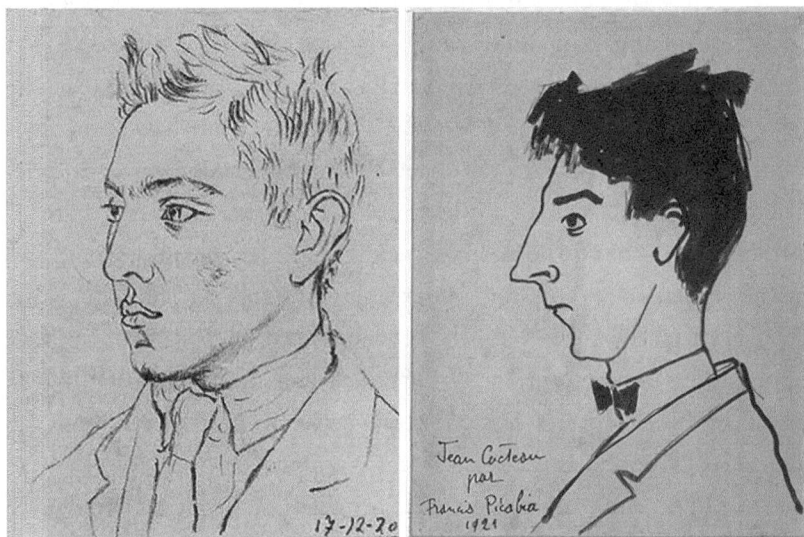

Raymond Radiguet by Picasso, 1920
Jean Cocteau by Francis Picabia, 1921

It is difficult to define what made Radiguet attractive to Cocteau and his crowd. There must have been other ragazzi around; it cannot have simply been the beauty of youth. Certainly, he was a precociously talented writer. (Radiguet's father, Maurice, a noted if typically impecunious cartoonist, had made the initial introductions to the Paris literary crowd.) The boy was not conventionally good-looking. Despite terrible eyesight, he apparently engaged intently with any interlocutor. He was small in stature but had a "stocky, well-built body".[17] He suffered a limp because one leg was shorter than the other. By all accounts, however, even as this sixteen-year-old boy, he had a certain aura, and chutzpah. Stravinsky, whose sexuality was entirely orthodox, found him "disturbingly handsome".[18]

Slowly, Radiguet became part of Cocteau's life. They started writing together. They went out together. They dabbled in Dada. They holidayed together. To the local scene, they were a couple. Maurice Radiguet wrote to Cocteau questioning the propriety of the relationship and Cocteau assured him it was entirely innocent: if the father believed this, he was alone in doing so.

Cocteau encouraged the boy to write, and write more. He mentored Radiguet and edited his work. Radiguet, who was always very self-contained and self-centred, gained in confidence and sometimes became cruelly inconsiderate to those around him. He drank too much, took drugs, and indulged himself. He affected a monocle and had long carried a cane. Radiguet took up with older women – Picasso's first choice for a wife, the bisexual Irène Lagut, being one; Beatrice Hastings, Modigliani's former muse, was another. The diminutive Perlmutter sisters, one blonde (Tylia) and the other brunette (Bronia), were a couple of very young crumpets who also took his fancy; indeed, he became engaged to Bronia. All this infuriated his mentor as, no doubt, was its intent. Hemingway cattily said that Radiguet "…knew how to make his career not only with his pen but his pencil." Radiguet's first novel – *Le Diable au Corps* ("The Devil in the Flesh") – a semi-autobiographical tour de force of adolescent lust and marital infidelity, was a triumph. It has stayed in the French canon to this day.

His second novel, *Le Bal du comte d'Orgel,* was in the can when he died a horrible death from typhoid fever in December 1923. Radiguet's sudden demise came as a great shock to everyone, and his funeral at fashionable Eglise Saint-Honoré-d'Eylan in the 16th arrondissement attracted all the artistic establishment: Misia and José-Maria Sert, Pablo and Olga Picasso, Brancusi, hangers on like Nina Hamnet (who allegedly had slept with the boy), Coco Chanel, the Dadaists, the lot. All except Cocteau, who was too distraught to attend. The saddest contingent was of course Raymond Radiguet's family – his parents, Maurice and Jeanne-Marie-Louise, and their six surviving children. The church itself was festooned in white drapes and flowers, and the clergy's vestments were white too – Radiguet was, after all, still a minor. He was dead at twenty. Misia had taken charge of the funeral arrangements; Chanel had decorated the church and dressed the priests, and she settled his medical expenses.

After a traditional service, a large crowd set off in the rain for Père Lachaise cemetery, led by the band from Le Boeuf sur le Toit – the same destination that huge congregation for Proust had headed for little more than a year before. And today Radiguet, a comet who burned out almost as soon as he appeared, rests there with Proust.

LUTETIA

In many ways the river Seine defines Paris: it flows around the site of the original settlement – those two natural islands in the centre of the city, the Île de la Cité and the Île Saint Louis – and today's residents identify themselves by where they live in relation to the river, either on its left or right bank.

The Seine has its source near Dijon in Burgundy, about 300 km from Paris. As it flows down to the sea it is joined by its tributary the Yonne (into which has already flowed the Aube) and then, in a major confluence, the river Marne joins the Seine just ten kilometres east of Paris proper. When the Seine arrives in the city, it initially runs roughly east to west, with Paris's *Left Bank* to the south and its *Right Bank* to the north. The river swings briefly south and then turns sharply north around the western edge of the Bois de Boulogne; thereafter it makes a series of sweeping turns before flowing on nearly 500 km to the English Chanel and the port of Le Hâvre.

On 1 January 1924, after weeks of rain and fog, the river had become a torrent, racing through Paris at more than ten kilometres an hour. Paris is in a flood plain – the Roman name for Paris, *Lutetia*, means swamp or marsh – and, in the first days of 1924, the city was seriously flooded. People feared a repeat of the record 1910 event, when Paris had been paralysed for months.

Sections of the metro were inundated. The Gare des Invalides suffered a major wall collapse, was closed for days and the station itself became "a walled-in lake."[19] Trains stopped running at the nearby Gare d'Orléans. Electricity was lost, cellars flooded. The yardstick by which the severity of a Paris flood emergency is measured is where the waters reach on the huge Zouave statue on the Pont de l'Alma. (Zouaves were the famously brave Berber soldiers from Algeria who were kitted out in an exotic "oriental" uniform.) The authorities usually start worrying when the water reaches the statue's feet. Its height is 5.2 metres or 17 feet. In 1910 the flood had reached the statue's neck. In the first days of January 1924, the Seine was already at its waist.

Boulevards and streets filled with water, only the lamps of the lampposts could be seen in some places, the pissoirs were flooded (with obvious consequences), people took to dinghies and canoes to get around and to deliver bread and other essentials. Lampposts and telegraph poles became handy spots to tether a boat. A dozen huge bears at the Jardin des Plantes, the Paris zoo, were trapped in their pen; they could not be rescued and were forced to tread water for twelve hours rather than drown. Eager citizens "rescued" hundreds of barrels of wine that had been swept from the cellars of Bercy. Police apparently ignored that wine liberation but otherwise kept civil order from rowboats. The entrances to many metro stations were bricked up or protected behind sandbags. Horse-drawn vehicles and large lorries sloshed through the streets of the less-affected areas. Boardwalks were erected everywhere.

A naval detachment had been sent from Cherbourg with collapsible boats and another lot soon arrived from Toulon. And then the sun came out, the rain stopped, and by 8 January the water level was falling, and buses and trams were starting to get back on the roads. After a couple of weeks, the boardwalks were removed and Paris returned to its cold winter.

The last of Paris city walls, the "Thiers Wall", was built between 1840 and 1845. These fortifications were ineffective during the Great War – German cannon could hit Paris from far away – so they were gradually torn down from 1919 to 1929. Thirty years later, the governments of Charles de Gaulle and Georges Pompidou built the Boulevard Périphérique on the route of the old Thiers Wall. The "Périph", circling Paris's twenty arrondissements, is France's busiest road – and it defines what today we think of as Paris.

One of the great attractions of Paris is that it is still recognisable as a city of the nineteenth century: its layout and major sites have remained largely unchanged for nearly one hundred and fifty years. The key tourist attractions from the 19th century and before are still there: Notre-Dame (now in restoration after the fire of 15 April 2019), the Eiffel Tower, the Opéra, the Madeleine, Les Invalides, Montmartre, the Arc de Triomphe, the Champs Elysées, the Louvre, Sainte-Chapelle, the Haussmann boulevards, the Bois de Boulogne, the Luxembourg Gardens and so on. All these landmarks were part of the Paris that Langston Hughes and every other visitor saw in 1924.

The Paris that Langston Hughes experienced was the result of perhaps the most comprehensive and successful urban redevelopment in modern history. In 1853, Napoleon III had appointed Georges-Eugène Haussmann "Préfet de la Seine", and he authorised Haussmann to remake the city's road system and its shape. With the political and financial support of the Emperor and the administrative clout of his own office, Prefect Haussmann transformed the city. In the next twenty years the built environment of Paris was changed more than it had been in the three previous centuries. The Prefect did work around the great ancient landmarks, but almost everything else was eligible to be torn down to conform to his new grand plan. Great new boulevards were built to provide easy circulation across the city, north/south and east/west. These thoroughfares opened up new vistas to the historic monuments and were linked to the great railway terminals – largely built in the 1840s – which themselves were further enhanced. Haussmann's wide boulevards also had a military purpose. Troops could move along them quickly and, as they typically radiated from a circular rond-point, the Emperor's cannon could readily fire down them on any rioters.

The Bois de Boulogne and the Bois de Vincennes were opened to the public and landscaped for public enjoyment. These two huge new parks, located on the city's outskirts to the west and east respectively, provided new lungs for the growing city. Public squares were extended or created, the Parvis de Notre-Dame among them. Improvements were made around the Arc de Triomphe such that the Étoile became the centre of a series of major new roads and vistas. And Haussmann built a huge sewer system that serves Paris to this day.

The streetscape on the Grands Boulevards was transformed with new apartment blocks. The classic Haussmann apartment building comprised five or six stories: a ground floor that might have a retail shop or two, a mezzanine floor for small business, upper floors of apartments and a roof space of some sort. Most buildings were finished in dressed limestone, which provided an attractive uniformity; and adjacent blocks had their facades, including the balconies, aligned. These new structures were typically built by speculators and rented to the bourgeoisie, an arrangement that encouraged the maintenance of a consistent style. (Many are now owned by insurance companies.) These 19th century Haussmann buildings have stood the test of time – adapting as necessary to modern conveniences – and are an essential part of the city's identity.

The three million residents of Paris in 1924 enjoyed a wonderful public transport system. Trams went everywhere, buses almost everywhere, and the Métro was nearly as extensive as it is today.

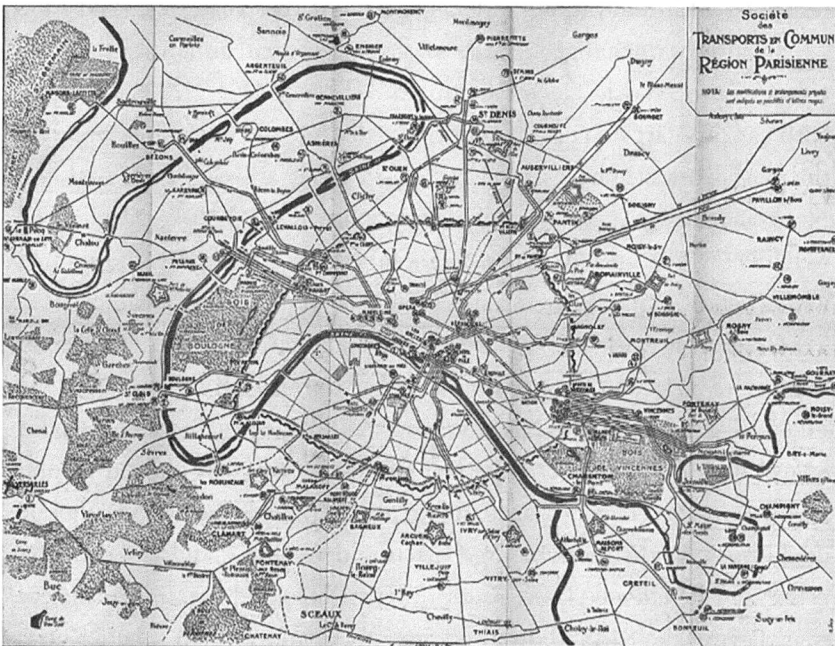

From 1914, all Paris trams were electric and there were more than 120 lines. The sound of the trams was the sound of modern Paris: *les watt-mans*, the tram-drivers, were "bell-clanging maniacs".[20] To maintain Haussmann's vistas, tram lines tended to avoid the Grands Boulevards, and they extended far beyond the Thiers Wall. For example, to get to the Olympic Stadium, way out in semi-rural Colombes, a spectator at the 1924 Olympics would take #35 tram or #36 from the Madeleine/ Boulevard Malesherbes terminus, changing once at Porte Champerret (at the Thiers Wall) for #64, and be at the stadium in about an hour.

The Métro's carriages have changed over the years and have been modernised. Electronic ticketing has now made unnecessary the clumsy discourse that was a feature of many a foreign traveller's attempts to be understood at the ticket counter. The new ticketing paraphernalia has none of the attraction of the old ticket counters, however, albeit that some are still allowed exist. Stations have been improved and some nastily sterilised but, in general, the original features of the Métro have been respected with renovation; and some, such as the great Nord-Sud Line 12, are almost unchanged. Many metro stations still announce their entrances in the classic Hector Guimard *MÉTROPOLITAIN* calligraphy with cast iron art nouveau plant ornamentation and curving lampposts; the most exotic still have a steel and glass canopy as well. For its part, the Nord-Sud line created a new totem signpost in the 1920s: a capitalised METRO, white on red, encased in a fancy cast iron frame and topped with a yellow globe. Most are still there.

Consistent with the *égalité* of the national motto, there are no longer two classes in the Métro. They went out in 1991. In the era of the nineteen twenties, though, those who paid a modest increment could enjoy comfortable leather seats (as opposed to wooden ones in second class), an uncrowded carriage, and an aura of social distinction. No one could miss the distinction: large lettering declaring 1 and 2 – première classe and deuxième classe – and different coloured cars made sure of that. Paying the extra allowed one to rub shoulders with a better class of person.

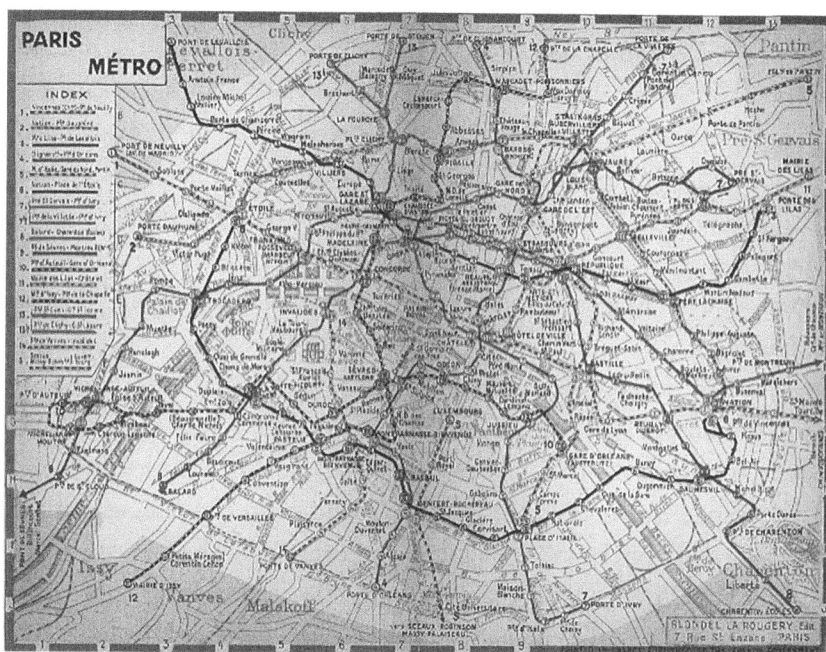

"Cut and cover" had been the construction method commonly used to build the Métro; this means cutting down into the existing road system, building the underground railway, and then restoring the road above. This had caused much disruption over the years but by the 1920s the lines were effectively complete and Paris had, as it has to this day, one of the world's great rapid transit railway systems.

The trams and the Métro linked to eight mainline train terminals, of which six are still in use. The twenties were the heyday of long-distance train travel and, for most travellers, humble and high-and-mighty alike, a grand Paris railway terminal was their first experience of the city. With their soaring vaults of cast iron and glass and their vast arrival halls teeming with people, these cathedrals to progress and architecture can rarely have disappointed the novice traveller or veteran alike. Five such terminals were on the Right Bank and three on the Left, each with its own particular character.

Manet and Monet both painted the Gare Saint-Lazare, the oldest of the stations, and thereby recorded the hustle and bustle of the 19th century that continued into the 20th. As the terminus for the Paris-Le

Havre railway Saint-Lazare carried passengers to and from the transatlantic cruise ships and therefore provided the first glimpse of Paris for many Americans. And before private cars became common place, it was the starting point for tourists and holiday makers setting off to fashionable resorts like Deauville on the Normandy coast. The station was an important terminus for commuters too, and it provided easy access to the nearby Grands Magasins and to the commercial centre of Paris – just as it does today.

The Rothschild-developed Gare du Nord was (as it still is) the busiest train station in Europe. It was the terminus for the Low Countries and, connecting with the cross-Channel ferries, it was the train route to the UK. Despite its wonderful Beaux Arts architecture – a famous statued façade, a good pitched roof and fine iron columns – the Gare du Nord has never really been loved like other terminals, probably because access from the station to the city has never been as good as from the other stations. (Haussmann failed in his attempt to drive a new boulevard to it.)

Le Départ des poilus août 1914 by Albert Herter, 1926

Just a ten minute walk from the Gare du Nord is the Gare de l'Est. In the Great War, it was the major staging post for getting troops to the front; the huge (12 x 5 metres) painting *Le Départ des poilus, août 1914*, which celebrates that effort, has dominated the station's vestibule since 1926. The station provided routes to Strasbourg and Mulhouse, and it has always been the starting point for the famous Orient Express. The juxtaposition of these two stations, du Nord and de l'Est – with their extensive train tracks cutting into the hillside to the north and running so close together – had caused the working-class suburb of La Chapelle and the adjacent Goutte d'Or to be neglected over time and left to decay, a situation that has continued to this day.

The fourth terminus on the Right Bank was the Gare de la Bastille. Built for strategic military purposes mid-19th century and then connected to Strasbourg and Mulhouse, the Bastille station was very busy indeed in the 1920s, both for long distance trains and for its interconnection with Paris trams. It complemented the Gare de l'Est. By the 1960s, however, with competition from the metro and the need to accommodate longer trains on main lines, the Bastille became redundant. It was a fine building and its demolition to provide the site for a new opera house was contested. In the event, however, the Opéra Bastille opened to much applause in 1989, and its elevated tracks were reborn as the marvellous Promenade Plantée in 1993.

The Gare de Lyon has a distinctive clocktower and has existed in its present elegant form since 1900. It is the road to the south – to Lyon (of course), to Marseille, Switzerland, Italy and Spain. From 1920, the luxurious *Le Train Bleu* originated here and the station's famous Second Empire-style restaurant now carries that name. (The famous platform scene in *Casablanca* – where, in the heavy rain, Rick receives Isla's note telling him that "I cannot go with you or ever see you again…" – was shot in Burbank, California not on the Marseilles platform; if it had been shot at the real Gare de Lyon everyone would have been undercover.)

Moving to the Left Bank, the Gare Austerlitz had lost much of its relevance in the 1920s because in 1900 its owner had extended the main line through it and beyond to the new Gare d'Orsay. Up to that point the Gare Austerlitz had served Bordeaux and Toulouse, a responsibility taken up by the new station. That setback was reversed in 1939 when the Gare d'Orsay was abandoned as a main line station and Austerlitz became a terminus again. (Visitors to the Musée d'Orsay, which has been created out of the old station and the associated Hotel Palais d'Orsay, will appreciate the Beaux Arts splendour of the original buildings.)

Gare Montparnasse, circa 1924

And finally, the Gare Montparnasse, a neo-classical building with art deco additions, sat happily on a busy square at the heart of Montparnasse. It has always served the south west and Brittany, and in the 1920s provided an important link to Paris' tram network.[21] An unsuccessful 1960s redevelopment, which includes the intrusive and unpopular Tour Montparnasse, has ruined the site and plans are now afoot to rectify this.

André-Gustave Citroën and Louis Renault were contemporaries, Citroën having been born in 1878 and Renault in 1877. Both became giants of the French automobile industry. Both made their names and early fortunes during the First World War when their factories produced munitions with great efficiency; but the two men were not alike.

Citroën, born of Jewish parents, earned an engineering degree at the elite Ecole Polytechnique. He was outgoing, liberal, progressive and popular. The vast Citroën factory, developed from 1915 in the 15th arrondissement, was a paean to the latest mass-production techniques, and – with playgrounds and nurseries – an exemplar of social responsibility too.[22] André Citroën followed the example of Henry Ford in producing lower-priced, tough and lighter cars that appealed to a wide public. A favourite in 1924 was the yellow Type C or 5HP – "la Petite Citron" – which appealed to women and those who enjoyed the play on words; and at that year's Paris auto show André Citroën stole the headlines with his all-steel B12. Citroën lived well and had a weakness for gambling. He was an inventive and agile marketer: from 1919 Citroën led the charge to display cars in a dedicated showroom on the Champs-Élysées; the firm organised exotic car rallies; and, for ten years from 1925, the word CITROEN lit up the city from a huge moving advertisement running vertically up the Eiffel Tower. (It was used as a beacon by Lindbergh in his historic 1927 transatlantic flight.) By the mid-1920s, André Citroën's car company had become the largest in France, producing almost one-third of all cars on French roads.[23]

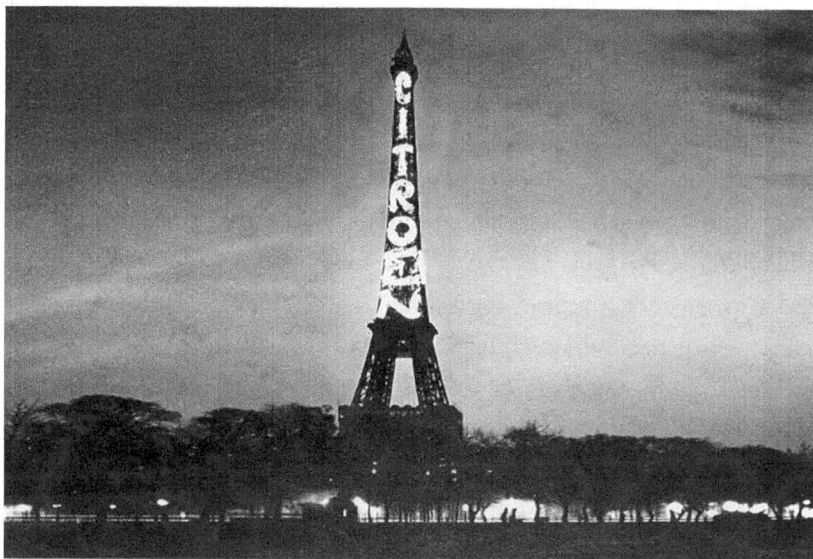

Louis Renault came from a wealthy bourgeois family and was educated at the fashionable Lycée Condorcet. The Renault firm produced a number of vehicles in the early 1900s, and Renault's AG 1 – little four-seaters with running boards and a driver's seat under a canopy up front – soon became the default Parisian taxi. It was a PR coup for Renault and a great succour to the war effort when the Paris taxi fleet answered the call to take troops to the front in September 1914. (Misia Sert had suggested the idea to the military governor of Paris, General Gallieni. That only about 5,000 troops were moved by the convoy – when the army comprised about two million Poilus – is rather beside the point: it made Renault's name as a national icon.)

Having specialized in buses and commercial vehicles pre-War, the firm produced tanks for the war effort. After the war, Renault developed a full range of vehicles – from trucks and tractors, to luxury cars – at its huge factories on the banks of the Seine at Bologne-Billancourt (until 1924 "Boulogne-sur-Seine"). Vertical integration of the supply chain made Renault a very profitable enterprise indeed: it owned foundries, glass works, sawmills and more. Louis Renault himself became notorious as a cold, vulgar and loud reactionary. He had a grand house on (what is now) the Avenue Foch and a country estate. His right-wing views did not endear him to his workers and Boulogne-Billancourt often suffered industrial unrest. Renault's anti-Semitism also grated; a short man, he saw no irony when he referred to his rival as "le petit Juif".

The French had been pioneers in the development of the motor car. Indeed, in the early 1900s the country produced more cars than any other. While Peugeot was the largest manufacturer pre-War, Renault and Citroën took the lead soon after. It was time for the glamourous *fiacre* – those horse-drawn buggies that had epitomised the Belle Epoque and featured in countless novels and paintings – to make way for the motor car. The auto lobby successfully argued that fiacres slowed down traffic flow and, in 1922, the authorities did not renew their licences to operate. The speed limit of 30 kph was suspended at the same time, and Haussmann's boulevards had no difficulty accommodating the increased motor traffic.

In 1923 the first mechanical traffic lights, red and green, joined electric signs in lighting up the night, but it would still be a few more years before motor vehicles exceeded the number of horse-drawn vehicles; and with that transformation the city gradually lost the reassuring sound and smell of horses, the familiar clip-clop of their hooves and their distinctive bouquet.

Shopping was a well-established recreation for the bourgeoisie in 1924, and the Grands Magasins continued to re-invent themselves. Le Printemps maintained its brilliant exterior and art nouveau rotundas with an internal rebuild, re-opening in 1923 with its now signature multi-coloured stained-glass cupola and a new restaurant. Its "young" neighbour, Galeries Lafayette, already famous for its Dome foyer, established *La Maîtrise*, an in-house arts workshop for the manufacture of household goods such as furniture, wallpaper and the like – a workshop theme it maintains to this day. La Samaritaine expanded its existing art nouveau building so that it now covered a whole city block with an art deco extension. And in 1924, to great excitement, Au Bon Marché, never to be outdone, opened its new Annexe – which today houses the incomparable food hall, La Grande Épicerie de Paris.

Au Bon Marché, one of the largest department stores in the world and certainly one of the best, had always identified itself as "respectable". It followed rather than led fashion. Its fashion items were reserved – the store always had a close association with the Catholic church – and provincials felt comfortable visiting Au Bon Marché rather than its racier cousins across the river on the Right Bank. By keeping its prices competitive, it also provided a vehicle for the lower middle class to aspire to the values and lifestyle of the next rank up the social scale. Au Bon Marché's catalogues and brilliant advertising reinforced this attraction, and a calendar of events – not just sales but specific promotions for particular departments like linen or whatever – provided a rhythm for the year, to which many subscribed. Au Bon Marché had long allowed goods to be returned or exchanged. Customers could spend the day at the store: there was a reading room with stationery where bored husbands could retire, and a buffet serving wines with a meal.

Yet there was a large population which the traditional Grands Magasins did not serve well: workers. True, Au Bon Marché had started to sell some work clothes; these were limited, however, to such items as uniforms for the household staff of its existing bourgeois clientele – for valets, housemaids, chauffeurs and the like. This was not an invitation to the common man.

Au Bon Marché d'Eté by René Vincent, 1924

But there was a store that catered to the working class – Les Grands Magasins Dufayel. Appropriately based in the lower-class Goutte d'Or district of the 18th arrondissement, it aped everything Le Printemps, Galeries Lafayette, BHV, La Samaritaine and even Au Bon Marché provided – only with a rather vulgar flamboyance. The store was housed in a huge glamorous building, topped with a dome and a searchlight that lit up the neighbourhood at night. It came to include a winter garden, theatre and concert hall and was decorated to the gills with pillars and paintings, statues and staircases.

With all this, the Dufayel store brought shopping as a social activity to the hoi polloi. Notwithstanding its location, Les Grands Magasins Dufayel became a tourist attraction. And it had one innovation that made the store an even greater success.

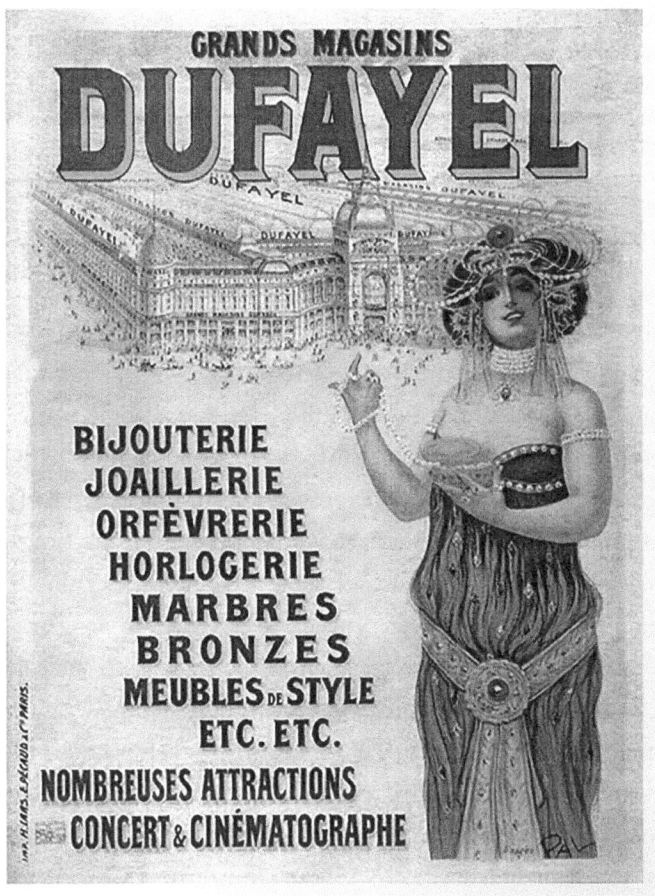

The traditional grand magasins only took cash. Dufayel provided credit. Thirty-three-year-old Georges Dufayel had taken over an existing enterprise in 1890; by 1904 he had 3.5 million instalment plans in place. Dufayel's credit collectors became a common sight in the city, kitted out in their blue military-style uniforms and carrying large money sacks; there were hundreds of them. Dufayel died in 1916 and, in 1924, Au Bon Marché acquired Les Grands Magasins Dufayel. The concern of Bon

Marché's shareholders that standards would be lowered and its reputation endangered, by being associated with Dufayel's instalment plans and lower-class clientele, proved unfounded. Upmarket Au Bon Marché kept the businesses separate and, in due course, credit became an important aspect of every department store's retail offering.

We all know from photographs and movies what people wore in the 1920s. As in many things, so it was with fashion: Paris was the centre of the world.

For women, fashions drew upon female post-War liberation. Clothes were looser, less formal. The boyish silhouette was celebrated and straight tops flattened women's figures. Shifts were soon popular, drop-waists came in, and arms and legs were exposed to accommodate the movement required for the "flapper" dances that were popular at the time. Chanel promoted trousers for women and they became an acceptable part of the female wardrobe. Cheaper synthetics, like rayon, were introduced. "Ladies" still wore silk and velvet and satin, of course, but cotton and wool came into their own. Somewhat ironically, French designers developed the "cocktail dress" for the American market, where Prohibition was still in force. Shorter skirts exposed shoes, so shoes joined hats and gloves as essential items for a complete ensemble.

Men too had their fashions. Military uniforms had formed part of many men's recent experiences; those uniforms influenced new high-buttoned suits, and lapels thinned noticeably. For evening wear, it's not that white-tie disappeared, that was still required for formal occasions, but dinner jackets – velvet, or white or black ("the tuxedo" in American) – became a less formal option. Some gentlemen still wore spats; socialist leader Léon Blum was one. Only politicians and aristocrats continued to wear tail coats. Casual clothes such as blazers and sweaters became acceptable on social occasions, with Hollywood movies promoting the change. Shirts with attached collars soon became the norm.

Nothing has changed more than the wearing of hats, particularly among men. In the 1920s, your hat was a representation of your identity and social status.

A hat of some sort was a near-necessary part of every man's wardrobe. When the factory whistle went off, a sea of flat cloth caps would walk out the gates. That was the uniform of the worker and newsboys. (The upper and middle classes adopted similar peaked caps for country pursuits and golf, but that hat did not represent their identity since they only wore such caps when they were at play.)

Known as a "derby" in the US, the bowler – the hard felt hat with a rounded crown – was the chapeau of choice for the bourgeoisie. (Charlie Chaplin lampooned the middle class by wearing one. Quechua women in Peru wear them to increase their fertility, and the marching Orange Order in Northern Ireland wear them to intimidate the local Catholics.) On formal occasions top hats, in black or grey silk, were worn by politicians and by high society.

The straw boater, which had originated as the hat worn by boatmen on the Seine, enjoyed popularity in the summer with all classes. (In the USA, 15 September became "Straw Boater Day", when it was expected that a boater would be replaced by a felt hat; hoodlums sometimes enforced the convention.) Chanel and Collette even popularised the boater for women.

The woollen beret – soft, round, comfortable and capable of being pushed or pulled to make a personal style statement – was the bohemian choice. Writers, artists and non-conformists of all sorts wore a beret in Paris; as, of course, did the Breton "onion johnnies" and countless others throughout the provinces. And the *kepi* – that circular cap with a flat top and a stiff peak or visor – was the standard headdress for the French Army. Kepis came in multiple variations of colour and enhancements for the different Army units, and officers' hats always had gold or silver braiding. The national police wore kepis too.

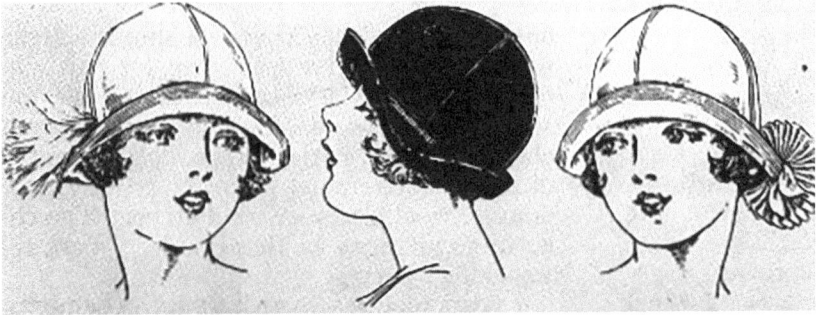

The hat provided a means of social elevation at a relatively modest investment vis-a-vis a suit or a coat. An aspirant to the middle class could readily wear a bowler – and might get away with it. Such social blurring can go either way, of course – both Lenin and Keir Hardie gravitated to cloth caps – although it needs to be said that such ruses were less common in France than elsewhere.

For women, the cloche hat was a must. Bell-shaped – "cloche" means bell – it was usually made from felt and came with no end of variations and enhancements to the fundamental shape. Feathers were a popular addition, as were flowers. Never really out of fashion, the twenties were the heyday of the cloche. It suited the new short hairstyles too. Yet it was no indicator of social class or station: the cloche was as popular with ladies of leisure as it was with ladies of the night.

Newspapers were a mixed bag. *Le Petit Parisien* was enormously popular and published nationwide from Paris. It appealed to a mass market and covered a wide range of interests, from finance to fashion. Every Sunday a new good-quality illustration was featured on the front cover; the drawings were sometimes risqué or even scandalous, and they were linked to a human-interest story inside. *Le Petit Parisien*'s circulation ultimately topped two million. The similar name of *Le Petit Journal* did not confuse readers. It was always a voice for conservatism and it stuck with its anti-Dreyfus stand as readers moved from it to *Le Petit Parisien* (which had avoided taking any stance on the scandal). *Le Petit Journal* had once been the largest newspaper in the country, but post-War its circulation faded badly. *Paris-Soir*, which was first published in late 1923, was the new boy. It lacked any political agenda and followed the example of London tabloids with sensational reporting. In due course it had the largest circulation of all.

Among the more respectable dailies *Le Figaro* had always been moderately right wing; it suffered a decade of relative unpopularity from 1922 when it was owned by the controversial right-wing perfume millionaire François Coty. *Le Temps* continued as the serious newspaper of record; often referred to as the "semi-official newspaper of the Third Republic", it was deliberately serious, indeed sometimes tediously so, like its successor *Le Monde*. *L'Humanité*, which the communists had taken control of from the socialists in 1920, was the newspaper of the Left. And *Action Française* catered to the loony Right.

The *Paris Herald* and the *Chicago Tribune*'s European or Paris edition were long standing English language rivals. In 1924 the *Paris Herald* became the *New York Herald Tribune* when it was acquired by the owners of the *New York Tribune*. (The *Chicago Tribune*'s Paris edition was sold to and merged with *The New York Herald Tribune* in 1934.) Before the year was out, and for the next few years, there were four English language newspapers when a group of American newspapermen started a new paper, the *Paris Times*, and London's *Daily Mail* also established a Paris edition, the *Continental Daily Mail*.

Radio was in its infancy. Television did not exist.

Telephones made a slow start in Paris. More than three-quarters of the connections were on the Right Bank, presumably reflecting commercial use and the distribution of relative wealth, but there were only about 100,000 connections in 1924. What did flourish, however, was the wonderful Paris Pneumatique.

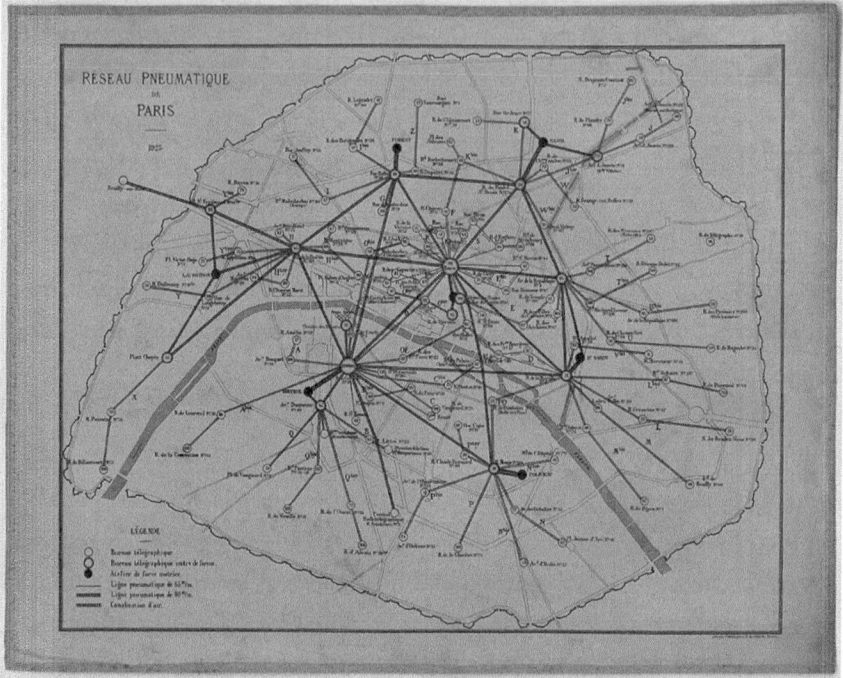

The Pneumatique was a mail service that delivered messages across the city by pneumatic post. Compressed air was pumped through tubes, pushing or pulling the message in a small metal cylinder – in a fashion similar to that employed in department stores at the time.

By 1924 the network reached every corner of the twenty arrondissements; more than 400 km of tubing was involved – through sewers and the Métro, across bridges and along railway lines – and Le Pneu would stay in service for another sixty years.

A message became known as a "pneu". (The "p" is sounded.) It was dropped off at a post office by the sender or by a servant or office staff; the message was then put in its cylinder and pushed or pulled along the tubes to a hub, switching to another hub as necessary, and ultimately onto the post office nearest the recipient; from there a messenger boy would deliver the pneu by foot or bicycle. Customers could be certain that their message would reach its destination within two hours; as the system created speeds of up to thirty km per hour, it was not uncommon for a message to be delivered within thirty minutes.

Over the years various cards and envelopes were accepted by Le Pneu. Commonly these were the "petit bleu", which was made of light-weight blue paper, and measured just 9.5 cm by 6.5 cm. The most famous petit bleu was a discarded, torn pneu which established the innocence of Dreyfus in 1896.

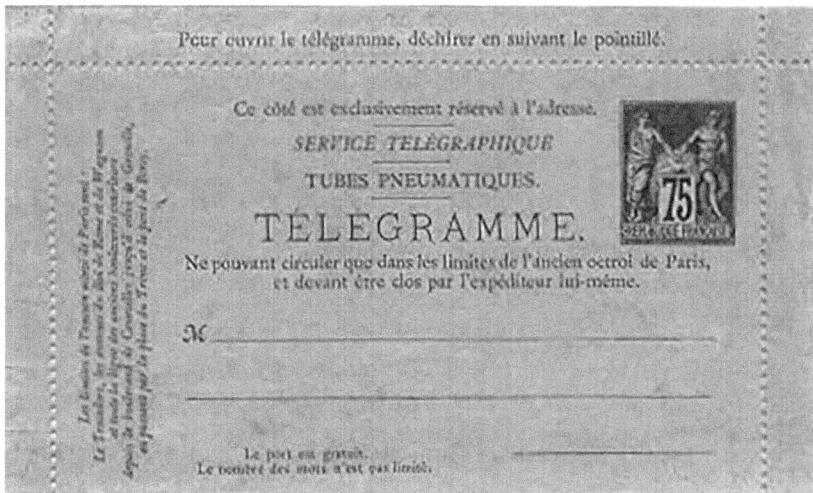

The pneu was part of everyday life, as references from Proust et al attest. ("[M]other ... you only have to send me a pneu."[24]) A pneu answered the need for speed and certainty of delivery. It was ideal for paying a bill or delivering a theatre ticket, and the pneu came into its own for sending that message you didn't want to give in a personal visit or a telephone call. Lovers broke off their affairs by pneu. Politicians warned each other of plots by pneu, and withdrew or confirmed their support by pneu.

CITIUS, ALTIUS, FORTIUS

A t the heart of the Bois de Bologne there is a garden, *le pré Catalan*, the Catalan meadow, a bucolic circular lawn surrounded by trees and flower beds – a centrepiece of the fabulous new public garden that had been created by Haussmann out of a former royal hunting estate. On 23 June 1894, a thirty-one-year-old French nobleman hosted a sumptuous dinner at the restaurant Le Pré Catalan in that meadow; they were celebrating the creation of the International Olympic Committee ("IOC"). The young man was Pierre de Coubertin. Thirty years later, he brought the Olympics to Paris for the second time. It was his swansong.

Pierre de Coubertin was born Charles Pierre de Frédy on 1 January 1863. He was also known as Pierre de Frédy and Frédy de Coubertin before he settled on the style by which we now know him. Notwithstanding his being only the third son (and fourth child) in the family, under the incomprehensible system of French titles, he was entitled to be known as Baron de Coubertin. His father – Charles Louis de Frédy, Baron de Coubertin – was a fashionable academic painter, and the family had considerable means. (The family maintained four establishments: a five-story townhouse at 20 rue Oudinot in the seventh arrondissement; the paternal estate, Château de Coubertin, near Versailles; another château in Normandy (Château de Mirville); and a "chalet" 25 km away in

56

the artist colony of Etretat on the Normandy coast.) Pierre was a good student and, in 1886, he graduated in law and public affairs from the recently-established elite Ecole Libre des Sciences Politiques ("Sciences Po"). A political or diplomatic career could be expected of him.

Instead, de Coubertin chose education and, in particular, advocacy of the beneficial link between education and organised sport. The catalyst to this vocation had been his first visit to England, in 1883. There, among the schools and universities, he came upon Rugby School and its headmaster Thomas Arnold. It was the first of seven visits to the UK and each reinforced his conviction that organised sport could add moral fibre to youth, and that sport's solid implantation in the English education system was a reason Britain and its Empire flourished.

De Coubertin's attempts to have the French education curriculum emulate this aspect of British life were not successful but, by 1890, he (and others) had succeeded in harnessing all the French athletic associations into a unified body – Union des Sociétés Françaises de Sports Athlétiques (USFSA). As Secretary-General or President of USFSA, he controlled and promoted amateur sport and the idea of reviving the ancient Olympic games. In the week before his 1894 Pré Catalan dinner, de Coubertin had organised a huge seminar in Paris to discuss amateur sport and his idea of reviving the games in a modern form. Two thousand worthy people – ministers of state, sportsmen, musicians, priests, even peace advocates – attended the opening session in the grand auditorium of the Sorbonne. Over the next few days, they resolved to establish the IOC, and to stage in 1896 the first Modern Olympics, in Athens.

Thereafter, the Olympic Movement became Pierre de Coubertin's life. He served as President of the IOC from 1896 to 1925, steering it through difficult times. The 1900 and 1904 Games, in Paris and St Louis respectively, were little more than sideshows for World Fairs; the 1908 Games, scheduled for Rome, were abandoned in 1906 because an eruption of Mt Vesuvius put too great a strain on Italy's resources, and London had to quickly stand in for the Eternal City. The 1912 Games in Stockholm, if modest and spartan in the Scandinavian manner, got things back on track and were a considerable success. Then Berlin's scheduled 1916 Games were aborted because of the Great War. At short notice Antwerp scrambled together an admirably decent effort in 1920.

Pierre de Coubertin was a person you noticed. Short, just 161 cm tall (5' 3"), his hair had turned white with age and that, together with his huge flamboyant moustache, made him a character that could not go unnoticed. He was a strange combination of the aristocrat and democrat: his parents were keen royalists but he himself was a staunch supporter of the Third Republic; a Catholic, he married a Protestant when, in France at least, those things mattered; he celebrated and encouraged participation in sport by all classes of society. His passion for the Olympic Movement was boundless and his opinions, such as limiting female participation, were certain. He became autocratic, and this necessarily aroused some opposition.

Almost from its creation, membership of the IOC was in de Coubertin's gift. The first appointments were for life. There were fifty-one members in 1921, representing forty countries. Three countries – France, the UK and the USA – had three representatives; Brazil, Hungary and Sweden had two; the rest had one. Many were aristocrats and most were plutocrats. (IOC Members are not their country's delegate within the IOC but rather representatives of the IOC in their respective countries. Political turmoil has sometimes produced strange results; for example, Prince Léon Ouroussoff, the Russian member from 1910, lived in Paris from the 1917 Russian Revolution until his death in 1933.) Whatever democratic principles de Coubertin promoted in sport itself, and he did, he was also a snob: he was happy to include the lower classes in the common purpose of sporting competition, but he was not one of them.

On 2 June 1921, the IOC assembled at Lausanne's Casino de Montbenon to decide which city should host the 1924 Olympics. There were six candidates: Amsterdam, Barcelona, Los Angeles, Paris, Prague and Rome.

Pierre de Coubertin had exhausted much of his and his wife's fortunes in promoting the Olympic Movement. Their family life had been strained because their two children suffered from debilitating disabilities. His colleagues on the IOC were vividly aware of all this. To their surprise, on 17 March 1921, de Coubertin sent a pre-emptive letter to all IOC members, announcing that he intended to stand down in 1924. The letter included a special request and assertion: "At this moment when the reviver of the Olympic Games judges that [my] personal task to be nearly at an end, no one will deny that [I am] entitled to ask that a special gesture should be made." He wanted them to vote for Paris. Whatever faults the President might have had, however difficult he had become, his colleagues could not deny him his request. The vote was not unanimous; four IOC Members opposed. But Paris it was, for 1924. De Coubertin later described his manoeuvre as a "coup d'état".

The IOC estimated the cost of staging the Games to be 30 million francs, of which 20 million would be needed for a stadium and accommodation. This is a not inconsiderable amount, perhaps as much as US$2 billion in today's currency. After the usual argy-bargy, the French Government agreed to contribute 20 million francs and the City of Paris 10 million.

The best site for a stadium was thought to be the Parc des Princes, which then housed a velodrome to the west of the city on the Thiers Wall. Unfortunately, the City of Paris would not allow it to be redeveloped. Second choice was the Pershing Stadium, to the east in the Bois de Vincennes. It had largely been built by the US Army in 1919 to stage the Inter-Allied Games, which had been a series of ad hoc sporting contests among Allied troops. This was not to be, as the cost of converting the stadium to Olympic standards was deemed prohibitive.

This was when Racing Club de France, the country's most prestigious sporting club, stepped up. Racing had provided its Croix-Catelan field in the Bois de Boulogne for the 1900 Games, and it now proposed that it build a new stadium for the 1924 Games at Colombes. The Club would own the stadium and, for the Olympics, it would receive a share of the ticket sales. Colombes was not an ideal site. A rather unattractive industrial suburb, it was way out in the banlieue to the north west – fully 14 km as the crow flies from central Paris. Previously a hippodrome, the chosen site accommodated a modest arena, "Stade du Matin"; it was sponsored by the newspaper Le Matin and had recently hosted rugby, football and athletic events. Racing Club's new Stade Olympique de Colombes would hold 45,000 spectators, of whom 20,000 would be undercover. It was well served for transport by trams, buses and trains, and, as it transpired, the new stadium proved to be an excellent venue for a number of sports.

Symbols have always been important to the Olympic Movement. The iconic five rings – blue, yellow, black, green and red – on a white background had been proposed for the IOC's stationery and a flag in 1913. The story is that de Coubertin himself created the symbol.

Baron Pierre de Coubertin and the Five Olympic Rings

With the hiatus of the Great War, however, it was not until the Antwerp Games of 1920 that they were adopted by the IOC. It is certainly true that Pierre de Coubertin proposed the Olympic motto *Citius, Altius, Fortius* – faster, higher, stronger – as far back as 1894. Persistence was one of his great qualities and, with 1924 being his swansong, the IOC adopted the now famous hendiatris as its motto.

The Opening Ceremony was planned for 5 July 1924, and the

traditional events would be concentrated in the three weeks that followed, to 27 July. Rugby would precede that Olympic period with a two-week tournament starting on 4 May, as would Football with a tournament to be staged from 15 May to 9 June.

The IOC has always been self-important, self-centred, even pretentious. One pretension has been the wish to see its philosophy of so-called Olympism – itself a pretension – embrace the arts. Pierre de Coubertin himself had showed the way at 1912 in the Olympic Arts Competition at the Stockholm Games, when his poem "Ode au Sport" won a gold medal for literature. He had entered the poem in French and German versions under dual pseudonyms, one French and the other German, and in the two languages. An English translation of the first verse reads:

"O Sport, pleasure of the Gods, essence of life! In the grey dingle of modern existence, restless with barren toil, you suddenly appeared like the radiant messenger of a past age, when mankind still smiled. And to the mountaintops came dawn's first glimmer, and sunbeams dappled the forest's gloomy floor."

Perhaps it resonated more vividly in 1912 than it does now.

Consistent with this arts theme, the 1924 Games organised five artistic contests: for architecture, literature, music, painting and sculpture. Twenty-three nations were represented in 189 entries. The contests would start the Olympic celebrations from 15 March, for a month, with the entries for architecture, painting and sculpture exhibited in the Grand Palais. IOC members Count Clary and the Marquis de Polignac thought they knew enough about each discipline for them to serve on all five judging panels; dramatist Jean Giraudoux served on four (not music). Whatever the quality of the entries, the juries included many of the good and the great. Literature boasted Gabriele d'Annunzio, Maurice Barrès, Paul Claudel, the Countess de Noailles (not the socially-prominent young countess, rather her mother-in-law who was a noted novelist), Marcel Prévost, Paul Valéry and even Edith Wharton. They awarded the gold medal to Charles Louis Prosper Guyot, whose poem

"Jeux Olympiques" apparently evoked the hammer-throw and footraces; an English translation reads:

> *"The runners bend, tense flowers…A shot: a violent word! And suddenly, Necks extended, forward, Like stalks, Faces like pale snatches, Apples, Teeth and jaws rushing into, Space"*

Music had a distinguished panel that included Bela Bartok, Gabriel Fauré, Maurice Ravel and Igor Stravinsky; that jury found insufficient merit in any of the entrees to award prizes. The painting panel included Foujita, John Singer Sargent and Vuillard; the gold medal was awarded to Luxembourg's Jean Jacoby (who won again in 1928). And, to the delight of the subscribers to the philosophy of Olympism, Alfréd Hajós, who had won two swimming gold medals for Hungary in 1896, completed his medal tally with a silver in the architecture competition.

Things warmed up in May. Paris would hold the Olympic rugby tournament, a special exhibition on sport which would run through to July, and the Olympic football competition would kick off.

De Coubertin's affection for rugby is well documented. His USFSA was the governing body of French rugby union from 1890 until 1919, when the FFA – Fédération Française de Rugby – was formed. Back in 1892, on 20 March, de Coubertin himself had refereed the first French rugby championship between Racing Club and Stade Français. (Racing won 4-3.) And he was lyrical about the game's virtues in 1896:

> *"What is admirable in [rugby] is the perpetual mix of individualism and discipline, the necessity for each man to think, to anticipate, take a decision and at the same time subordinate one's reasoning, thoughts and decisions to those of the captain…[rugby] is truly the reflection*

of life, a lesson experimenting in the real world, a first-rate educational tool."

Rugby was not played at the 1896, 1904 or 1912 Games. In the 1900 Paris Olympics the competition was among just three teams, France, Germany and the UK. France won. In 1908 there were but two teams, Australia and the UK; Australia won. Again, there were only two competitors in 1920 at Antwerp, France and the USA; to the surprise of most, the USA won. Naturally, de Coubertin was hoping for a better competition in 1924. This was not to be.

The British unions were planning a British Lions tour to South Africa, and it was scheduled for July to September 1924; they also argued, on this occasion at least, that rugby was a winter game and it was inappropriate to play in the summer. So Britain was out, as were the South Africans. The All Blacks from New Zealand were scheduled to make an extensive tour of the British Isles from September 1924 to March 1925, and Paris was a long way away from Oceania (as it was for Australia); so New Zealand and Australia were out too. Insofar as that 1924/25 All Black team – "The Invincibles" – did not lose a game on their British tour, the Kiwis would certainly have started favourites had they turned up in Paris. But the USA would defend its title, and the French rustled up Romania as a third team.

France had not done well in the Five Nations championship of 1924. England had won each of its four games, Scotland and Ireland won two each, and France (against Scotland) and Ireland (against France) had both won just one. Even so, France could expect to start favourites for the Olympic tournament.

The Americans paid their own way. A squad of thirty lost all four practice games in England. A key player was Dan Carroll, originally from the St George rugby club in Sydney, who had won a gold medal playing on the wing for Australia in 1908. He emigrated to the USA and studied at Stanford. As an American citizen, he then played fly-half for the USA in Antwerp and coached that winning team. Carroll was again a US coach in 1924. Nine of his charges attended Stanford, and all the others came from California teams. Although five players were returnees from Antwerp, they were certainly not expected to win.

Things did not go well in France for the Americans from the start. The crossing from England had been stormy and, on 27 April, there was a kerfuffle at immigration on arrival at Boulogne. The French cancelled trial games and denied the Americans access to proper training grounds; in response, the Americans marched to the just-completed Colombes stadium, scaled the fence, and practised there on the virgin soil. It didn't take long for the French press to brand them "streetfighters and saloon brawlers".

The tournament would be a round-robin, with each of the three teams playing the other two. All games would be played at the Stade Olympique. On 4 May the French slaughtered the Romanians 59-3. Their star, Basque winger Adolphe Jauréguy, an excitement machine from Stade Français, scored four of France's thirteen tries. The following week, the Americans prevailed against Romania, 37-0. The Americans were powerful athletes and they had come to develop good rugby skills and coordination on their tour. They were physical but they were also now skilful. The French crowd refused to be impressed, and they booed the Americans no matter what.

All was set for the France v USA game on 18 May, which would effectively be the final. (Finishing third, albeit of three, meant that the Romanian team won the bronze medal – the first Olympic medal in the country's history.) France was expected to win by at least twenty points. Tensions between the Americans and their hosts were not lessened when the Americans were robbed of clothes and money while training.

More than forty-thousand partisan French supporters came to Colombes for the game. At four o'clock sharp the teams came onto the field. The Americans looked spic in their V-necked white uniforms with the American shield, blue belts and white stockings hooped in red and white. *Les Bleus* wore white shorts and their famous blue guernsey badged with the French cockerel. It did not start well for the French. Jauréguy was flattened by his opposite number when he was seemingly in the clear; the same player flattened him again, perfectly legally. When US Rhodes Scholar Alan Valentine, a huge forward, sprinted the width of the field and took down centre Jean Vaysse, the Frenchman was carried from the field. It was only 3-0 at halftime, the USA's way, but they were clearly on top. The partisan crowd was getting restless.

The Olympic Rugby "final": USA (in white) v France, 18 May 1924

These were the days of no replacements. Vaysse started the second half but Jauréguy did not. The Americans scored three quick tries before *Les Bleus*, who were becoming increasingly frustrated, finally scored. Vaysse soon left the field permanently, so the French were now down to thirteen players and in a very difficult position. Late in the game, the Welsh referee wanted to send off French captain René Lasserre for twice "slugging" the big US captain, its star centre Dick Hyland; Hyland persuaded the referee to reverse that decision.[25] This did not placate the crowd at all, and the final score was 17-3. The French supporters were not happy. In fact, they went wild. Some American fans were said to have been beaten up. Bottles and rocks were thrown onto the pitch, and one of the American reserves was struck and knocked down by a spectator's walking stick.

Few could hear the playing of the *Star-Spangled Banner* for the booing and noise of the mob. No-one could disagree with the Chicago Times reporter: "America [had] outfought, outplayed and totally outclassed the French [team]...."[26]

Police had to escort the US team to their changing room. It had not been an auspicious start for the Olympics of 1924.

"Football" evokes a different game largely according to where one lives. For the IOC, which was based in Lausanne in 1924 and is still based there – albeit now in considerable splendour – it means "association football", or "soccer". That is the game the IOC recognized as football in 1900 and has done ever since.

The common element in all football codes is that kicking a ball to score a goal is part of each code. Sometimes kicking is essential, sometimes less so. In the USA, football is undoubtedly that game whose ultimate competition is the NFL. Canada has its own version of the same game. In Australia, the most popular football game – and it is called football by all its adherents – is Australian Rules Football, a development of Gaelic football. Gaelic football is played in Ireland; there it is "football", and it is certainly not soccer. Rugby league football is the brilliantly skilful and physical game played largely in Australia, England, New Zealand and Papua New Guinea (where it is the national game). And, not least, there is rugby league's forebear, rugby union football, Pierre de Coubertin's favourite, which is played in many places around the world.

Football was a particular problem for the IOC in that the IOC insisted on competitors at the Olympics being amateurs. More often than not, this was ignored. The UK, home to the most extensive football competitions, wanted the situation clarified for 1924. They could not get satisfaction. Nor could Denmark. And Austria, with one of the best teams in the world, simply didn't enquire. There were also political vetoes: against de Coubertin's wishes, Germany was not allowed to compete in Paris at all, effectively as a punishment for losing the Great War, and the IOC simply didn't recognize the Soviet Union.

Stade Olympique de Colombes, set up for the
Olympic Football competition

In the event, twenty-one teams competed in the tournament, all from Europe, save the USA and Egypt – and Uruguay. This small country of just 1,600,000 inhabitants had won the 1923 South American *Copa América* (beating Argentina in the final), thereby qualifying for the Olympics. The team was the first from their continent to compete in a major football competition. It would not be the last.

Atilio Narancio, the president of the Uruguay football association, had promised to take them to Paris should they win the Copa. To do so, he mortgaged his house. The team travelled third class, stopping in Spain to play a few friendlies to raise money, but they got there. No one in Paris thought they would be any particular challenge. Yet the Uruguayans had thought it through and were well prepared.

The team travelled with a doctor. This was an innovation. They were super fit, being trained by their goalie, Andrés Mazali, a former rowing champion. And they took a villa across the river from Colombes, in Argenteuil, which kept the team away from the temptations of central Paris (at least for the tournament) and allowed them to concentrate on their preparation. When tipped off that their first opponent, Yugoslavia, would have a spy at training they put on a show: tripping over, passing poorly, bumping into each other and missing shots at goal.

On 26 May, the Uruguayans ("La Celeste") stepped out for their first game in black shorts and socks and their soon-to-be famous light blue jerseys trimmed in white. The band played the Brazilian national anthem and the Uruguayan flag was raised upside down. That was the end of their humiliation because *La Celeste* soon put on a football demonstration. Short passes were executed perfectly; they glided around the pitch, cutting up the Yugoslavs and humiliating *them*. The South Americans won 7-0, putting all the other teams on notice.

Victories followed against the USA (3-0), France (5-1) in the quarter finals, the Netherlands (2-1) in the semis—before the team prevailed against Switzerland (3-0) in the final on 9 June. They were humble, young working men who simply enjoyed playing the game. And they were popular. At the final whistle, La Celeste circled the ground, thanking the crowd and accepting their applause, thereby inaugurating what is now the traditional victor's "lap of honour" at such events. In their five wins the Uruguayans had scored twenty goals with only two scored against them. The competition's leading scorer was Uruguayan striker Pedro Petrone, who was a grocer back home. He was not yet nineteen, 1.73 cm tall (5'8") and 74 kg, and dubbed "El Artillero" (the gunner); he was probably the fastest player in the tournament. The star, however, was 23-year-old José Leandro Andrade.

Uruguay was unlike most colonised nations in that, although the first settlers had exterminated many of the original native population, Uruguay had developed into a very tolerant country. There was no overt racism; education and sport were entirely integrated. La Celeste had long included black players. And Andrade was one.

He was also poor. Born to a voodoo-practising mother and (allegedly) a 98-year-old father, he grew up in the barrios of Salto, Uruguay's second city. With his obvious football talent, the young Andrade moved to Montevideo. There, he found his position at "wing-half". He was very handsome and a great womaniser. Andrade played at 77 kg, and stood a relatively tall 179 cm (5'10"). Never trying to match those who were physically stronger, he was technically brilliant, fast and dynamic.

Back home he had been a carnival musician and a bootblack. In Paris, he became *La Merveille Noire* (the black marvel), a sobriquet he would carry for the rest of his career. As result of his talent and charisma, José Leandro Andrade was in many ways the first international football idol.

La Celeste, the 1924 Olympic Football champions

The tournament ran from 15 May to 9 June, and had been an enormous success. Four grounds had been used – Colombes, Stade Pershing, Stade Bergeyre (now gone) and Stade de Paris (now usually known as Stade Bauer) – and the crowds had been excellent. The competition was the talk of the town. Every sports enthusiast who could manage it attended a game. The future Chinese leader Deng Xiaoping, twenty years old and living in La Garenne-Colombes at the time, may well have been one; this has never been definitively confirmed. Whatever, the final at the Colombes stadium attracted a capacity crowd of more than forty-five thousand spectators, and the total ticket sales amounted to a handsome 1.8 million francs.

When the news of their win reached Uruguay, the people were ecstatic. According to essayist Eduardo Galeano, it was the defining moment in shaping nationhood: "The sky-blue shirt was proof of the existence of the nation: Uruguay was not a mistake."[27] Atilio Narancio was hailed "The Father of Victory". In 1929 Uruguay completed the huge Centenario Stadium in Montevideo's Parque Batlle with Narancio's statue erected outside in pride of place. FIFA – Fédération International de Football Association – the world body that had supervised the Olympic competition took notice of the event's popularity. As a result, FIFA organised football's first World Cup in 1930. In Uruguay.

In this Olympic year, Paris had now seen a rugby tournament, the March/April artistic contests, and the successful football competition. It was also enjoying the surprisingly well-received sports exhibition, l'Exposition Internationale des Sports, somewhat incongruously located at the often louche Magic-City, an entertainment centre on the Left Bank at the Pont de l'Alma, which was well-known as the venue for annual Mardi Gras drag balls.

The official Opening Ceremony of the Games was less than a month away. It would herald nearly three weeks of competition for the signature events of all Olympic Games – those in track and field and swimming – and more.

LA REPUBLIQUE

While rugby aficionados may have had their focus elsewhere and football fans too, the important national event in France that spring was the General Election. The two-stage process took place on 11 and 25 May 1924. A return of the conservative Bloc National was widely expected but those expectations proved to be wrong: a new left of centre coalition – Le Cartel des Gauches – prevailed.

The new Prime Minister was Edouard Herriot, the long-standing Mayor of Lyons. Aged fifty-two, a graduate of the elite ENS (*Ecole normale supérieure*), he was scholarly and physically thick-set, with a hearty manner and an appetite appropriate to his home city. He was a fine orator, and he was trustworthy. Herriot's party affiliation was with the so-called Radical-Socialist Party, which was widely acknowledged to be neither radical nor socialist. (A "mis-named party of laissez-faire middle class Frenchmen..."[28]) The second of several parties making up the Cartel was the Socialist Party, which was indeed socialist. While they backed Herriot to lead a government, political purity kept the Socialists from taking seats in the Cartel des Gauches' "bourgeois" cabinet.

It was an important handover. The Bloc National had won the 1919 election in a wave of popular support for post-war stability. France had been traumatised by the Great War, probably more than Germany and certainly more than Britain (which, per capita, had suffered half France's casualties). Perhaps 1.5 million French people had died in the war and, of the six million surviving combatants, about 50% suffered some form of continuing disability. It would have been difficult to find an extended family that had not experienced a war death. The psychological damage was all-pervading. "Spanish flu", the viral pandemic that spread at the close of the Great War and took 250,000 French lives, simply added to the sense of uncertainty.

— Je suis le Président de la République...
— T'es pas tout?

Edouard Herriot
L'Humanité, 25 May 1920

The conservative Bloc's leaders were three: the impossibly aggressive George Clemenceau, still bathing in the glory of leading the nation to victory and signing the Treaty of Versailles; the austere, elegant and aloof Raymond Poincaré; and the ever-present Aristide Briand, who was "never trusted, always admired, rarely loved".[29]. They traded on the fear of Bolshevism, the Russian revolution having taken place just two years earlier than the 1919 election, and their nationalist slogan: "Germany will pay!". The three worked together against the Left, but they were not friends.

Clemenceau had expected to be elected President in 1920. Briand denied it to him, backing Paul Deschanel and harnessing Catholic supporters against the avidly anti-clerical war hero. Clemenceau retired in a sulk. Public debt, both domestic and that owed to the USA, was immense and put a heavy hand on the economy; the north east, where the country's most advanced industries and agriculture had been located, was still to recover from its occupation and destruction. As Prime Minister, Poincaré may have been the bankers' favourite, but he had gone too far when, in 1923, with Germany in arrears on its reparation payments, he invaded and took control of the Ruhr.

The Cartel des Gauches policies had resonated with the public in 1924, as did Herriot himself and Socialist leader Léon Blum. Herriot and his allies campaigned: "for peace" (in contrast to the posture of "Poincaré-la-guerre"); "for the ordinary people"; and, "against the power of money". President Deschanel had been quickly embarrassed into resignation (see below) and his replacement, Alexandre Millerand, had campaigned for the Bloc National. Once victorious, Herriot and his majority in the National Assembly simply wouldn't work with Millerand, so he had to resign too, well short of his seven-year term. Gaston Doumergue was a happy new choice for President, and he served out his full seven years from 1924 to 1931.

Herriot and his supporters in the National Assembly soon:

- gave amnesty to wartime pacifists;
- allowed the civil service to unionize, importantly including the teachers;
- recognized the Soviet Union;
- reinstated striking railway workers who had been sacked; and
- with a more conciliatory attitude towards Germany, agreed to a new reparations plan, the "Dawes Plan", which also terminated the French occupation of the Ruhr.

Despite the obvious differences on domestic public policy, almost all parties – from socialists on the Left to nutters on the far Right – were agreed that the French Empire was a good thing: it brought civilisation – *la mission civilisatrice* to the natives. Algeria was a départment of France, fully integrated into the nation since 1848, and therefore technically not part of the Empire. But the Empire was extensive: it included the French colonies of Indochina, concessions in China (not least the

French Concession in Shanghai), protectorates in Tunisia and Morocco, the colony of Madagascar, mandates over Syria and Lebanon, colonial entities throughout much of Central and West Africa and colonies in the Pacific and the West Indies.

France's Third Republic does not get good press. In its seventy-year history, from 1870 to 1940, it had more than one hundred separate administrations or governments. Governments were formed in the National Assembly, France's lower house, where there were upwards of 600 deputies; they enjoyed four-year terms. Counter balancing the National Assembly was an upper house Senate of 300 senators, each elected indirectly for nine year terms by local governments and other ex-officio electors; in effect, the Senate was a conservative brake on the National Assembly. Women were not enfranchised; even among progressives support for female suffrage was not universal, because many believed they would be under the thumb of priests and the Church. (Women had to wait until 1944, when General de Gaulle's brief first government enfranchised them.) A joint sitting of the two houses elected the President.

It is standard belief that the constant changes of government in the Third Republic made for instability. Yet the opposite can be argued. Governments had short lives, to be sure, but they drew from the same cast of characters; and the civil service was talented, remained in place with the changes of government, and was committed to the common good. This provided a sort of stability. That the Third Republic was the longest-lived of all French governance regimes since 1789 speaks for itself. Only Hitler's War terminated it.

Some of the Third Republic's Presidents were colourful. The most famous, in a way, was Félix Faure. President from 1895 to 1899, he died from a heart attack aged fifty-eight. He died "on the job", as they say, in the arms of 30-year-old Marguerite Steinheil who, according to reliable reports, had been fellating him. The circumstances provided much material for cartoonists and political opponents; for example, French slang for oral sex is "pomper" and the word went around that "[Faure] voulait être César, il ne fut que Pompée." (He wanted to be Caesar but ended up as Pompey.)

Faure's demise provided some relief, if that is the correct word, from the Dreyfus Affair. Simply put, in the early 1890s, military secrets were leaking from the French General Staff to the German Embassy in Paris. Alfred Dreyfus was one of the few Jews on the General Staff, and he was set up. Documents were forged, the true spy was protected and, in 1894, Dreyfus was found guilty of the leaks, stripped of his rank and sent off in ignominy to Devil's Island in French Guinea. It took twelve years for the Dreyfus family to prove his innocence, for Dreyfus to be completely exonerated and for him to be reinstated in a position in the General Staff – albeit a broken man.

The Dreyfus Affair became much more than the fight to exonerate an innocent man. It became a metaphor for the divisions in French society. Some "Dreyfusards" – those who supported Dreyfus – found in the campaign an opportunity to attack many aspects of the roles conservative forces continued to play in the Republic. For the anti-Dreyfusards – who included many in the Church, some notable anti-Semites, monarchists and elements of the Army – the Dreyfusards were unpatriotic, and it was more important to defend the honour and integrity of the Army and the glory of France than to seek out the truth of the matter.

For decades the Affair continued to poison public affairs. Prominent Dreyfusards, like Clemenceau, found that ultra-conservatives never forgot any historic support for Dreyfus. It probably made the difference between Clemenceau's success and (ultimate) failure when he sought the Presidency in 1920.

The victor in that contest, Paul Deschanel, served only eight months as President, from 17 January 1920 to 21 September 1920. In March, when a speech in Nice was well received with copious applause, Deschanel was so flushed with joy that he repeated it, word for word; then, when schoolgirls presented him with flowers, he threw the flowers back, one by one. The British Ambassador is said to have been received by Deschanel with the President clothed in his sash of office, but otherwise naked. On the evening of 23/24 May, when travelling on the train at Montargis near Orléans, he fell out of the Presidential carriage's window.

Bleeding and bruised, barefoot and dressed in smart pyjamas, his rescuers first thought they were dealing with a madman – "I am the President of France" – albeit that they quickly deduced that he was a gentleman, because he had clean feet. (Deschanel's fall from the Presidential train was not unique. The otherwise very sober Gaston Doumergue repeated the feat in 1926 when, travelling to Germany on the Orient Express, he opened an external door and fell from the train. When he identified himself as the President to a signalman, the incredulous worker replied: "And I am Napoleon Bonaparte.") And finally, on 10 September 1920, President Deschanel adjourned a cabinet meeting at the Château de Rambouillet and walked into the lake fully clothed, where he disrobed and gambolled naked. He resigned a week later.

By 1924, the many parties in the National Assembly had formed into two identifiable groups: the conservative Bloc National and the progressive, but certainly not radical, Cartel des Gauches. True, they regularly changed leadership and established new alliances and factions within their two groups; by and large, though, politicians fell into one or the other. Aristide Briand was Prime Minister ten times and Poincaré five. The Bloc National were hard on Germany, seeking revenge. Their supporters came from the Church, from established elements such as the armed forces, bankers and big business. The Cartel de Gauches was softer on Germany, albeit keenly patriotic, had the support of small business and professionals such as teachers – and they were implacably anti-clerical. One result of this alignment was the marginalisation of anti-democratic elements from the Left (such as communists) and the Right (royalists).

L'Humanité, 1 August 1914
Jaurès's catafalque at the Panthéon, 1924

Herriot and his Radical-Socialist Party were keen to lock in support from their Socialist supporters. The tenth anniversary of Jean Jaurès' assassination provided the perfect opportunity.

Jean Jaurès is one of the iconic heroes of the French Left. An anti-militarist and a prominent Dreyfusard, he had co-founded the socialist newspaper *L'Humanité* in 1904, and had led the Socialist Party or elements of it from 1902. He was a provincial, coming from a middle-class family in the south western city of Castres. He was a brilliant student, topping the entrance exam for the ENS. After graduation he returned to his native south west, lecturing at the University of Toulouse before entering politics. Born in 1859, he was physically unprepossessing. By the early 1900s Jaurès was a stocky, untidy man in a frock coat – bowler-hatted, be-suited and bearded – with a fervent following among the Left. He was a compelling orator and intellectuals and workers alike fell for his captivating erudition, charisma and passion.

Jean Jaurès had been dining at a Paris café on 31 July 1914 when a right-wing political zealot shot him dead. In the month following the earlier assassination of Franz Ferdinand in late June, Jaurès had been campaigning against any form of retaliation on the part of the Triple Entente (Russia, France and Britain) – reaching out to fellow socialists and pacifists in Germany and Belgium, and arguing for negotiation and reconciliation rather than war. It seems an entirely sensible proposition now but it was anathema to the conservative Right. (Poincaré, for example, had received considerable financial support from Russia prior to and during the 1914 election – which had taken place in April and May and Russia was very keen indeed to show support for their co-religionists and fellow Slavs in Serbia.)

In the wake of the Great War and the Russian Revolution, the French Socialists split. At an historic meeting in Tours in December 1920, two-thirds of the members chose to follow the Bolshevik line led by Moscow; they soon styled themselves Communists. The minority followed Léon Blum – he argued that the revolutionary ideas and practices of the French party were "incompatible" with Bolshevism – and came to be known as Socialists. As a result of the vote, the Communists took control of the party newspaper, *L'Humanité*. Over the next few years, the Communists lost members and support, however, and the Socialists prospered. The relations between the two arms of "socialism" were bitter and uncooperative. Both claimed Jaurès as their own, but the Socialists seemed to have the greater claim.

So, exactly ten years on from the assassination of Jaurès, on 31 July 1924, the new government resolved to acknowledge his importance: he was to be "pantheonised", that is, interred in the Panthéon. A grand event was planned. On 22 November, Jaurès was exhumed from his grave in Albi. A large crowd of local and national dignitaries saw the coffin off by the Paris train; miners from Carmaux travelled with it. (Jaurès had made his name by supporting the Carmaux miners in 1892.) On arrival at the Gare d'Orsay, the hero's remains were transferred to the Palais-Bourbon, the seat of the National Assembly that Jaurès had graced with such distinction, which itself was festooned in black and purple. There his body lay in state.

The next day a grand procession took Jaurès' huge hearse to the Panthéon on a march along the boulevards St Germain and St Michel. The hearse was truly dramatic: a strange rectilinear shape, it had the dimensions of a small battleship; bowls of incense burned on its four corners, and it was shrouded in red and gold.

Seventy-two Carmaux miners carried the hearse along the route, a large but necessary contingent such was the size of the bier; in celebration of their heritage and Jaurès' famous support, the miners wore their work clothes and carried pick axes. The leaders of the Socialist Left followed behind them. Crowds cheered and threw flowers. At the Panthéon, under a huge red and gold portière, Blum gave a eulogy, as did Herriot. The accompanying music was inspiring and theatrical. It was all the government could have hoped for.

Even so, the Communists tried to spoil it all. *L'Humanité* carried front page articles arguing that the event was a bourgeois disgrace, "a second assassination". (To this day the newspaper proclaims "Fondateur: Jean Jaurès" on its masthead.) The Communists organised an alternative march. *L'Humanité* published military-style maps on that front page, showing assembly points for the alternative march, and their march did attract the Communist faithful. The neo-fascist Action Française also organized an event in protest to the pantheonisation itself, and it was a fizzer. Then the people spoke over the next few days, with thousands coming to the Panthéon to pay their respects, before Jaurès' final re-internment.

The pantheonisation of Jean Jaurès had two results. It strengthened the cooperation among the Cartel des Gauches partners, and it amplified the rupture between the Communists and Socialists.

There was almost universal support for the Third Republic's two great legacies: free secular education and *Laïcité* – "secularity", the concept and implementation of the separation of church and state. From the 1880s, free secular education had been available – indeed it was compulsory – for all children, boys and girls, from ages six to twelve.

And from its inception, the separation of church and state had been a key tenet of the Third Republic. Removing the Catholic Church from education was fundamental to this effort. Over time:

- divorce became a civil matter;
- a civil ceremony was required for a marriage to be recognised;
- work on Sunday was permitted;
- prayers were abolished at the opening of Parliament;
- religious references were removed from judicial oaths;
- seminarians became subject to conscription;
- state schools were secularised, in that priests were no longer teachers; and
- religious instruction was banned in public schools.

The breakthrough in the separation of church and state and the insti-tutionalisation of the concept of Laïcité had come with the Combes Laws of 1905. These laws guaranteed religious freedoms but withdrew all government funding of religion, nationalised all churches and other religious buildings, made religious buildings open to the public, and pro-hibited religious signs on public buildings. In summary, the reforms pro-tected religious observance while strictly excluding religion and religious expression from state institutions; rather than discouraging religion, the reforms allowed all faiths to prosper under the watchful eye of an agnos-tic motherland.

With the elimination of clerical influence in schools, teachers started to come from modest social origins, and they were strong supporters of the republican ideal: they drummed into their charges progressive thought, respect for science, freethinking and nationalism. Over time, *les instituteurs*, the teachers, became a powerful force in French politics, even more so once they were allowed to establish their trade union in 1924: the Syndicat National des Instituteurs. Les instituteurs, whether Socialists or Communists, and they were typically one or the other, were keen supporters of Edouard Herriot and his winning Cartel des Gauches in the 1924 elections.

To this day, French leaders promote and protect the separation of the sacred from the secular. Thus, when in 2003, almost one hundred years after the Combes Laws, President Jacques Chirac spoke against "ostentatious displays of religiosity" in schools and other public buildings – crucifixes, skullcaps, head scarfs and veils were his targets – Chirac was reinforcing a fundamental tenet of the French Republic. So too, in 2020, when Islamic fundamentalists were found to be opting out of public edu-cation in favour of home-schooling, President Macron promoted new laws to address this "Islamic separatism". In doing so, Macron argued that "secularism is the cement of a united France" – because Laïcité, the great reform of the Third Republic, is an enduring gift to the nation.

LE BOEUF ET AL

Fashion house Hermès has been located on the same corner of rue du Faubourg St Honoré since the 1880s. By the 1920s, Hermès Frères still advertised themselves as simple *selliers* (saddlers); they were makers of high-end saddles, to be sure, but also of golf bags and a wide range of fancy leather goods.

Next to Hermès, there is a small one-way street, rue Boissy-d'Anglas, which works its way up towards the Madeleine. In 1924, if you walked just one hundred metres up that street to number 28, you would be outside the new unofficial headquarters of the Parisian avant-garde – Le Boeuf sur le Toit.

Everyone who counted, but everyone, went there. It was a bar, a restaurant and the venue for new music. Chic and fashionable, there has never been anything like it before or since.

In 1920, Louis Moysès had been running a small piano bar, La Gaya, at 17 rue Duphot. Jean Cocteau and his entourage were occasional customers; they included Darius Milhaud and other members of Les Six. The piano player, Jean Wiéner, did not appeal to many of La Gaya's clientele – but Cocteau and his friends liked his music. An admirer of Satie and a friend of Milhaud's since their time together at the Conservatoire, Wiéner was into jazz. He was inventive and open to new music. One such tune was Milhaud's *Le Boeuf sur le Toit*, a Brazilian-influenced ditty that was the centrepiece of a successful pantomime/tango-ballet that Milhaud and Cocteau had recently created. (The theatrical piece was the development of a story wherein a baby calf was temporarily housed on a roof top, but as it grew the roof became its permanent home because, when it became a fully-grown ox, it could not be removed.)

Moysès was a young, demobbed soldier – fair-haired, charming and well-liked – but the business was not going well, and he attributed this to Wiéner's musical tastes. When Moysès confided to Cocteau that he thought he should move Wiéner on, Cocteau demurred: "Keep your pianist and send your customers away."[30] This he did, and young artists quickly adopted La Gaya as their own.

With his newfound success, Louis Moysès needed more room and, in late 1921, he moved about four minutes' walk away, to 28 Boissy-d'Anglas; it had previously been a quiet local restaurant, the Taverne Anglaise. You couldn't miss it. His new venue was a double-fronted shop, boldly marked – LE BOEUF SUR LE TOIT – in capital letters above two of the three windows, with a smaller "Restaurant" sign under the porte-cochère.

Licensed for fifty, it had a capacity of one hundred. To one side was a club-like bar and, on the other, the restaurant. They were separated by a series of narrow sparkling black pillars and somewhere in between was a tiny dance floor. It was a classy, inviting set-up.

Every night was a party for the beau monde. And everyone dressed up, if they could. Dinner jackets were expected for men, the latest couture – Chanel, Lanvin, Vionnet – for women. It attracted high society and high bohemia, partly, no doubt, via Moysès' ample extension of credit to those in need. For Cocteau, who could rightly claim some paternity, Le Boeuf was "not a bar at all, but a kind of a club, the meeting place of all the best people in Paris, from all spheres of life – the prettiest women, poets, musicians, businessmen, publishers – everybody met everybody at the Boeuf."[31] According to Jean Hugo, Le Boeuf was "the crossroads of destinies, the cradle of love affairs, the hearth of discords, [and] the navel of Paris."[32] And the beautiful young people who were attracted to Le Boeuf, men and women, did not always come free.

A new enterprise does not survive unless it delivers what it promises and what its prospective clientele expects. The restaurant of Le Boeuf looked very spic with white cloths on black tables. Its handwritten menu was ambitious: caviar, soups, truffled eggs, fish, fowl, beef and lamb – and, apparently, notably good Alsatian dishes. Late night suppers included sandwiches of all sorts, terrines and foie gras. Champagne was the default beverage.

A night at Le Boeuf sur le Toit

But the bar was the centre of the show. It was there that music prevailed. Wiéner's piano stood at one side. The house band was led by black American saxophonist Vance Lowry. By 1924, Clément Doucet, a fat Walloon pianist, joined up too; with his left hand he would play stride piano while he drank beer with the other. His speciality was a parody of (or tribute to) Chopin that he called his "Chopianata". Wiéner and Doucet "played like angels and looked like Mutt and Jeff."[33] Together, and separately, they played Gershwin and Cole Porter, "Aint She Sweet", Bach, Satie, Strauss, "Yes, we have no bananas", jazz tunes of all sorts and Mozart. Customers quaffed fashionable Manhattans and Alaskas – and champagne – into the night.

L'Oeil Cacodylate by Francis Picabia et al, 1921

Wiéner once described a scene from his seat at the piano: "At one table…
André Gide, Marc Allegret and a woman. Alongside them, Diaghilev,
Kochno, Picasso and Misia Sert. A bit farther on, Mistinguett, Volterra
and Maurice Chevalier. Against the wall, Erik Satie and René Clair and
his wife. Then I saw Picabia arguing with Paul Poiret and Tristan Tzara.
Cocteau and Radiguet were saying hello at every table. Fernand Léger

got up and asked me to play 'St Louis Blues' and, in passing, Moysès, the owner, told me that Artur Rubinstein would be in after his concert."[34]

Over in the bar area, the bartender always stood out in his crisp white jacket. Hanging from the ceiling, randomly placed, was a series of translucent multi-coloured "lanterns"; among the lanterns, to one side, was a small "Le Boeuf sur le Toit" sign designed by Jean Hugo. A classic long bar commanded the back wall, with wines, glasses and bottles of every known spirit and digestif populating the wall itself. Apart from the ubiquitous champagne, the house speciality was a potent cocktail of half gin, one quarter plum liqueur (Trimbach being the recommended brand) and one quarter curaçao (Cointreau preferred). There were a couple of stools at the bar, and small white-clothed tables, with chairs, in front of that. Over on one wall was the now-famous Dada painting *L'Oeil cacodylic* – a concoction started by Picabia, which had been enhanced and completed by graffiti, signatures and aphorisms from his artist friends. (The painting is now in the Centre Pompidou collection.) The other walls housed photographs by Man Ray, paintings lent by Picasso and various artworks by regulars. [35]

Cocteau (with Radiguet) was a regular. He held court almost every night. Late at night Cocteau would play drums with Lowry's band – and castanets, wine glasses and klaxon horn. Behaviour became more exuberant as the night wore on; it was not unknown to observe a lady allowing a paid admirer to bury his face under her skirts. Le Boeuf had become a true mecca of Parisian nightlife. Proust even paid a visit in his last year; a late-night altercation with a young hearty resulted in an exchange of addresses, but the prospective duel was mercifully called off the next morning, with profuse apologies, when the young man worked out that he was dealing with the legendary Proust.

Moysès moved Le Boeuf from Boissy-d'Anglas in 1928, and it has moved again several times since. The original site is now a smart ophthalmologist and spectacle store.

At the foot of Montmartre, the Moulin Rouge's business flourished with its near-naked romps, light snacks and expensive champagne. It and the other great cabaret, the Folies Bergère, had a responsibility to maintain the nightlife that had made Paris famous. Meanwhile, up on the Butte Montmartre – the high flat hill to the north of the city dominated by the Sacré-Coeur – lived artists of all sorts, notably black musicians. By the 1920s, jazz was the go in the small "boîtes" that employed these artists – together with the hostesses essential to what the Japanese euphemistically call the "water trade".

When Langston Hughes arrived in Paris on 23 February 1924, he was told that "most of the American coloured people" lived in Montmartre.[36] So he walked there. He was looking for a place to stay, and to work. He saw some fellow black Americans. "Well, what instrument do you play?" they asked. None. When pressed, they asked if he tap-danced "or what?". In many ways, it was Harlem in Paris. As it transpired, Hughes was picked up by a girl, a professional Russian dancer, and she soon found work at Zelli's.

Zelli's was the top nightclub in "Montmartre" which, as noted earlier, included at the time both the Butte Montmartre and the area south of Place Pigalle that would today be called Pigalle. The proprietor was Joe Zelli – an Italian by birth, French by persuasion and American by adoption. He was now thirty-five. As a teenager he had worked in New York, reportedly establishing a bar in the headwaiter's name because licences were not granted to fifteen-year-olds. And he was an Italian artilleryman during the Great War. Soon after, he worked out how to get post-midnight entertainment licences in Paris and, in 1922, he established Zelli's at 16 bis rue Fontaine.

Joe Zelli was a terrific host – a warm personality, he greeted everyone with a smile and a handshake. He remembered names. The nightclub was on two floors. You entered via a balcony floor that overlooked a cavernous dance floor; here, on the balcony floor, was an American bar and a series of comfortable cubicles – dubbed the "royal boxes". Below was the bandstand and dance floor, and many lesser tables set amongst atmospheric pillars and mirrors. Langston Hughes' friend worked as a "danseuse" – a good looking girl who would sit at a table with the patrons, dance with them if that was desired and, most importantly, induce them to drink champagne or whatever. A danseuse would receive a commission on every bottle.

Zelli's with Joe Zelli at centre

Zelli pushed the envelope and made a fortune. Photographs of his legitimate entertainers filled a street window half a block from the venue. A huge neon sign attracted customers to it, where they would also find photos of topless danseuses and Zelli's nearby address.[37] His danseuses were famous: "...everyone [was] affectionate, hungry, thirsty and broke...". The contemporary *Pleasure Guide to Paris*, which advised men not to bring one's wife – unless she was "very resolute or very lenient"– promised "all sorts of attractions", and "many pretty women". Zelli's opened late, about midnight, and was regularly raided.

Apart from the hostesses and gigolos, and there were both, Zelli's had top class entertainment. Indeed, Zelli induced the incomparable "Hutch" to move to Europe and take up a residency at Zelli's in December 1924.

Born in the West Indian island of Grenada, Leslie Hutchison was just twenty-four. He had already made a name as a musician and a singer in New York, and he would go on to capture the stages of London and Paris. Endowed with a rich baritone, handsome and charming, he is alleged to have been endowed with a very large penis. Lovers apparently included Lady Mountbatten, Merle Oberon, Cole Porter and Ivor Novello. He married just once but, over a forty-year period, fathered eight children by seven different women.

Less louche and more legitimate than Zelli's was Le Grand Duc. Langston Hughes had won a job there as a kitchen hand in early 1924. Two minutes away from Zelli's, around the corner at 52 rue Pigalle, Le Grand Duc was owned by a French aristocrat of mixed reputation, Georges Jamerson. The manager was Eugene Bullard and the star was chanteuse, Florence Embry. It was small and intimate and exciting.

Gene Bullard was twenty-nine. He had already enjoyed a most extraordinary life. His father was a black man from Martinique and his mother a Creek Indian. As a boy of perhaps fifteen he stowed away to Scotland; there he learnt to box, fought, and learned to play the drums. By late 1914 he had signed up as a "poilu" in the French army, and saw service in the Somme and at Verdun; wounded, he studied to be a pilot, and then made twenty combat missions for the Lafayette Flying Corps. Demobbed, Bullard worked as a jazz drummer at Zelli's for four years where he also managed the club's musicians. Then he had a couple of further boxing bouts – and he was a good boxer – before taking up the manager's position at Le Grand Duc.

Florence Embry was a princess. "She was very pretty and brown, and could wear the gowns of the great Paris couturiers as few other women could."[38] By 1924, Florence was thirty-two. Married to the pianist Palmer Jones, who was employed elsewhere, she was loved by her work colleagues, but adopted a severely aloof air for Le Grand Duc's patrons. She starved them of songs, perhaps only a couple an hour, and would only really open up if and when her husband arrived at the club after his own work. Customers were famous people and almost all were white: "It was the first time I had ever seen a coloured person deliberately and openly snubbing white people", wrote Langston Hughes, "so it always amused me no end to watch Florence move away from a table of money-spending Americans, who wanted nothing in the world so much as to have her sit down with them."[39]

Florence fell out with Bullard and moved down the road. Le Grand Duc had a very good chef who dished up established American favourites – chicken Maryland, Boston baked beans, corn fritters and corn bread and the like – but this could not hold the patrons. They moved with Florence. The management tried tap dancers and transvestites, until they concluded that they needed a new singer. This is where Bricktop came in.

Ada "Bricktop" Smith was thirty. She had been born poor, dirt poor, in Virginia, and finished high school in Chicago, before her mother let her out on the road. She sang in a wistful way, danced a little and was warm and liked. Light skinned, short and a bit plump, she had freckles and red-gold hair – hence the nickname by which everyone knew her, "Bricktop"; hers was a pale and unspoilt beauty. She described herself as "one hundred per cent American Negro with an Irish temper." (The freckles may have derived from a long-forgotten Celtic forbear, and few found her temperament anything but temperate.) By the time Le Grand Duc put out feelers, Bricktop was happily working in Harlem at the new but already successful Connie's Inn. On a whim, she accepted the French overture. She arrived at Le Havre on 11 May 1924, to be greeted by a "tall, handsome American Negro", Gene Bullard.

It was not a happy arrival. Bricktop had lost her money. And when she was taken to the nightclub no-one was there except the staff, the danseuses and the band. No customers. And it was tiny. Bricktop had been used to a twelve-piece big band at Connie's, lots of lights, and a big crowd. Le Grand Duc could only manage a three-piece ensemble, the bar was perhaps eight foot long, there were few tables and the dance floor might accommodate a dozen couples. The night wore on and still no one arrived. Bricktop was reduced to tears.[40]

Bricktop by Man Ray, 1928

Langston Hughes and the chef tried to jolly her up: "Life's a bitch, but you can beat it if you try." She said she would, and she did.

Bricktop buckled down. The Charleston was new to Europe but Bricktop knew the dance steps and she helped people out. She was pleasant. Human. She sang well, in a light attractive voice, and the word got around that Le Grand Duc was fun. And Bricktop started to take on the role of hostess as well as performer. The menu was soon enhanced by dishes she knew from the Harlem clubs: corned-beef hash, a club sandwich, creamed chicken and so on. Soon she was teaching Cole Porter the

Charleston and doing private parties for him. (Scott Fitzgerald said "my greatest claim to fame is that I discovered Bricktop before Cole Porter".)

Langston Hughes by Winold Rein, 1925

Bricktop had grace. She was kind and considerate, and she had good business skills. Within a year or so, and for the next fifteen years, this small, pleasantly plump woman was the toast of the town:

> *"When…I arrived there the place was crowded. One drunken Frenchman wanted to get away without paying his bill. At another*

table a French actress in her cups was giving her boyfriend hell and throwing champagne in his face. In the back room several Negroes were having an argument. Brick sat at the cashier's desk keeping things in order. With a wisecrack she halted the actress in her temper, cajolingly made the Frenchman pay his bill, and while she was adding up accounts, calling out to the orchestra to play this or that requested number…She began to sing "Love for Sale", while still adding up accounts. Halfway through the song there was a commotion in the back room where the argument was taking place, which meant that the coloured boys had now come to blows. Brick skipped down from her stool, glided across the room, still singing. She jerked aside a curtain and stopped singing long enough to say, "Hey you guys, get out in the street if you want to fight. This ain't that kind of joint!" Then she continued the song, having [missed] but two phrases, and was at her desk again adding accounts."[41]

The arrival of Bricktop in Paris was not the only new show in 1924. Over in the backwoods of the 15th arrondissement, a putative politician from Martinique had been organising a run for the May 1924 French elections. Jean Rézard de Wolves was eligible to stand for an Antilles seat in the French Parliament. In the 19th century, 33 rue Blomet had been a farmhouse; by 1924 it was a working class bar/tabac owned by an Auvergnat, Alexandre Jouve, and he was happy to let out the back room to de Wolves. There de Wolves set up his campaign headquarters. After his Saturday night political gatherings, de Wolves organised dance parties for the Martiniquais and Guadeloupians who he hoped might vote for him. Many worked in the Renault and Citroën factories nearby. They loved the beguine, the rhumba-like foxtrot of the Antilles that de Wolves featured on his piano.

De Wolves was a better piano player than politician. He was not successful in his political ambitions, but the parties were a success. His Caribbean melodies worked. De Wolves pumped out the beguine and, enhanced with accordion and cabrette, his parties soon attracted many new expatriates, particularly black francophones. Colonial soldiers from the nearby École Militaire joined them, as did some of the many Spaniards and Poles who had come to Paris seeking work. The bar was a little far away from the heart of Montparnasse for the mainstream Montparnos – but it was exciting, and the word was getting around. Saturday night parties stretched to Saturday and Sunday. Wild black Senegalese soldiers added spice. North African workers from a nearby residential block joined in. Soon, the Bal Nègre was born. It attracted everyone from Nancy Cunard to the Prince of Wales. Jean Rézard de Wolves gave up his political ambitions, and stuck to the beguine. In due course, every visitor to Paris wanted to spend at least a night at the Bal Blomet or Bal Nègre – either name would work – and every taxi driver knew where to go.

Le Bal de la rue Blomet by Georges Goursat ("Sem"), 1928

For as far back as anyone could remember, the most elaborate, luxurious and prestigious brothel in Paris had been Le Chabanais. In 1924, it faced a rival.

Napoléon the Great had established the rules in 1804. *Maisons de tolérance* or *maisons closes* were authorised, prostitutes were required to be registered and have regular health inspections, and the brothels had to be run by women. (This last requirement was designed to eliminate pimps.) Most madams were ex-prostitutes. It worked satisfactorily for nearly one hundred and fifty years.

With men away from their wives or away from home for the first time, it was natural that demand peaked during the Great War, when Paris supported perhaps forty major brothels (plus 5,000 licensed street-walkers). By 1924, the number of brothels was probably about thirty.

Le Chabanais was located in a six-story building at 12 rue Chabanais, just off the avenue de l'Opéra. The lobby was a generous and theatrical stone cave – proclaiming, in English, "Welcome to the Chabanais. The House of All Nations." (English seems to have been the *lingua franca* of the trade.)

The clientele included the top level of French society. Indeed, it was always accepted that members of the Jockey Club de Paris had helped finance setting up the enterprise back in the 1870s, and that some continued as silent partners. For English milords Le Chabanais was an essential stop on their Grand Tour. There were always thirty to forty "ladies" on duty, together with a number of sous-madams who orchestrated the transactions.

Rooms were extraordinarily luxurious. There was a Moorish suite designed to evoke the eroticism of Andalusian Spain, an Indian suite introduced the Kama Sutra, the Louis XVI room glistered with mirrors and chandeliers, a Japanese suite apparently won a design prize at the 1900 Paris World Fair – one wonders what category it entered and what the display arrangements might have been – a "Pompeii" room that celebrated the thrills of the ancient world, and so on. Everyone of consequence knew of Le Chabonais and, even if they did not wish to participate in its offerings, wanted to inspect the premises; the diaries of visiting heads of state often used the euphemistic entry "Visit to President of the Senate." A double elevator was specially configured to give privacy to those coming and going.

Its most celebrated client was Edward, Prince of Wales – the future Edward VII. He owned an apartment at 39 avenue de l'Opéra – now the Hotel Edouard VII – which was just a five minute walk from Le Chabonais. (Not that someone of his rank and girth would have walked.) The importance the proprietors and Edward both attached to the place can be gleaned from the fact that he had special furniture built for his needs: both an exotic upholstered *chaise de volupté* with bespoke stirrups and handles that apparently enabled the very heavy prince to enjoy three-somes at ease, and a huge gilded copper bathtub in the shape of a sphinx that he would fill with champagne and his chosen courtesan.

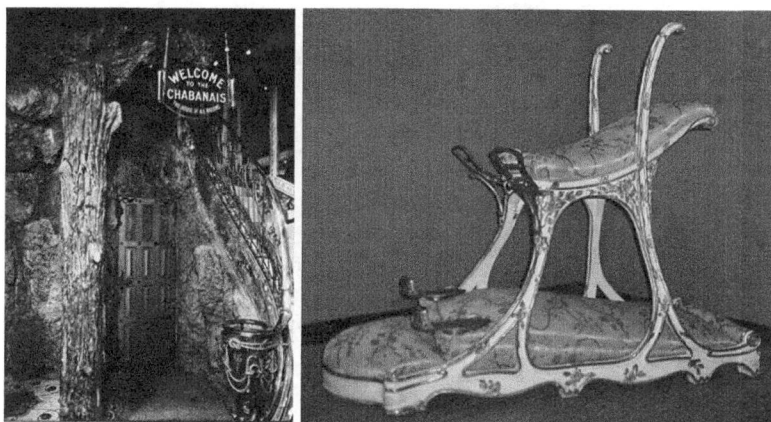

Le Chabanais and Edward VII's *chaise de volupté*

The major competitor to Le Chabanais was Toulouse-Lautrec's old fa-vourite, La Fleur Blanche. It had been at 6 rue des Moulins since the Second Empire, and its success probably encouraged the many lesser establishments to locate themselves on that street. In the 1890s, Lautrec essentially moved his atelier to La Fleur. He was known to the whores as the "coffee pot" because he was small and, such was his ardour, he would keep them up all night. A luxurious house, La Fleur was themed – again, a Moorish chamber was a feature. Its top room was the "ducal" suite which featured a lavishly carved mahogany bed. Lautrec's "Salon de la rue des Moulins" of 1894 preserves the ambiance forever.

Aux Belles Poules ("Beautiful Chicks"), in the second arrondissement, was an innovator. Apart from the basics, Aux Belles Poules put on small erotic shows – tableaux vivants – where, among other excitements, couples were welcome to witness the ever-popular and skilful vulva coin harvest whereby the girls could earn an extra coin (or many) from the clientele. The house produced its own currency, redeemable for personal services; its address – 32 rue Blondel – was on one side of the coin and a cute chicken motif on the other.

It was an attractive set-up with brightly-coloured tiles – faiences – which, together with the staircase and hallway are now protected by law. Down the road at 16 rue Blondel was the Brasserie du Moulin. It had a large and dramatic Art Nouveau floral façade; all gone, it is now a Vietnamese restaurant.

No one suggested that Le Chabanais, as top dog, was losing its allure or lowering its standards. Business must have been good at this high end of the market, however, because in 1924, Le Chabanais was faced with a formidable new competitor. The new bordello, located at 122 rue de Provence, was known simply as *One-Two-Two*. In English. (Again, the *lingua franca*.)

This former townhouse of Prince Joachim Murat was a handsome three-story building just north of the boulevard Haussmann near Galeries Lafayette. It would later be extended to seven stories. (Allegedly, the higher a client went up the building the more fetishistic the décor and services became.) Fernande Jamet, known as Doriane, and her husband Marcel were behind the new enterprise. She was a former Le Chabanais favourite. What they created at *One-Two-Two* was something special – twenty-two rooms that would take you on a trip around the world: their historical and geographical allusions topped Le Chabanais' efforts for exotica, luxury and fetish. *One-Two-Two* had enhanced Indian, Moorish, Egyptian, African and Asian rooms – plus igloos and straw barns. The Orient Express room reproduced the cabins of the famous train; it shook and bounced, had a railway soundtrack and, on request, the occupants could have a conductor interrupt the coitus. The Pirate Room reproduced the movement of a vessel at sea; a tempest would engulf the room and, since this is what they had chosen, the occupants would be drenched with a shower of salt water; further showers were at a client's discretion.

In the kitchen of Le Boeuf à la Ficelle

The Jamets were inventive and considerate. There was a refectory for the forty to sixty girls usually working at any one time. On Thursdays, wounded soldiers – "broken faces" – would be granted a visit, gratis. And there was an adjacent restaurant, a very good restaurant by all reports, Le Boeuf à la Ficelle; the female servers there wore only aprons and high heels and, when the diners plates were cleaned, the plates revealed erotic scenes from around the world. Clients were free to go next door, or move off into the night.

The lower classes had their own establishments, often called *maisons abattage* ("slaughterhouses"). Most were pretty sordid affairs: for the client, it was very much take your ticket and take your turn. It cannot have been much fun for the service providers. An exception of sorts was the *Lanterne Verte* in the Goutte d'Or (on the corner of rue de Charles and rue de la Goutte d'Or). It had no rooms.

> "*The Lanterne Verte was a brothel; it was declared as such, and in its large hall, furnished as a café, naked girls served the offer of the house. A shoppen white wine cost a franc and who wanted to fuck with girls or wank one, the waitress was paid forty sous. Everything happened on a bench or a chair of the establishment: there were no rooms. Customers entering were usually surprised at two or three pairs who were just in full swing.*" [42]

Paris catered to all tastes in 1924. Non-conformists had their own establishments. Records of and reports on the exclusive lesbian brothel Les Rieuses ("The Merry Women") are hard to find. Originally housed in a mansion on the Champs-Elysées, it is said that three Parisian actresses hosted events at Les Rieuses once a week. And, although it was an entirely correct set-up, Natalie Barney's Friday salon at 20 rue Jacob was a convenient venue for lesbians to establish romantic liaisons. Gay men had bathhouses, such as the one in the Passage de l'Opéra that features in Louis Aragon's *Le Paysan de Paris* (1926), and there were several brothels that catered to their tastes. Perhaps most notable was the Hotel Marigny, a small townhouse at 11 rue de l'Arcade, near the Madeleine. Proust was a regular.[43] He helped furnish the premises in 1917 with chairs, sofas and carpets from his parents' flat; and he may have helped finance the venture. The proprietor, a seedy character named Albert Le Cuizat, was the inspiration for the tailor Jupien in *In Search of Lost Time*, and it was allegedly at the Hotel Marigny that Proust undertook his research for Baron de Charlus's flagellation.

The usual sadomasochist specialists rounded out the extraordinary array of options available to a visitor or resident. Chez Christiane, housed in an elaborately attractive townhouse at 9 rue de Navarin, was perhaps the pick for S&M. Dominatrices – with handcuffs, whips, chains and the like – were available opposite Chez Christine at the not cheap and extensive (five story) Hotel Amour, which had the reputation of being a happy place for prostitutes to work; an alternative was the Medieval on the second floor of 32 rue de Navarin. (It would seem that rue de Navarin was enjoying a concentration of high-class brothels at the time.) The brothel at 15 rue Sant-Sulpice, opposite the famous Saint-Sulpice church on the Left Bank, was run by a madam named Alys; the mosaic floor there still carries her name. Perhaps the most interesting offerings, however, were just down the road at 36 rue Saint-Sulpice where, in a thin several-story building, Miss Betty's gave dominance on the second floor, and l'Abbey catered to priests on the sixth – somewhat like a department store.

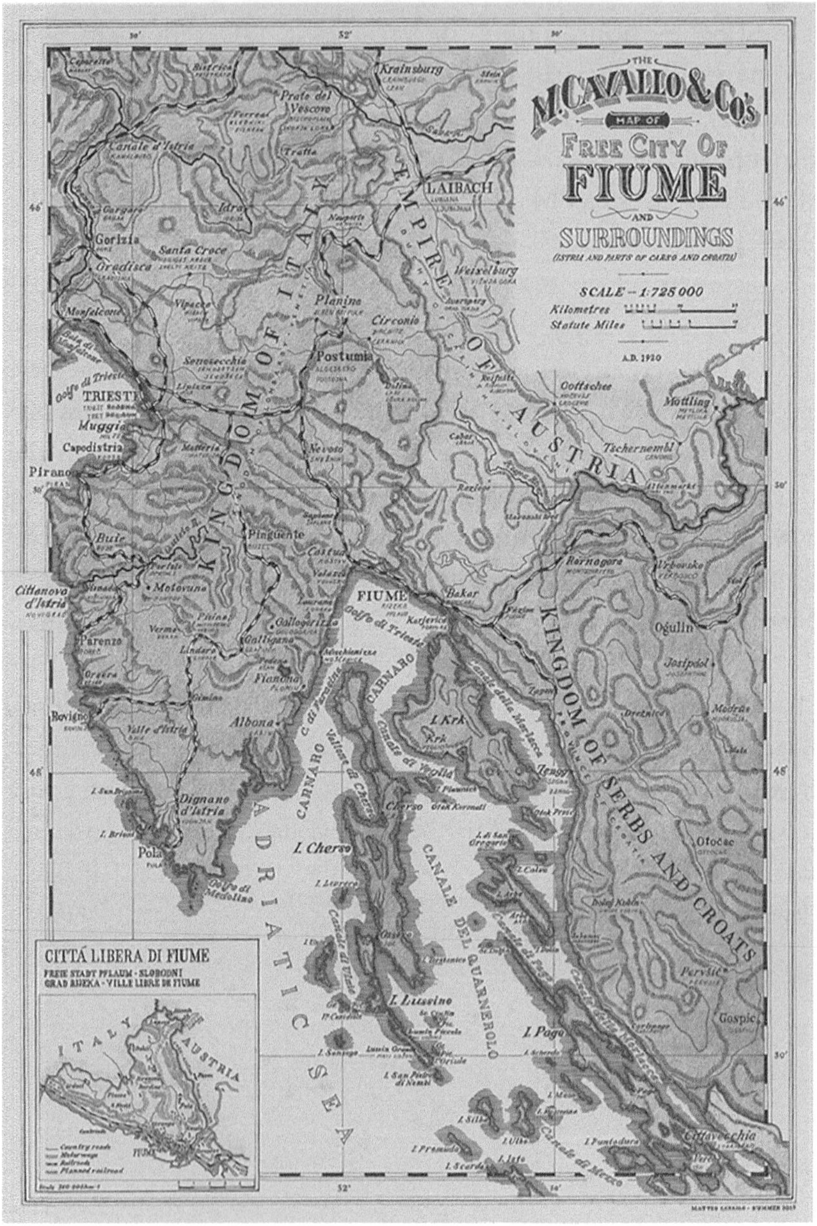
THE
M. CAVALLO & Co's
MAP OF
FREE CITY OF
FIUME
AND
SURROUNDINGS
(ISTRIA AND PARTS OF CARSO AND CROATIA)
SCALE – 1:725 000
Kilometres
Statute Miles
A.D. 1920
KINGDOM OF ITALY
EMPIRE OF AUSTRIA
KINGDOM OF SERBS AND CROATS
ADRIATIC SEA
CANALE DEL QUARNEROLO
CARNARO
FIUME
TRIESTE
Gorizia
Gradisca
Santa Croce
Monfalcone
Muggia
Capodistria
Pirano
Buie
Cittanova d'Istria
Motovun
Parenzo
Rovigno
Pola
Dignano d'Istria
Albona
Fianona
Pinguente
Castua
Postumia
Planina
Circonio
Idria
Laibach
Krainsburg
Weixelburg
Gottschee
Möttling
Tschernembl
Bakar
Ogulin
Josipdol
Otočac
Gospić
I. Krk
I. Cherso
I. Lussino
I. Pago
Cittavecchia
Zengg
CITTÁ LIBERA DI FIUME
FREIE STADT FLAUM · SLOBODNI
GRAD RIJEKA · VILLE LIBRE DE FIUME
ITALY
AUSTRIA

OUTREMER

A tiny city-state on the Adriatic, now largely forgotten by the world at large, was the centre of political attention in 1924.

At last, after five years conflict and controversy, the Fiume Question had been resolved by the Treaty of Rome which was signed on 27 January 1924. A Lilliputian country, the Free State of Fiume – barely 28 square kilometres in size, with fewer than 50,000 citizens – was to be carved up between Italy and Yugoslavia. It had been a member of the League of Nations, and had existed for little more than three years.

This all started during the Great War when both sides were seeking Italy's support. Italy aspired to annex the Austrian Littoral – that stretch of land from Trieste and its hinterland on the upper Adriatic coast, to the port of Fiume and beyond. Italy had long had influence there, many Italians lived there, and the war gave Italy the opportunity to put its foot on this part of the Austrian Empire. In the secret 1915 Treaty of London the Allies promised most of it – but not Fiume – to Italy and, as a result, Italy entered the war on their side. At the Paris Peace Conference, where Woodrow Wilson's principles of self-determination wrestled with the claims of victorious imperialists, Fiume was a flashpoint. In Fiume itself there were apparently 22,488 Italian-speakers and 13,251 speakers of Serbo-Croatian; across the river that ran through the town, however, the suburb of Sušak was estimated to have only 1,500 Italians and 11,000 Yugoslavs. In total, therefore, out of less than 50,000 people, Italian-speakers represented a statistical minority. On this basis, Wilson asked the Italians to put aside their claim to Fiume. His 23 April 1919 "Fiume Appeal" was supported by Lloyd George and Clemenceau, but completely misjudged Italian sentiment. Italian Premier Orlando was moved to tears and he and his delegation left the Conference.

Gabriele d'Annunzio, Italy's most famous contemporary poet, a desiccated sensualist sliding into his late 50s, was among the many Italians who were outraged like the Premier. D'Annunzio had been a war hero, a man of action, and he was going to do something about it. On 12 September 1919, he perched himself in a large open-topped red touring car, and set off from Ronchi, near Trieste, for Fiume. D'Annunzio led a convoy he dubbed the *Impresa di Fiume* ("the Fiume Endeavour"). It comprised just 186 members of the elite Arditi and twenty-six army lorries that the Arditi had commandeered from the local military depot. Defecting Italian soldiers soon joined up, schoolboys too, as the caravan swept down the one hundred kilometres to their destination. By the time the convoy reached Fiume it numbered perhaps as many as 2,000. Fiume was "liberated" without bloodshed, and the Italian-speaking residents welcomed them with enthusiasm: "Viva Fiume Italiana!", was their catchcry.

Gabriele d'Annunzio with his followers, Fiume 1920

The Arditi, "the Daring Ones", were in the vanguard. Created in 1917 and known for their bravery and skill in hand-to-hand combat, the Arditi were Italian shock troops who had made their name in the Great War. They eschewed "cumbersome rifles", typically ambushing the enemy with hand grenades before springing upon them with daggers. They were widely celebrated and had flashy black uniforms with a distinctive skull-and-dagger badge; they carried themselves with an equally flashy swagger and wore their hair ostentatiously long in strange styles. (Mussolini's fascists later highjacked the Arditi symbols and their name, thereby diminishing the elite corps' heritage.)

Italy was embarrassed by d'Annunzio's gambit. The new government did not want to alienate its allies, and refused d'Annunzio's gift of Fiume.

D'Annunzio was a libertine. An outrageous and flamboyant hedonist, he did his best to promote that image. His lovers and love life were extensively documented – by d'Annunzio himself. He was a great poet, and a national hero. With this Fiume adventure, d'Annunzio came to personify Italian irredentism. At Fiume, he let loose all his extravagant personality. A small man, he claimed to be 164 cm tall, less than 5' 5", but looked much shorter. (The consummate egotist, he was keen to have it known that, despite his slight figure, he was large where it counted.)

He was bald, with a goatee beard and a curled moustache. D'Annunzio often clothed himself in extravagant costumes – in his Fiume days, the costumes were military uniforms – and he was given to wearing distinctive headwear, often a Tyrolean hat. In Fiume he self-designated himself the "Commendatore". There, he perfected the passionate long rambling speech, ideally delivered from a balcony. He promoted the Roman (fascist) salute, black uniforms, distinctive symbols, great public events and rituals. All these initiatives were later picked up by Mussolini, who dubbed d'Annunzio "the John the Baptist of Fascism".

The new government of Italy blockaded the port city. Yet Fiume survived – with porous borders and support from the Italian people and its military. Several Italian navy ships mutinied and joined d'Annunzio. In December 1919, Italy proposed a solution – a "modus vivendi" – which essentially gave d'Annunzio everything he asked for. The results of a local referendum, which overwhelmingly supported Italy's proposal, were ignored by the Commendatore; he and his mad louche colleagues rather liked running their nascent mini-state.

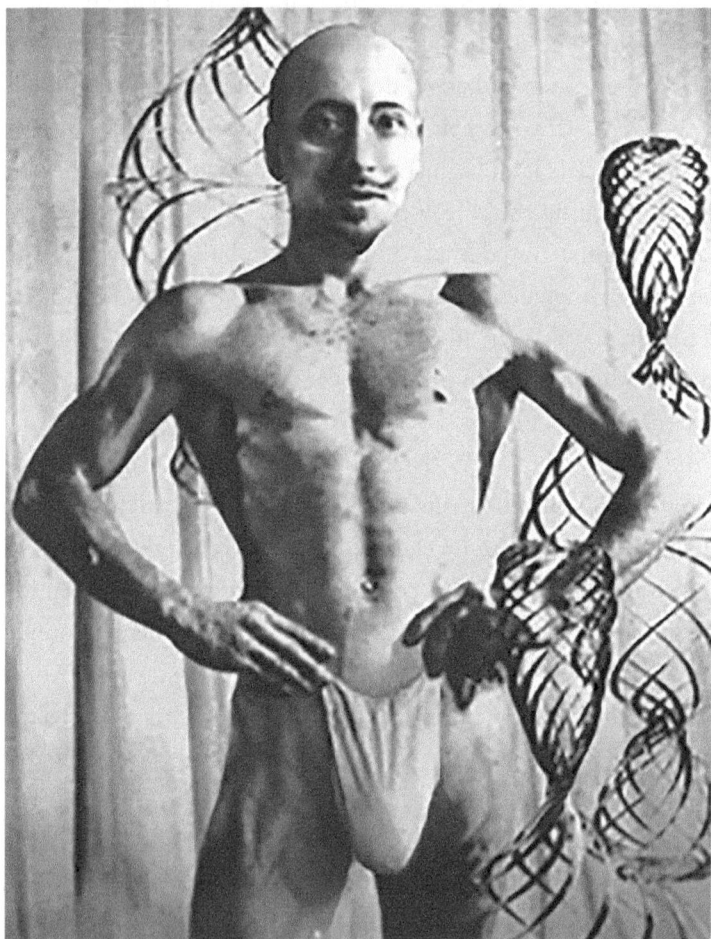

D'Annunzio at leisure, and on display

In the fifteen months that d'Annunzio was in control of the Lilliputian state it attracted a wide range of interested parties: anarchists, futurists, traditionalists, fascists, authoritarians of the left and right, loonies of all sorts, necromancers, the Sinn Féin and Flemish nationalists. Toscanini and Marconi checked it out, as did Mussolini. Fiume became a magnet for non-conformists and an earthly paradise for sensualists. It embraced d'Annunzio's lifestyle. Free love was encouraged. Homosexuality was tolerated, "as in the time of Pericles".[44] Every morning d'Annunzio read announcements and poetry from the Governor's Palace; there was a concert and fireworks almost every night. At first, the blockading Italian navy would allow officers ashore to participate in an evening's carousing.

But it couldn't last, and the squeeze was soon on from the new Italian government. The cabbage-covered beef and pork *sarma* pockets and the fried *bisato* eels for which Fiume was famous were becoming scarce. By March, food rationing became necessary. Chocolates and caramels, cakes and biscuits were banned. There would be no more delicious walnut and poppy-seed *oresgnaza* rolls. Residents were put on 300 grams of bread per day, 300 grams of flour and sugar a month, a kilo of potatoes a week and 2.5 litres of [cooking] oil a month.[45] There was no obvious objection. The Arditi started to go home; those who remained bashed up opponents of the regime and, in a lesson well learnt by their fascist successors, forced dissidents to drink castor oil. D'Annunzio's mad offsider, Guido Keller, an exhibitionist and keen naturist, would appear naked anywhere at will; as support for the administration waned, Keller advocated the establishment of a Committee of Public Safety without any sense of irony.

D'Annunzio had decided to get rid of the local provisional government and take explicit charge. By early summer he had largely completed work on the creation of an "Italian Regency of Carnaro". It was, like d'Annunzio himself, a most bizarre concept.

A new philosophy and constitution were developed for the prospective Regency, led by the loony anarcho-syndicalist Alceste de Abris. De Abris' draft Charter of Carnaro included anarchist, democratic, libertarian and proto-fascist elements, which were then tricked up with d'Annunzio's prose. The democratic breakthroughs, such as universal suffrage, were tempered by authoritarianism and a sprinkling of Aleister Crowley Thought, elements of the Mad Hatter's Tea Party and Dada. Divorce would be authorised, as would nudism and the use of drugs. Music was designated a "religious and social institution", and was to be central to everything: "in every province there will be a choral society and an orchestra subsidised by the State"; "the College of Aediles will be commissioned to erect a great concert hall"; "the great orchestral and concert celebrations will be entirely free…". In anticipation of Mussolini's future fascist Italy, the legislature was to embrace the corporate state: Fiume identified nine different sectors of the economy – seafarers, teachers, etc – which were joined by a tenth sector for "superior individuals" (such as d'Annunzio).

On 8 September 1920, d'Annunzio launched the Charter of Carnaro and announced the establishment of the Regency. He was to be Duce. Although the Regency recognized the Soviet Union, the first entity to do so, no country recognized it.

Meanwhile, on 12 November 1920, Italy and Yugoslavia (technically the "Kingdom of Serbs, Croats and Slovenes") signed the Treaty of Rapallo under the auspices of the League of Nations. Its most important element was the agreement to form a new independent state, the Free State of Fiume: free of Italy, free of Yugoslavia, an independent entity.

D'Annunzio would have none of it, saying he would resist the solution to the end. In answer, Italian forces – the army, navy and air force – attacked Fiume on 26 December. After a few days of extreme violence, d'Annunzio conceded, and his military occupation of Fiume came to an end. D'Annunzio's adventure had lasted fifteen months. He retired to his new estate on Lake Garda and was never prosecuted.

The Free State of Fiume quickly joined the League of Nations as its smallest member. Just about every country recognised it and, although there remained Italian dissidents who still aspired to annex the city-state, at first all seemed well. The Free State existed *de jure* for little more than three years, but *de facto* it lasted about eighteen months; from mid-1922 actual control reverted from the de jure government to Italian insurgents.

When Benito Mussolini came to power in late 1922, his supporters revived Italy's claim to Fiume; and on 27 January 1924, Italy and Yugoslavia signed the bilateral Treaty of Rome which dissolved the independent entity. The Treaty, recognised by the League of Nations, gave most of the former Free State of Fiume to Italy – it excised the suburb of

Sušak and a few small villages, which went to Yugoslavia – and created a narrow seaside corridor linking Fiume proper to the rest of Italy.

In the wake of this victory, and with a great deal of intimidation and violence, Mussolini's National List easily won the 6 April 1924 Italian General Election. It was the last multi-party election in Italy for twenty-two years. On 10 June, Socialist leader Giacomo Matteotti was assassinated by fascist Blackshirts. And Fiume remained part of Italy, as the Province of Carnaro, until it was ultimately absorbed into Yugoslavia in 1947, when the city assumed the name by which it is now known, Rijeka. In 1991, with the breakup of Yugoslavia and the creation of an independent Croatia, Rijeka emerged as Croatia's principal seaport and the country's third largest city; while D' Annunzio's bizarre shenanigans and the Fiume Question disappeared into the mists of time.

Outremer translates simply as "overseas". For the French, however, it tends to mean *Overseas France*, that is, the Francophone world. In the mid-1920s, metropolitan France ("La Métropole") had a population of about forty million; the French colonial empire – its colonies, protectorates and overseas territories – added a further sixty million. By any measure it was vast. With Canada, Australia and "white" South Africa, Britain had the comfort of like-minded souls as constituents in its huge empire; in contrast, France's empire did not comprise many people who looked like French men and women. Its jewels were Indochina, Africa and the French Concession in Shanghai.

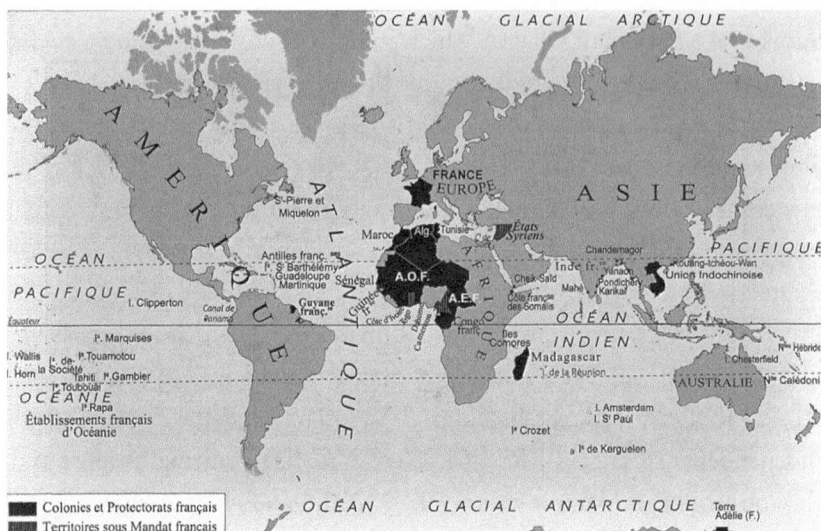

Like all colonial powers, the French continued to exploit their empire. It was an entitlement. And when not exploiting the constituent parts, France treated them with a degree of benign neglect. France expected its dependencies to supply France with raw materials, workers and soldiers. After all, they were getting the benefit of *la mission civilisatrice* – France's civilising mission. While the role of Minister for the Colonies was often seen as a second-rate job, the colonial civil service itself had a grand time. To be Governor-General of Indochina or Resident-General of Morocco meant that you could live like a king. And they did. (When still a subordinate to his mentor Joseph Gallieni in Madagascar, Hubert Lyautey wrote: "I am Louis XIV and it suits me.")

Few criticised the set-up. Calls for independence were virtually non-existent. What discontents typically asked for were basic human rights: equality before the law, equal access to education, to employment, to public facilities and so on; French citizenship would be nice but not necessary. Overwhelmingly, those who lived in the French Empire saw merit in maintaining their connection to the mother country. They were happy to assimilate. But there were anomalies and gaps between social and legal status throughout the Empire: why should Antilleans and some Senegalese be French citizens when Malagasies were not? And so on. Should you seek an independent national identity or acceptance as a French citizen?

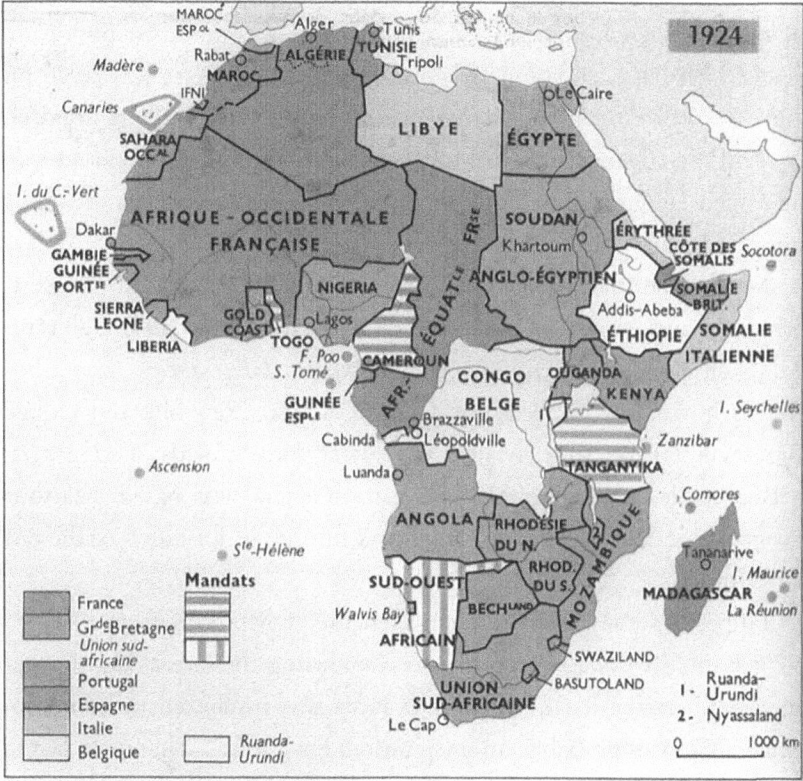

René Maran (left), Hubert Lyautey (right)

In Paris, René Maran, a black colonial functionary, surprisingly won the 1921 Prix Goncourt for his novel "Batoula". It was not about French colonialism, but it did criticise the system; the novel was soon banned throughout French colonies. Marcel Cachin, a communist politician, attacked French occupation of Morocco and, in 1923, he was jailed for doing so. A prominent colleague, journalist and author Albert Londres, also had a go – exposing working conditions in North Africa, notably the forced labour in prisons. But these commentators were not widely supported. Paris was not interested.

Meanwhile, in Africa, one radical voice emerged. André Matsoua formed a movement seeking French citizenship for all inhabitants of French Equatorial Africa – *Afrique équatoriale française* or AEF – what is now Chad, Gabon, the Central African Republic and Congo (Brazzaville). Over time, Matsoua attracted large crowds of supporters in Brazzaville, where the AEF Governor-General was based; Matsoua was gaoled in 1929, a situation he found himself in for much of the rest of his life.

Hubert Lyautey was Resident-General of Morocco from 1912 to 1925. Based in Rabat, except for service during the Great War, he was empathetic to the local customs. Lyautey was rumoured to be homosexual and was probably an inspiration for Proust's character Baron de Charlus. Clemenceau, who truly hated him, once cattily observed: "There is an admirable and courageous man who always has balls up to his ass. It's a pity they are not always his."[46]

Lyautey publicly deferred to the Sultan, thereby maintaining the fiction that the Sultan was in charge of the Protectorate. The product of a traditional Christian upbringing, he kept his own religious beliefs private. Indeed he was seen to support the population's near universal adherence to Islam, and enthusiastically absorbed the country's culture and art. Lyautey was strategic, establishing good relations with the various tribal leaders, with the spiritual brotherhoods and with the Berbers; thereby not upsetting the local power structures and effectively supporting the established order and customs. That done, he still ran the show. Nearly 50,000 Moroccan troops served France's cause in the First World War. They saw that the war had been fought between white people, by people ostensibly superior to them, fighting for no cause other than one country's dominance over another and their competition for imperial expansion. Even so, when the soldiers came back from the war, there was still no opposition of any consequence during Lyautey's many years in charge. He encouraged the economic development of Morocco while preserving the local culture; when new European-style urban developments were undertaken, they were built outside the ancient Moroccan cities. In many ways, as Resident-General, Lyautey was an exemplary representative of the French Empire. When the grand Paris Colonial Exposition was staged in 1931, he was given the honour of serving as its Commissioner. Hubert Lyautey had been created a Marshal of France in 1921; he died in 1934, by which time he was a keen supporter of the fascist movement, and he is prominently entombed near Napoleon in Les Invalides.

Elsewhere in Africa, the French really did exploit their subjects. Algeria was part of France. Morocco and Tunisia were Protectorates. In Algeria, with perhaps six million people in 1924, French settlers controlled everything. The local Arabs had next to no political status or power, nor did they have much of a participation in the country's economic progress. Algerians were French subjects but fewer than 100,000 Arab Algerians were French citizens. About 300,000 Algerians had gone to France to support the war effort, nearly 200,000 of them having been combatants. On their return, there was a widespread expectation that combatants would be granted French citizenship; but this was not to be. Many of these returnees, the celebrated Zouave soldiers included, felt they had been used by the mother country. That said, many returned to France proper to work: "In France they love us, they teach us to work, and they pay us."[47] Migration to France reached 100,000 in 1924 and each year up to the 1939-45 War emigration from Algeria was never less than that number.

In Tunisia, the bourgeoisie had been the only voice for civil rights. This changed in 1924, when dock workers went on strike for two months. West Africa was the worst off. The several territories known as French West Africa – *Afrique occidentale française* or AOF – had a total population of little more than three million. Collectively known to the French as "Senegalese", French West Africa had sent about 175,000 men to the Great War and they suffered 30,000 fatalities. These soldiers returned to work in the AOF's coffee and banana plantations with no improvement in basic human rights; they were oppressed by African chiefs, compliant collaborators with their French masters, who enforced colonial rule, taxation and labour laws.

Only in French Indochina – *l'Union indochinoise* – essentially today's Vietnam, Cambodia and Laos, was there any real nationalist effort and success. Indochina had committed about 100,000 people to the war effort, half in factories, and post-war there was much local pamphleteering and agitation for civil rights.

A twenty-nine year old Ho Chi Minh had famously made an effort to be heard at the Paris Peace Conference – travelling to Versailles dressed in a borrowed bowler hat and black suit – only to be turned away without meeting any of the decision-makers. Ho was not asking for independence, just civil rights. Without a hearing from France and its allies, he turned to Communism.

Ho Chi Minh, 1920

In 1922, a Senegalese boxer, Battling Siki, defeated Georges Carpentier in a world title bout; whereupon Ho Chi Minh adopted Siki as an anti-colonial icon, and published a short essay on the subject. While Ho was attending the Fifth Congress of the Comintern in Moscow in June and July 1924 (as a representative of the French Communist Party), a fellow patriot, a Vietnamese student, took decisive action...

Martial Henri Merlin, the Governor-General of Indochina since 1923, was visiting Canton. Merlin was a conservative reactionary, and he was not popular. (Among other early initiatives, he had taken a knife to the education budget, believing that a primary school education was quite sufficient for the indigenous population.) On 19 June 1924, Merlin survived an assassination attempt by the patriotic student. Merlin reacted viciously, with renewed support for the shocking conditions in Vietnam's mines and rubber plantations. A particular grievance was the oppressive labour contracts, and at great risk Vietnamese workers abandoned colonial plantations in increasing numbers: in 1924 there were 847 recorded desertions, and by 1928 this had risen to 4,484.

Not all manifestations of independence and nationalism involved violence or explicit opposition to the status quo. Just as the Mormons emerged as a home-grown religion in the 1830s when the USA was feeling its oats and Joseph Smith discovered Latter-day Saints, so the Vietnamese found a new religion too.

The prophet was Ngo Van Chieu, a forty-one year old civil servant who, at a spiritualist séance in 1919, received word from an agent of the supreme being that he, Chieu, would be the vehicle for a new religion. It would bring all the world's religions together. After much prayer by Chieu and others, the supreme being – the Cao Dei – finally communicated the definitive arrangements to Chieu and fellow mediums on Christmas Eve 1925.

Caodaism was to be monotheist and embrace elements of three great Asian faiths – Confucianism (from which it drew ethics), Taoism (occult practices) and Buddhism (karma and reincarnation); the absence of Hindu elements may relate to its polytheism. The organisation structure was to be hierarchical, largely following that of the Catholic church. Caodaism has a Pope, Cardinals and priests of various ranks. Their silk robes are red, yellow and blue – the three colours of the religion – and white. Women can be ordained but are not eligible for the top two jobs. Adherents are vegetarians and are expected to abstain from alcohol.

The Great Divine Temple, Tây Ninh, Vietnam

Caodaism believes in heaven and hell, access to the former requiring a virtuous life. The Holy See was established in Tây Ninh, about 90 kilometres north west of Saigon near the much-revered Black Virgin mountain that dominates the landscape for miles in all directions. Caodaism's predominant symbol is the Divine Eye, representing God's left eye; it reminds adherents that God sees everything, everywhere. The Great Divine Temple, set apart in a huge public square in the centre of the

Holy See, looks somewhat like a very large Hollywood cinema with twin towers and balconies; closer inspection reveals garish oriental flourishes, Divine Eyes and over-colourful frescoes.

Inside, the Great Divine Temple shares the elements of a Christian cathedral – a nave, apse, altars, a high vaulted ceiling and galleries – but the decoration is incredible. The ceiling itself is relatively sober with white clouds on a light blue sky, but the rest of the grand chamber presents a cornucopia of bizarre design features: the floor-to-ceiling dragon-encrusted columns look like a petrified forest of candy-floss; over the main altar there is a huge blue-ish orb with a Divine Eye; bright murals cover the mainly yellow walls; and further Divine Eyes and representations of the Venerable Saints fill out the Disney-like fantasia. When populated with priests, the Great Divine Temple creates a truly spectacular scene; something visitors can share during the daily rituals and through the year which has an established calendar of annual celebrations.

The religion seeks universal peace, and its desire to reconcile and synthesise all religious views and is confirmed by a list of Cao Dai's Venerable Saints; these include the Buddha and Confucius, of course, but also Muhammad, Jesus Christ, Julius Caesar, Pericles, Jeanne d'Arc, Louis Pasteur, Shakespeare, Moses, Lenin, Sun Yat-sen and – perhaps because of his interest in spiritualism – Victor Hugo. When Norman Lewis visited the Holy See in 1954, a young man explained that he was the reincarnation of a member of the great poet's family. He went on to explain that some of Hugo's most sublime work had been written after his death – since disincarnation – and that he, the young man, was official editor of these posthumous works.[48]

Caodaism caught on quickly, resonating with Vietnam's need for national identity. It was never popular with the colonial authorities because of the religion's consistently strong nationalist stance; by 1940, however, perhaps one-quarter of the population were adherents to the sect. In the 1950s, the Caodaists had a considerable private army which controlled an area around the Holy See. It had been established in 1943, during the Japanese occupation, and the French authorities tolerated this situation because Caodaists were by then ant-Viet-Minh and this split the nationalist cause.

France's most important foreign policy issues all related to Germany. Germany had suffered hyper-inflation in the years 1921 to 1923, largely as a result of its own mismanagement, and it could not keep up the onerous reparations imposed by the Treaty of Versailles. When Germany defaulted on the delivery of coal and timber in late 1922, France (and Belgium) occupied the Ruhr in order to claim control of those commodities. This deeply offended the Germans, and an undeclared war of resistance and civil disobedience resulted in hundreds of Germans being killed in the streets. The occupation was not universally supported in France, and in Britain there was sympathy for Germany's travails.

German politics were becoming increasingly polarised, albeit with multiple parties across the political spectrum. Even so, by 1923 "the failure of democracy...seemed far less probable than its consolidation."[49] There were two general elections in 1924 and although the Social Democrats won both, their best result was just 26% of all votes. The top four or five parties won between 70 and 80%, and the resulting governments were all coalitions.

With goodwill from German foreign minister Gustav Stresemann, in August 1924 US envoy Charles Dawes was able to get agreement to the Dawes Plan. It dramatically reduced reparations and had France agreeing to withdraw from the Ruhr.

Britain had been encouraging such a compromise, but was more concerned with its own affairs. The first Labour Government, in power since December 1923 and initially propped up by the Liberals, lost a vote of confidence. The Tories were brought back in the ensuing 29 October 1924 election, helped partly by the forged "Zinoviev Letter". (The 1924 General Election was the Liberal Party's last hurrah. From this point British politics became a contest between the Left and the Right, between the Conservatives and Labour. The 1923 election had proved to be the last genuine three-cornered contest, and after the 1924 election the Liberal Party was never again a serious contender to win government. Oswald Mosley, hitherto a Conservative and an Independent member of Parliament, stood as a Labour candidate against Neville Chamberlain in that 1924 election, and came within 100 votes of defeating Chamberlain in the Chamberlain family's Birmingham stronghold.)

Lenin died on 22 January 1924. The Soviet Union had already been recognised by Germany, in July 1923. Ramsay MacDonald's new Labour Government recognised the Soviet Union in February 1924, as did Italy, and then Herriot's French government followed in October 1924.

In August 1923, the colourless Calvin Coolidge had succeeded Warren Harding as US President, and Coolidge would be the Republican nominee for the 1924 election. Woodrow Wilson died on 4 February 1924. In July 1924, in New York, the Democrats finally settled on a candidate for the forthcoming Presidential election. It had taken the Democratic Convention no less than one hundred and three separate ballots and more than two weeks to find a candidate acceptable to the Ku Klux Klan; the Klan held an effective veto, and John W Davis emerged as someone acceptable to its adherents. In November, Coolidge won easily. The French had been bitterly disappointed that the US Senate had refused to ratify the Treaty of Versailles and its guarantee to preserve the frontier with Germany. By 1924, however, with the USA going into an isolationist mode, their only real concern was the attitude a US government would take towards France's large war debt.

Adolf Hitler was released from Munich's Landsberg prison on 20 December 1924, in time for Christmas. He had been imprisoned throughout the year.

Thirteen months earlier, on the evening of 8 November 1923, Hitler had crashed a right-wing political rally which was taking place in Munich's Bürgerbräukeller, and there he launched an insurrection, "the beerhall putsch". His brownshirts, perhaps three hundred of them, surrounded the building, with Hermann Göring manning a heavy machine gun at the main entrance. The attempted coup reached its climax the next day at the Munich town hall with a shootout between the brownshirts and the police in which twenty-one people died, sixteen Nazis, four policemen and a bystander.[50] Hitler was quickly arrested and charged with high treason. His much-anticipated February 1924 trial lasted a full month and the presiding judge allowed it to become a propaganda platform for Hitler's obsessions: he spouted virulent anti-Semitism almost without interruption, and ranted on and on about the "November Criminals", by which he meant those politicians who negotiated and signed the November 1918 armistice, and ultimately anyone associated with the Weimar Republic.

It would be wrong to think of the failed putsch as a minor piece of history. Indeed, it had sufficient notoriety for the foreign press to send many reporters to cover the trial. On April Fools' Day 1924, Hitler was pronounced guilty of high treason, but he received only the minimum sentence of five years; what's more, he was recommended to be eligible for parole after six months.

Hitler's incarceration was not uncomfortable. Together with fellow putschists, he was housed in a small wing of Landsberg prison which was designed to accommodate political prisoners and the like. His room had a bed, blankets, a nightstand with lamp, two chairs, a small writing table, a wardrobe and an open (if barred) window which gave out onto a view of the rolling countryside beyond the prison walls. The privileged prisoners shared a sitting room with a table for six, at which meals were served on a white table cloth. Hitler's personal chauffeur, Emil Maurice, was held in an adjacent cell and effectively served as a valet; Rudolf Hess moved in next door to Maurice, and thereafter sat at the feet of the Tribune (as Hitler was temporarily known) while he poured out his *völkisch* meanderings and anti-Semitic venom. They all shared a bathroom.[51]

If he wasn't pontificating to his fellow prisoners or reading the newspaper in one of the sitting room's comfortable wicker chairs, Hitler was writing his magnum opus: the appalling *Mein Kampf.* Rarely did he take advantage of the walks in the garden to which he was entitled. He became obsessed with his book, with putting into writing his "philosophy" and wild interpretations of history.

1924: Hitler with colleagues in Landsberg prison;
Rudolf Hess, second from right

Hitler had a stream of visitors, largely political allies and supporters such as Richard Wagner's daughter-in-law Winifred. They brought gifts of clothing, liquor, books, sausages, many flowers, a typewriter, a gramophone and his favourite cakes. A record twenty-one visitors were welcomed on his thirty-fifth birthday, and three thousand true believers celebrated this special day at the Bürgerbräukeller. Mail arrived in such volume that it was delivered in laundry baskets. It was clear that, even in these early days, well before he came to power in 1933, Hitler already had widespread support from the *völkisch* nationalist movement and some of the Bavarian establishment.

After thirteen months in prison, the future Führer was paroled by a Bavarian court – and released on the world.

FROM MONTMARTRE
TO MONTPARNASSE

Montmartre ("Mons Martis", the Mount of Mars) is a large hill north of downtown Paris. For more than a century it has been dominated by the Basilica du Sacré-Coeur, a huge white-domed Catholic church. In the wake of France's defeat in the Franco-Prussian War and the disruptions of the 1870-71 Paris Commune, the National Assembly voted to support the church's construction.

Catholic clerics saw the new basilica as a monument of penance for the national disgrace in losing the war and an atonement for the "crimes" of the subsequent Commune. A sub-plot was the promotion of Catholic virtues versus the Protestant ethos of victorious Prussia. The Church further argued that Sacré-Coeur's construction was a necessary redemption for the one hundred years of moral decline since the French Revolution. Since Montmartre was one of the Commune's last redoubts and traditionally a centre of working class dissent, the proposal naturally attracted resentment and disdain from the Left.

Sacré-Coeur's foundation stone was laid in 1875. Given the state's secular constitution, no state funds were explicitly contributed to its construction. The faithful coughed up as the huge edifice was built. It was an outlandish and intrusive design – a huge neo-byzantine structure reaching up from a Romanesque base. And it used imported stone, not the local Paris variety, this being not only whiter than the stone traditionally used throughout the city but a variety that became whiter with age. The Great War delayed Sacré-Coeur's completion, and it was finally consecrated in 1919.

The juxtaposition of the new basilica with traditional Montmartre was incongruous and intrusive. While no longer the bucolic village depicted by Van Gogh in the 1880s, Montmartre still had windmills and narrow streets, small gardens and run-down shacks in which real people lived. Le Moulin de la Galette was a community dance hall, not corrupted by the water trade down the hill. Le Lapin Agile cabaret still attracted many artists, local and foreign, albeit that it had lost some cutting edge after 1914; but well into the 1920s, the bourgeoisie checked the venue out in the hope that they might come across its famous clientele such as Picasso or Max Jacob or Guillaume Apollinaire (the last being unlikely since he had died in 1919). Montmartre's artists' colony, the Bateau-Lavoir, continued to accommodate emerging artists, their families and lovers. And through the 1920s, the Butte de Montmartre continued to house and welcome, permanently or periodically, such luminaries as Virgil Thompson, Josephine Baker and her Revue Nègre colleagues, Nadia Boulanger, Max Jacob, Langston Hughes (briefly), most of those black musicians at Zelli's and the other nightclubs, Man Ray, Tristan Zara, Emma Goldman and Salvador Dalí.

But Montparnasse was the new thing.

Métro route 12 is a metaphor for the migration of the artistic community from Montmartre to Montparnasse. Completed in 1912, it was a new north/south subway specifically built to link Montmartre with developing Montparnasse (at the Gare Montparnasse); the route ran conveniently via the Gare Saint-Lazare railway terminus. Picasso moved from Montmartre to Montparnasse in that very year.

Other early adopters of Montparnasse included Léger, Brancusi, Chaime Soutine and Foujita. By 1924, many future great artists (or passing stars) were all somewhere in Montparnasse (or, like Picasso, had moved on): they included each of the above plus Marc Chagall, Flossie Martin, Ezra Pound, Max Ernst, Marcel Duchamp, Robert McAlmon, Henri Rousseau, Nina Hamnett, Juan Gris, Man Ray, Kiki, Diego

Rivera, Albert Giacometti, Cocteau (briefly, he was really a Right Bank man), Joan Miró, André Masson, Hemingway, and many others.

Montparnasse has never had the village charm of Le Vieux Montmartre. It has never been a really distinct district. Montparnasse has always lacked the concentrated location that was part of Vieux Montmartre's charm. It was grittier than Montmartre, and covered a lot of territory. For tourists it was the Carrefour Vavin, its cafes and bars, and perhaps the nearby music halls such as the Bobino on rue de la Gaîté. For others it covered most of the 15th arrondissement, which is one of the city's largest. Artists embraced this wider definition. The rent was cheap and there were lots of places with room for a studio.

It was not difficult to find somewhere suitable to work and live. In the 1920s, although Montparnasse was becoming increasingly suburban, in parts it was still semi-rural. There were plenty of workshops, and it still had market gardens. As is the way with urban development, this was gradually changing; open space was being filled in. Almost wherever you lived, however, it was a congenial place to be. This included such artists' outposts as La Ruche (less than two kilometres from the boulevard du Montparnasse) and the Bal Blomet (two kilometres).

La Ruche ("the beehive"), in the south west outskirts of the 15th arrondissement, has always been something special. Originally built as a wine store for the Great Exposition of 1900, it was acquired by the sculptor Alfred Boucher at auction. He moved it to 2 rue Passage Dantzig, where, in 1908, he set it up as housing and studios for needy artists. The new name for the structure – La Ruche – was chosen to encourage a complex for artists in which they were all buzzing about with bee-like industry, and it quickly fulfilled that hope and intention. A fine piece of architecture in its original three-story circular design, La Ruche was enhanced by the addition of doorways and sculptures that had been acquired at that Exposition auction. In some ways La Ruche was the new Bateau-Lavoir, only much cleaner than that Montmartre icon and also refurbished for purpose. The clientele included lots of Russians – many of them Jews, who spoke Yiddish amongst themselves – as well as drifters and plenty of genuine new talent.

La Ruche

Camille Soutine, Marc Chagall, Jacques Lipchitz, Marie Laurencin, Modigliani, Brancusi, Léger, Max Jacob, Pincus Kremegne, Diego Rivera and Nina Hamnett were all alumni. Today it still houses about fifty artists as well as hosting events and exhibitions.

Also near the boulevard du Montparnasse were the studios and dilapidated housing complex of Joan Mirò, André Masson and surrealist poet Robert Desnos, at 45 rue Blomet. (It is now an attractive playground with a wonderful Mirò sculpture.) By 1924, this had become a quasi-frat house for a sub-set of Surrealists, where Hemingway had taught both Mirò and Masson to box, where Jean Dubuffet made his last paintings before his strange eight year sabbatical, and where everyone played cards, debated the meaning of life, danced and drank. Just up the road was the Bal Blomet or the *Bal Nègre* (as Desnos christened it): "In one of the most romantic neighbourhoods of Paris, where each carriage entrance conceals a garden and arbours, an oriental ball has settled. A true 'Bal Nègre' where one can spend, on Saturdays and Sundays, an evening far from the Parisian atmosphere. It's at 33 rue Blomet, in a great hall adjoining the Jouve tobacco shop..."[52]

Montparnasse was never much of a mountain. (The name derives from the French "Parnasse", for Mount Parnassus in Greece, and was allegedly the name given the hillock by French students reading poetry there in the 17th century.) Whatever mountain there might once have been was levelled by the building of the boulevard du Montparnasse in the 1800s. And, by 1924, a short section of the boulevard was headquarters for much of what today we celebrate about Montparnasse of the 1920s.

In 1924, the Gare Montparnasse was an attractive combination of neo-classical and Art Deco elements with a busy square facing the boulevard du Montparnasse; the square itself was an important interchange for trams and buses. It was a bustling scene, full of humanity, nothing like today's colourless wasteland of anonymous buildings and neon glitz. To the north east of the square was Joyce's favourite big spend, Les Trianons, and nearby, at 59 boulevard du Montparnasse, was the Chartier brothers' Bistro de la Gare, an Art Nouveau extravaganza; it was sold by the Chartiers in 1924, but seemed to be maintaining standards. (After nearly a century out of their hands, it has recently been bought back by the family firm and now trades as Bouillon Chartier.)

Diagonally opposite the Bistro de la Gare, on the southeast corner of the square, closer to the station, was the classy hotel and restaurant Lavenue. It provided a psychological or emotional bridge for visitors to the famous cafes down the road, as it was both a little bohemian – because it welcomed well-known artists – and also quite safe for middle-class tourists; they could have a taste of Montparnasse while dining either in the three small rooms of Lavenue or out the back in its courtyard. (The Lavenue name is still visible on the building at 68-70 boulevard du Montparnasse, although the corner is now occupied by a Hippopotamus steakhouse.)

Today the boulevard du Montparnasse is pretty featureless. Its core strip is the three or four hundred metres from the Gare Montparnasse to the carrefour at the boulevard Raspail – known in 1924 and still today as the "Vavin", but now officially Place Pablo-Picasso. (Picasso's studio in Montparnasse was ten minutes' walk away from the now eponymous crossroads, at 5bis rue Victor Schoelcher, overlooking the Montparnasse cemetery.) That stretch of the boulevard would have been livelier in the 1920s. There were lots of small bars then, and no health regulations prohibiting the display of seafood and oysters on the footpaths; it had personable street vendors who sold strawberries, lemonade and ice cream.

For decades Le Dôme had been the café of choice for visiting Anglos, both American and British; for Scandinavians too, and Germans before the Great War. It was an all-purpose bistro, perfectly located on the south west corner of the carrefour Vavin, on the corner of the boulevard du Montparnasse and the rue Delambre. From 1911, Le Dôme had competition across the road from La Rotonde at 105 boulevard de Montparnasse. Both were comprehensively renovated and expanded in time for the 1924 season.

Le Dôme in the 1920s

The new Dôme had been refurbished in bordello red:

> *"The famous café which has been the rendezvous of American Bohemians in Paris for the past thirty years is now as up-to-date, modern, shiny and completely equipped as the bathroom of an American "Babbitt"…Patron Chambon has chosen red as the basic color of his scheme: red flowers, red woodwork, red benches and last and the most apparent, red wall-paper with a wriggling design that needs only a little imagination to look like snakes. Green palms here and there make the red more red and the total effect is multiplied many times over by plate glass mirrors which take up all the space not occupied by red."*[53]

César, the oldest and cheekiest of the waiters was still there, still ostentatiously spraying stray cats (and clients) with his soda siphon. Le Dôme had quadrupled in size with the renovation. It now had an extensive set of tables on the sidewalk, flowing out and along the boulevard and around the corner into the rue Delambre. The billiard table in the back room had gone, but the same crowd still gossiped, drank, paid debts, borrowed and backstabbed as before. It was always busy. In the summer, tables were put together and moved around as American college boys on their summer holidays met up with their pals – all dressed up in their default uniform of straw boater, blazer and white flannel trousers.

Across the road, La Rotonde had a slightly racier crowd. It had always been so. It was rumoured to have been a haunt of undesirable revolutionaries, and Lenin and Trotsky had certainly been customers. Picasso too. La Rotonde served exotic foreign liqueurs and Turkish coffee – both suspicious – and it had Eastern European papers in the newspaper racks. Importantly for some, the food was generally thought to be better than that at the Dôme. By 1924, it was more of a "local" than its neighbour, which was seen as favoured by tourists. The original proprietor, Victor Libion, who had always been generous with credit and was happy to receive payment in artwork, had retired in 1920. The new owners were on trial but it seemed to be working. Although he came to be a regular, Hemingway was initially not a fan. In 1922, he wrote:

> "...the scum of Greenwich Village, New York, has been skimmed off and deposited in large ladles...They have all striven so hard for a careless individuality of clothing that they have achieved a sort of uniformity of eccentricity...You can find anything you are looking for at the Rotonde – except serious artists...for the artists of Paris who are turning out credible work resent and loathe the Rotonde crowd... They are nearly all loafers...talking about what they are going to do and condemning the work of all artists who have gained any degree of recognition."[54]

Café de La Rotonde, 1924 by Cedric Morris
La Rotonde circa 1925

La Rotonde too had expanded when it reopened in the spring of 1924. It had acquired the adjacent Café du Parnasse, at 103 boulevard du Montparnasse. The new red awning shouted LA ROTONDE in gold capitals. There was a large new upstairs dining room that turned into a dance floor and cabaret after nine. (Emmanuel Macron held his preliminary victory party there in 2017.) In some ways it was more democratic than the Dôme. A newcomer, who came to be known as Kiki de Montparnasse, liked the "nutty crowd" and, because she was down and out at the time, and was pretty and loose, she enjoyed "bathing privileges" in the ladies' lavatory: the staff delivered hot water to her there, where she washed.

By the end of the year, Le Dôme and La Rotonde had got a competitor: Le Select. Just a door up the street from La Rotonde, at number 99, it was the first to be open for twenty-four hours. And, like La Rotonde, it enjoyed the morning sun. Le Select undoubtedly had a more unkempt clientele than its rivals. With each round of drinks, there and elsewhere, the bill would come on a small plate. A new drink brought a new plate. Perhaps the patrons *did* stack up plates quicker than at the older establishments. It seemed so. In any event, Le Select itself looked crisp and clean with green and white woven chairs, art deco styling, white table cloths and correctly attired waiters; and the cursive sign over this new competitor – Le Select – was beckoning. The proprietors were Monsieur and Madame Select, that's what everyone called them. Monsieur Select cooked a great welsh rarebit, their brie de Meaux was first class, and the Croque Select a specialty. Madame Select, a severe bean counter, oversaw it all from the cash register; she wore fingerless gloves, and she looked capable of breaking up almost any brawl. (Tsuguharu Foujita's famous etchings of a street fight, *A La Rotonde* and *Le Café de la Rotonde*, from 1925 and 1927 respectively, look more like fights at Le Select than any that might have taken place at its sometimes more sober neighbour.) One of Le Select's most established clients was the American journalist, intellectual and racing tipster, Harold Stone; Hemingway was well-disposed towards the Select but not to Stone, so in *The Sun Also Rises* he pictured a pseudonymous Stone sitting there alone: "He had a pile of saucers in front of him, and he needed a shave."[55]

Le Select opened in 1924 and stayed open "toute la nuit"

Opposite Le Select and La Rotonde, at 102 boulevard Montparnasse, was a coal yard which sat behind a high wooden fence, a few doors up from Le Dôme, on its side of the boulevard. On 20 December 1927 there was a grand opening of a new café at that address: La Coupole. An art deco wonder, much bigger than the others, with two floors of dining and thé dansant in the basement, it was an instant hit. But it did not exist in 1924.

Often bracketed with these famous cafes, but separate from them both physically and in atmosphere, is La Closerie des Lilas. Originally an old inn on the route to Orléans, by 1924 it was well tarted up. In contrast to the excitement at the Vavin, La Closerie was "an island, a small, quiet island."[56] It was also a proper restaurant, in what was then a tranquil location on the way to the Latin Quarter, at the end of the boulevard, at Port Royal. As a matter of course, habitués of the three Vavin cafés – Le Dôme, La Rotonde and Le Select – did not venture there; they tended to circulate among themselves, hopping from one café to another. And La Closerie was a good six hundred metres away, along the boulevard. In any event, if the Vavin habitués were looking for a proper meal, they were unlikely to get beyond Le Nègre de Toulouse[57] and Monsieur Lavigne's splendid cassoulet or, on Fridays, his couscous special; it was sort of half way.

Serious drinking was done at the Dingo. It was around the corner from the Dôme, at 10 rue Delambre. In 1923, a Frenchman with a big moustache and a goatee, Monsieur Harrow, had bought what was an old workingmen's café. He had seen that the area was a magnet for American tourists, and he thought he might be able to cash in. Monsieur Harrow refurbished the café, put in a bar, and decorated the frontage with solid wooden-framed windows; he curtained the windows so as to add privacy and imply that something interesting was going on inside. Classic external wall advertisements said that the establishment served bière ("brune & blonde"), wines and spirits, "déjeuners" and "diners" (sic). The "Dingo American Bar and Restaurant" was born. Harrow didn't have a word of English; he even hired an interpreter who doubled as a barman. It didn't work until early 1924, when Jimmie Charters arrived as a barman and Flossie Martin discovered it. Harrow cashed in quickly in autumn of that year, selling to American Louis Wilson and his Dutch wife, Jopi.

When the Dingo started in business, *the* "American" bar for the local artists of Montparnasse was the recently-opened Jockey. It was a five minute walk away from the future Dingo, at 146 boulevard du Montparnasse on the corner of rue Campagne-Première, towards Port-Royal. On the walls outside there were striking stylised murals, of an American Indian on horseback and of various strange characters in un-explained costumes. Inside stood a wooden bar, a veritable American saloon.[58] Artists took to the venue and brought with them their new favourite, Alice Ernestine Prin – the aforementioned "Kiki". She and her single mother had moved from rural Burgundy to Paris in 1913, when Kiki was twelve; by age fourteen she was looking after herself. Living hand to mouth, it soon became apparent that her greatest attribute was her body and she became an artists' model – for Soutine, Utrillo, Modigliani, Foujita and many others. Almost all portraits of Kiki de Montparnasse were of her naked.

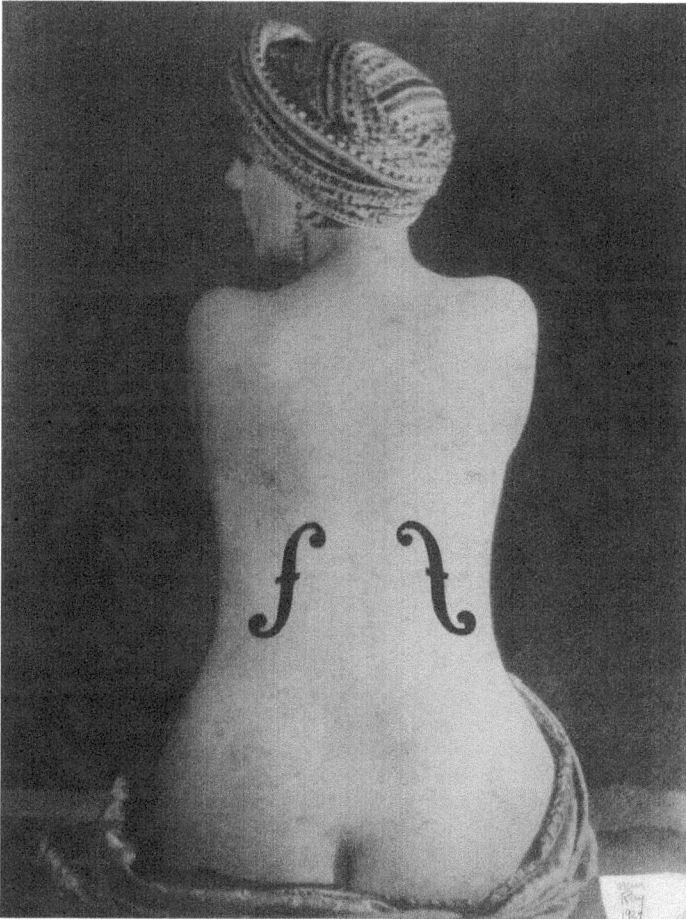

Le Violin d'Ingres by Man Ray, 1924 (Kiki)

Kiki teamed up with the American photographer Man Ray (né Emanuel Radnitsky) in 1921, soon after he arrived from Brooklyn. Notwithstanding her affection for La Rotonde and its bathing facilities, The Jockey was her favourite haunt. She would sit at the bar, sometimes singing Burgundian peasant songs, smoking and drinking something exotic – and always attracting attention with her personal presentation. Kiki had a cat-like translucent face, set off by her black hair. Man Ray "designed Kiki's face for her."[59] He would shave off her eyebrows and paint on new coloured ones; her eye-shadow was bright copper or blue, and she would wear wild ear-rings – gilt curtain rings being a favourite.

And then there was her voluptuous body. In 1924, Man Ray took his famous backshot of her – *Le Violon d'Ingres*. Always impecunious, Kiki was happy to show her breasts "for a franc or two". She did not wear underwear. This was apparent to those for whom she would lift her skirt, again "for a franc or two", in the Jockey and elsewhere.

The Jockey

Jimmie Charters was brought up in Manchester and Liverpool. A short, slight, pink leprechaun of a man, by 1924 he was twenty-seven. He had worked as a waiter and then barman at some of the great hotels and restaurants, largely in Paris after his arrival in 1921, but in London and elsewhere too. Jimmie was everyone's favourite bartender.

He was a charmer, listening, considerate and kind: the quintessential barman. Having seen all measure of human behaviour, he had insight and understanding and compassion. Jimmie Charters ran a great bar. And he seems to have been able to keep almost everything in order too – perhaps because, although Jimmie was diminutive, he was also physically tough, having been a successful professional boxer as a young man.

What's more, he seems to have never made an enemy in his life.

The Dingo's customers would start drifting in after noon. "What'll you have?" was Jimmie's habitual greeting. By five the Dingo would be in full swing. There would be more women than men, with all the half dozen tables taken up, and there would be standing room only at the bar. The Dingo served only simple food, so custom would fade a little during dinner time; and then, after that lull, the customers would return until closing about 3 am. There would always be a few gigolos accompanying older women (who were known as "the alimony gang"), and there was a semi-professional air to a cohort of the younger women too; genuine "poules", however, were not welcome. Jimmie later wrote: "I had never been in a madhouse before I went to Montparnasse. I had never seen people drink to get drunk; never seen artists, writers, nobles, American sailors, and doubtful women mingle on equal terms without reserve."[60]

Jimmie had a following. Laurence Vail wrote:

"Human beings can be roughly divided into two classes. There's the fellow who drinks and yarns at Jimmie's from cocktail to dawn. Then there's that other individual, that nobody, that man in the street."[61]

More often than not the people who came to the Dingo had plenty of money. Jimmie would look after them; he'd tell fibs to their wives or husbands, put them into a taxi when legless and even pay their fare. He listened to the stories of their love lives, their theories about art and sport, took countless watches as security for unpaid bar tabs, and allowed regulars to run up considerable credit. Sylvia Beach, who probably never went into a bar, knew many of his customers: "We have always served the same clients, you, Jimmie, with drinks, I with books."[62]

Lady Duff Twysden and Patrick Guthrie – the inspirations for Brett Ashley and Mike Campbell in *The Sun Also Rises* – were great pals of Jimmie Charters. He considered them a fine couple: theirs was "the most famous love affair and romance of the Quarter."[63] In 1924, Duff Twysden was an Englishwoman of thirty-three, about to be twice-divorced; the title, which she was about to lose, came from her second husband, a baronet. (Sir Roger Twysden, Bt; they were married in 1917 and finally divorced in 1926.)

Outside the *Dingo American Bar and Restaurant* circa 1924:
Jimmie Charters at centre, Duff Twysden seated at left
and Pat Guthrie behind on Jimmie's left

Somewhat androgynous in appearance, Duff was tall and bawdy, and was caricatured by Ernest Hemingway as an alcoholic airhead and nympho-maniac. She spent much of her life breaking men's hearts, Hemingway's included. According to Jimmie, Pat Guthrie had a certain style and dig-nity; a louche Scot, five years younger than his lover but not scrubbing up as well, he could apparently perform a great highland fling. Others simply found this would-be coupon clipper with his elusive fortune the epitome of "genteel, debauched poverty"[64], and a bad drunk.

Hemingway exchanged boxing talk with Jimmie, and together they would go off to the fights at the Cirque de Paris. Other followers of Jimmie were a heterogenous bunch: women in number, Robert McAlmon (who could drink, and fight), paedophile Norman Douglas (who was a "white winer"), future American diplomat Bill Bullitt, Brancusi, Ford Madox Ford, Aleister Crowley, Nancy Cunard (always with a young "coloured" male secretary) and Nina Hamnett.

Nina (Hamnett) by Amedeo Modigliani, 1917

By the time the Dingo got going, Nina was well into her thirties. An Englishwomen, she was a gifted painter, and had already lived in Paris for ten years. It is part of Montparnasse folklore that on her first day in the City of Lights, in 1914, she walked into La Rotonde and was greeted by a handsome youngish man who introduced himself: "Modigliani, painter and Jew". Soon she was a resident of La Huche. Nina's painting career did not take off at this point, however, perhaps because she lacked sufficient application and enjoyed the good life. She was a bon vivant, loved titled people, was happy to dance naked on a restaurant table and to sleep with whoever took her fancy – male or female.

"Hamnett was often out until 7am…People always seemed to be taking their clothes off. There was absinthe, whisky, wine, champagne, plums in kirsch, calvados, bol de cidre, hashish, cocaine, crème de menthe frappe and Pernod Suze, a drink invented by English expats who deemed French cocktails too weak."[65]

Nina played guitar and sang well, and had a repertoire of bawdy songs, with sea shanties a specialty. Her favourite rendition was perhaps *"She Was Poor But She Was Honest"*, although *"Bollocking Bill the Sailor"* was the most popular among the Dingo's clientele. Jimmie Charters was not enamoured of American sailors; they had a penchant for getting into fights. But Nina liked them.

Once Flossie Martin discovered the Dingo it really took off. "Flossie… knew every Englishman and American in Montparnasse, brought all her friends and within a few days the place was so crowded that there was rarely a table free at drinking hours."[66] An ex Ziegfeld girl, Flossie had been sent to Paris by an American admirer to take singing lessons. Singing was to be her new profession. The lessons lapsed and, although Flossie could hold a tune nicely, it was her loud mouth for which she became most famous. Her spoken voice was both piercing and childlike. From deep inside her substantial bosom, an unsuspecting man would be attacked:

"Give us a kiss. Tweetie-tweetie…I'm going to take this sweetie home and lose my virginity…You sweet thing. I'm scaring the [shit] out of you ain't I, pet.[67]

By 1924, she was probably in her mid-thirties. Everyone loved Flossie. She loved a drink, and many of her admirers were those much-valued "buy a drink for the bar" types. In order to cash in on her popularity, Joe Zelli paid Flossie to just turn up at his Montmartre nightclub. He believed she was sure to attract a crowd of touring American legionnaires. And she did; Zelli claimed that the six months he employed her was the best business he ever had.

But Flossie was in her element on the Left Bank, in Montparnasse. She ate (and drank) at the Dôme, and drank and drank at the Dingo. Whatever shenanigans she might have been up to the night before, she fronted up the next day seemingly fresh and clean – and cheerful. She had flawless white skin and a shock of orange hair, but had filled out from her Follies days. What had been a dish was now a tureen.

Flossie Martin, circa 1924
Duff Twysden, 1925

Flossie's favourite cocktail was allegedly the "Jimmie Special": 1/3 cognac, 1/6 Pernod, 1/6 Amer-Picon, 1/6 mandarin liqueur, and 1/6 cherry brandy. Jimmie advised that this combination should be shaken thoroughly with ice, strained into a highball glass with ice added, and served with or without a little soda.[68]

Charters believed the Jimmie Special had the effect of making women undress in public – apparently a common event at the Dingo. The establishment had a preponderance of female customers and, in the interests of moral tone, Jopi Wilson banned the drink from being served. This ban was not always observed, of course, and Flossie continued to be a much-loved drawcard.

Every visiting American knew of the Dingo and Flossie. As noted above, the premises were clearly marked "Dingo American Bar and

Restaurant". Nevertheless, one famous story has two American matrons peering through the curtains of the Dingo, not sure if they had arrived at the right address, when Flossie Martin sauntered by, spat out a vulgar expletive, and walked through the door; that settled it: "This must be the place, Helen." (It is now an Italian restaurant, l'Auberge de Venise. From the street it does not appear greatly changed from its Dingo heyday, and the bar inside is intact.)

A

Most visitors to Paris in the 1920s and 1930s had a Russian taxi driver story. Each driver claimed to be a grand duke or related to one, and each had a family palace back in St Petersburg that had been desecrated by the Bolsheviks. Heavily bewhiskered, sitting high up on the driver's seat, they were seemingly ubiquitous. In fact, they probably represented about ten per cent of the Paris taxi trade; and they had their own trade union – *Union Générale des Chauffeurs Russes*, numbering about 3,000 members. This Russian connection was, in its own way, a continuation of the long tradition of Russia's love affair with Paris: the most handsome bridge in Paris was the Pont Alexandre III; Russian aristocrats were original investors in The Ritz; there were Russian Orthodox churches – Picasso had married his Russian bride in the Cathédrale Saint-Alexandre-Novsky – and then there were the Fabergé eggs. Russian artists had flooded Paris before and after the Great War. Expatriate "White" Russians lived in Paris and (if they had got their money out) in Nice, and the expatriate Russian underclass worked at the Renault, Citroën and Peugeot factories. By 1924, there were perhaps 200,000 such exiles in France.

There were about 60,000 British permanent residents of Paris in 1924. Indeed, there may have been as many as 400,000 foreigners in total.[69] American expatriates numbered above 30,000 – and they were the most obvious. They had come in a recent rush; in 1921 there had been just 6,000 of them.[70] Their motivations to leave the USA included the favourable exchange rate, the city's toleration of non-conformity, the vibrant artistic environment and the absence of Prohibition.

The "American colony" had two cinemas dedicated to American movies, the American Chamber of Commerce thrived, American newspapers had their own Paris editions, and many young Americans, women in particular, were studying at the Sorbonne. Montparnasse had a particular attraction for these expatriate Americans; many made their lives in the district, while a good number of students and tourists adopted Montparnasse as their Paris playground. And for the summer of 1924, American tourists came in waves; first about 5,000 a week and, in one week in July, cruise liners delivered fully 12,000.

Ernest Hemingway and his wife Hadley had first come to Paris in 1922. He was twenty-three, and she thirty-one. They had introductions to Gertrude Stein and Ezra Pound, and lived off her relatively modest income. In 1923 they returned to the USA for the birth of their only child, before returning to Paris in January 1924. This is when all the Hemingway myths and legends started.

Rue Notre-Dame-des-Champs is a narrow, high sided and rather bland street; it winds its way from behind the Closerie des Lilas at Port Royal, and crosses the boulevard Raspail before terminating at the rue de Rennes. In 1924, the street was a mixture of simple housing, local workshops and the usual neighbourhood providores. The Hemingways rented a loft above a carpenter's sawmill, at number 113. Less than five minutes up the street, past Fernand Léger's studio at number 86, lived the Pounds, Ezra and Dorothy; theirs was a simple studio with good light, an annex to number 70 bis.

In March, the Hemingways had their baby christened, just as most other middle-class Americans would do. The venue was their local American church in rue de la Grande Chaumière, a tiny Episcopal chapel largely made of tin, known as St Luke's in the Garden; it was just five minutes around the corner from the Hemingway apartment. (The church existed from 1892 to 1929 in what are now the gardens of Reid Hall, Columbia University's Paris facility.) There were three godparents, including Gertrude Stein and Alice B Toklas; quite how these two Jewish women could handle their responsibility for the Christian child's spiritual welfare, God knows.

Gertrude Stein had adopted Hemingway two years earlier, when he had first introduced himself. Hadley and Ernest became regulars at Gertrude's Saturday evening soirées at the Stein/Toklas apartment (27 rue de Fleurus), drinking eau-de-vie and eating dainty cakes, and Gertrude became a valued mentor, friend and promotor of the fledgling writer.

By 1924, Gertrude Stein was fifty and she had lived in that apartment for nearly twenty years, first with her brother Leo, before Alice moved in (in 1909) and Leo moved out (to Florence, with many of the most valuable paintings). Despite their differing personas, Gertrude overbearing and Alice retiring and self-effacing, they were a devoted couple. As is often the case, their affectionate names for each other were embarrassingly cloying: Alice addressed Gertrude as "lovey" and Gertrude called Alice "pussy".

Gertrude Stein and Alice B Toklas by Man Ray,
1923 at 27 rue de Fleurus

The famous art collection – Cézanne, Picasso, Renoir, Gauguin etc – had been accumulated with Gertrude's brother, who was in fact the family art expert. Gertrude claimed similar insight into painting and painters to that of Leo on the basis of the two Steins having both been early sponsors of Picasso. Picasso enjoyed her, it is true; he painted a portrait of her in 1906, and he remained a friend for years. Gertrude Stein's real talent, however, lay in literature. Not in her own works – most people found them impenetrable, and volumes of her prose and poetry went unpublished. When they ultimately fell out, as Hemingway did with almost everyone, he wrote that "she disliked the drudgery of revision and the obligation to make her writing intelligible".[71] She is credited with inventing the term "the Lost Generation" and the maxims "a rose is a rose is a rose" and "there is no there there" (which is probably a reference to Oakland, California where she spent her childhood). Gertrude Stein's enduring contribution to literature was as a critic and mentor, however, and in that regard she helped Hemingway and others immensely.

From afar, it's difficult to identify Gertrude's attraction. Certainly, it was not physical. She was stout and plain, dumpy and dowdy; she wore leather sandals and "steerage clothes", which she was happy to justify with the advice to "buy your clothes for comfort and durability."[72] She was a political reactionary, not that she talked politics, and she had a compelling presence. Stein would sit in her armchair at rue de Fleurus and command the room. According to Janet Flanner, she had a laugh like a "roaring oven" and when she laughed "it was a like a signal" for all her audience to join in. She was pedantic, and she was always right. One thing she was certain about was the superiority of lesbian sex over gay male sex: "The main thing is that the act male homosexuals commit is ugly and repugnant and afterwards they are disgusted with themselves. They drink and take drugs, to palliate this, but they are disgusted with the act and they are always changing partners and cannot be really happy…In women it is the opposite. They do nothing that they are disgusted by and nothing that is repulsive and afterwards they are happy and they can live happy lives together."[73]

Harry and Caresse Crosby were the epitome of American expatriate indulgence. After a scandalous love affair in Boston when she was still Mrs Peabody, they arrived in Paris in May 1922. She had large breasts and had already patented the first modern brassiere.

Caresse was "Polly" at this point, albeit having been born Mary Phelps Jacob. (Americans, like their former colonial dependants, the Filipinos, often have an aversion to using their real names and adopt diminutives or nicknames instead.) By 1924, Polly had become "Caresse". Harry had been to war and hated what he saw; he was also rich. She was seven years older than he, privileged and well-connected, but not really rich. After Harry graduated from Harvard (Class of '21), he promised himself a life of dissolution. Polly, still married, was happy to join the adventure. In Paris, it was all self-indulgence: the best clothes, best drugs (cocaine, hashish, opium by preference) and the best champagne. Harry was a sexual adventurer, a serial seducer, and together (sic) they led an open marriage. In 1924, they lived in a cottage at 29 rue Boulard, south of the Montparnasse cemetery. A few years later, aged just thirty-one, Harry shot both himself dead and his latest inamorata too. By this time, he and Caresse had become distinguished publishers of the *Black Sun Press*, a new English-language imprint of the first rank. But it was too late; Harry and Caresse's lifestyle was rightly seen to have let the side down.

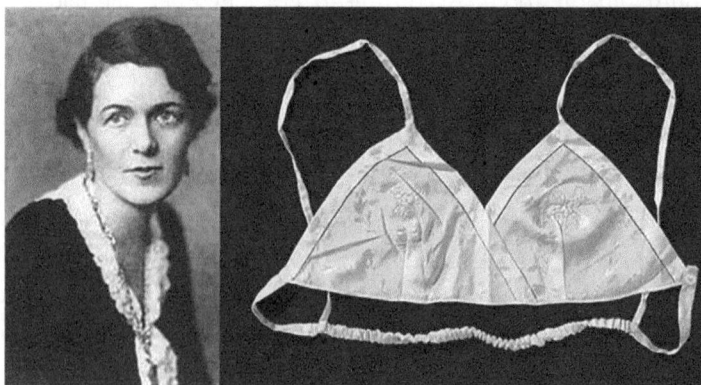

Caresse Crosby and her patented invention

Sara and Gerald Murphy were a complete contrast to the Crosbys. They were exemplary Americans. A good decade older than the leading American Montparnos, they had three golden children; he was handsome, she quite beautiful. "There was a shine to life [wherever] they were... [they had an] inherent loveliness."[74] Of course they were rich, both of them. His money came from the Mark Cross luxury goods business, hers – and it was considerable – from a revolutionary printing process. A graduate of Yale (Class of '11 and a Bonesman), Gerald was thirty-six in 1924; Sara was forty-one. He had found an interest and talent in painting and, on arrival in Paris in 1921, they became honorary members of the Ballets Russes design team.

"Every day was different," Gerald Murphy remembered. *"There was a tension and an excitement in the air that was almost physical. Always a new exhibition, or a recital of the new music of Les Six, or a Dadaist manifestation, or a costume ball...and you'd go to each one and find everybody else there, too."*[75]

The Murphys kept their distance from the Montparnasse crowd. They were somewhat Right Bank and curiously unpretentious. Even so, they were great party givers; their crowd included Cole Porter (Yale '13 and a fellow Bonesman) and Linda Porter, Rudolph Valentino, the Picassos and Douglas Fairbanks. The all-night party they gave on 17 June 1923, after the opening of the Ballets Russes *Les Noces*, was the party of the decade. There were only about forty guests, starting with the Serts and Winnaretta Singer; Diaghilev insisted on rank, so while the ballet principals were invited, the corps de ballet was excluded. The party was held on a *péniche*, a large barge, on the Seine near the Pont de la Concorde. Sarah herself did the décor; it being impossible to buy fresh flowers on a Sunday, she improvised with "bags and bags of toys – fire engines, cars, animals, dolls and clowns – and [she] arranged these in little pyramids at intervals down the long banquet table."[76] Picasso thought it sensational and famously arranged his own grand collage. Food and drink were plentiful. Every artist of note was there: Picasso, Cocteau, Stravinsky,

Tristan Tzara, Milhaud and the rest of Les Six, the lot. The elegance and sophistication of the Murphys was admired by everyone. "They had the gift of making life exceedingly pleasurable for those who were fortunate enough to be their friends."[77]

Having taken the summer holidays of 1922 and 1923 in Cap d'Antibes, the Murphys bought a modest villa there. By August 1924, after extensive improvements, "Villa America" was ready for occupancy. The newly terraced gardens overflowed with oleanders, jasmine, roses and cascading mimosas on a seven-acre site. Sara served delicious food, beautifully prepared and presented; Gerald whipped up exotic cocktails, cleared seaweed from the nearby beach, and gambolled there with their beautiful children.

Sara Murphy and Pablo Picasso on La Garoupe
Sara and Gerard Murphy, 1923

Gerald's "Bailey" was the house speciality cocktail: 3/5 gin (Booth's), 1/5 grapefruit juice, 1/5 lime juice, fresh mint and a great deal of ice. "First put the mint in the shaker, torn up by hand, then the gin – which should be allowed to stand for a minute or two – then the grapefruit and lime juice; this should be stirred vigorously with ice making sure not to dilute the mixture too much and served very cold with a sprig of mint in each glass."[78]

Villa America was a bucolic arcadia to which everyone sought an invitation. Picasso – like Léger, an admirer of Gerald's unheralded talent– was a regular, as was Hemingway with his complicated love-life. And Scott and Zelda Fitzgerald ruined things most of the time, just as he did with his cruel and inaccurate depiction of what everyone took to be the Murphys in *Tender is the Night*.

Back in Montparnasse, Dorothy and Ezra Pound were becoming restive. They were thinking of moving from the frenetic pace of Paris. After promoting James Joyce for years, Hemingway and TS Eliot had become Ezra Pound's new favourites. Pound's friendship with Hemingway was genuine and had become mutually supportive. They were odd companions, though: a bewhiskered bohemian who favoured dandyish velvet jackets, Pound spoke with a dull American accent and was wildly opinionated on almost any subject; to many he was pretentious and affected and, unlike his dashing young friend, he was carrying too much weight. But Hemingway admired Pound's work, and Pound – half a generation older than Hemingway – had been a mentor and promotor of the younger man since their first meeting in 1922. They enjoyed hanging out together; Hemingway wrote to a friend: "he's teaching me to write, and I'm teaching him to box." (In fact, Pound was a keen tennis player at this time; both Natalie Barney and Peggy Guggenheim, on separate occasions, shared a court with him.) The two men had visited Italy together in 1923. Now, the complicated and irascible Pound was preparing to move permanently to the relative calm of Rapallo on the Italian riviera.

Ezra Pound and Dorothy Shakespear left Paris for good in December 1924. Pound's latest lover, pianist Olga Rudge, was three months pregnant and quickly followed the Pounds to Rapallo. After the birth of Rudge's daughter, Dorothy scarpered off to Egypt, if only briefly, and returned visibly pregnant herself; the child was Pound's son. (The women hated each other. The children were adopted out. Pound stayed married to Dorothy, and Olga was happy to stay Pound's mistress for the rest of his life.) Pound and Hemingway maintained their friendship for another decade, until Pound finally went off the rails as a supporter of Mussolini and fascism.

When Harold Stearns graduated from Harvard in 1913, he was quickly picked up by the literary establishment in New York. Son of a single mother, he had earned his keep at Harvard writing for newspapers. On graduation, he was widely thought to be the next big thing, the great hope of American literature. But he did not take to his country's post-war development. In Paris he had found real civilisation. In 1921, he wrote of the Trump-like philistinism and intolerance of his home country; he despaired of "the emergence of inarticulate mediocrity, armed with self-assurance, a full stomach, and a tenacious determination to destroy anything better than itself…"[79] At first, Stearns was the great advocate and example of a successful American expatriate. But the drink got to him. Within years he was reduced to writing up horse racing tips as the *Chicago Tribune*'s "Peter Pickem", and asking acolytes to pay for his pile of drink saucers.

Hemingway, who had enjoyed discussing art with Harold Stearns, now dropped him. Stearns subsequently put his life in order, but to Hemingway he was of no more use. Ernest Hemingway found others more interesting – those he drank with, those he saw at the fights or the velodrome, those that could critique his work and help him become the great writer that he was determined to be. He was industrious and wildly ambitious. The Hemingway apartment in the rue Notre-Dame des-Champs was not suitable for writing; there was a constant buzz and whir from the courtyard below, as the saws of the carpenter's shop worked from seven in the morning to five in the evening. And their boy disturbed him. The answer was to take himself off to La Closerie des Lilas, just up the road, which was happy to allow him to sit out the back nursing a café crème or a glass of ice cold Sancerre. From April 1924, it became his de facto writing studio and it was here that he perfected the clean direct prose that became his signature style.[80]

The American colony did not take kindly to the rush of American tourists each summer. They did not want to be associated with visiting legionnaires from Topeka or Rotary members from Cincinnati, nor indeed the swarms of Ivy League boys and their girlfriends. If they could, they went off to the country or the seaside, like the French. In the summer of 1924, the Hemingways put together a team of eight cronies to go to Spain, where they drank and played at Pamplona's San Fermín fiesta for a week before a rump retired to fish in the tranquil streams of the Irati at Burguete. (The group included neither Duff Twysden nor Pat Guthrie; they were members of Hemingway's 1925 contingent, when they unwittingly provided much material for *The Sun Also Rises*.) Ernest and Hadley were away from Paris for a month and, as their absence coincided with the Paris Olympics, they probably sub-let their apartment to Olympic visitors.

In August, on their return, Paris was swept with torrential rains. Hemingway returned to work at La Closerie. Later, in the autumn, he wrote outside the restaurant, either under the shade of the trees in sight of Marshall Ney's statue or at one of the square tables under the awnings on the boulevard side. His infectious charm and charisma had already made him a social prize, and within two years he was the famous writer of *The Sun Also Rises* – and he was on his way.

That summer, Flossie Martin had entertained her compatriots at the Dôme and the Dingo. As usual. In the first ten days of June 1924, eleven transatlantic liners had docked at Cherbourg; the passengers wasted no time in packing themselves into Paris-bound trains. Then there was the US fleet: Navy vessels SS Pittsburgh, SS Memphis and SS Detroit each came to France for protracted visits, and "all Montparnasse was infested with sailors and petty officers moving in groups around Flossie and Nina [Hamnett]."[81] Nina was particularly fond of a sailor, in or out of uniform. One night she borrowed one – a uniform, perhaps the sailor as well – and took to the streets of Montmartre and Montparnasse in sailors rig.

Yet, years later, as Flossie reflected on those raucous and hedonistic days, not simply the year 1924 but all the years, she said her happiest memory was of:

"just sitting outside Le Select with a good long drink, and nothing to do but drink it"[82]

DIVERTISSEMENTS

Paris had more than two hundred cinemas in 1924.[83] They still showed "silent" movies. Talkies did not arrive until 1927, although nothing in the city's picture theatres was silent. Every cinema had a piano, some had an organ, even a grand organ, and the smartest establishments had small orchestras.

Cinemas were everywhere. The grandest were on the Grands Boulevards, such as the Aubert-Palace (at 24 boulevard des Italiens), the Madeleine (14 boulevard de Madeleine), and the Louxor (170 boulevard de Magenta). These were people's palaces, with baroque ornamentation, galleries and balconies, and seating for up to two thousand. A typical programme would comprise a newsreel or short documentary, an episode from a serial and, after an interval, the feature film.

Although the movie-houses were typically owned by French investors – Gaumont, Aubert or Pathé – American films now dominated the screens. It has been estimated that French movies may only have accounted for ten or twelve per cent of footage shown at the time. Charlie Chaplin (known to the French as "Charlot") was top dog, although his fellow United Artists founders Douglas Fairbanks and Mary Pickford were close behind. Douglas Fairbanks' swashbuckling extravaganza *The Thief of Baghdad*, the big event of 1924, cost more than $1 million to make. Fairbanks was the writer, producer and star. His athleticism, plus the movie's special effects – rope tricks, flying carpets – and the exotic Arabian Nights sets, all helped make it one of the great silent films.

Charlot directed a film – *A Woman of Paris* – in which he didn't appear, which was not a good idea because the public had expected to see him in it. The critics, however, were full of praise. Mary Pickford's contribution for the year was *Dorothy Vernon of Haddon Hall*.

French films tended to be more avant-garde and experimental. René Clair's films of 1924 were *Paris qui dort* and *Entr'Acte*; one featured freeze frames in dramatic views from the Eiffel Tower, and the other synchronisation of music with the movie's action. For its part, Fernand Léger's *Ballet mécanique* (also 1924), was littered with visual puns.

The wonderful Aubert-Palace cinema (1915-1987)

Among the important cinemas of the era, some are still operating. Ciné Max-Linder at 24 boulevard Poissonière has a most wonderful interior; it first opened in 1912 and was subsequently remodelled in the art deco style. The Louxor, a neo-Egyptian extravaganza built in 1921, has been refurbished and revived. The Studio des Ursulines (1925), which was subjected to one of André Breton's ridiculous disruptions in 1928, is still intact, inside and out, at 10 rue des Ursulines; and the Gaumont Opéra at 2 boulevard des Capucines, although renovated inside, still has its classic exterior.

Ordinary folk celebrated a night out at a bal musette, simple dance halls with an accordion band. The high society of the Beaumonts and the Noailles had their fancy balls. Gays had drag balls at Music-City and elsewhere. Music halls featured Mistinguett and Maurice Chevalier. And the art students from the École des Beaux-Arts had an annual event, an extraordinarily licentious bacchanal: the Bal des Quart'z'Arts.

In 1924 it was held at Luna Park on Tuesday, 17 June.

The Bal des Quart'z'Arts had taken place every year for thirty years. Located in a splendid Beaux-Arts building on the rue Bonaparte, the national art school had four seperate faculties – painting, architecture, sculpture and engraving – *quatre arts*, that is "four arts". Each of the faculties would put on a party of some sort during the year to which almost anyone was invited; they charged for attendance, and any surplus was put into the pot to help finance the annual Bal des Quat'z'Arts. It was the climax of the year for the students, marked the start of the summer holidays for many and, since the students tended to take over the town, it gave some more sober Parisians a good reason to get out into the country early.

Typically, participants would dine somewhere cheap with a crowd of fellow students and then set off for the designated party venue. The theme for 1923 was "Bacchanale in Pompeii", and it too was held at Luna Park. An enthusiastic observer reported this scene in front of the Gare Montparnasse:

> *"Under the low, grey sky of a rainy end of the day, the sudden appearance of a theory of helmeted warriors and half-naked dancers, as if one had suddenly broken, on the pavement of the square, some precious vase from our museums or a millennial vase, whose frescoes would suddenly have been animated…these blue men, these red bestiaries, these yellow dancers, all this masquerade radiated an unknown beauty…"*[84]

No doubt the 1923 revellers behaved as we know their successors did in 1924. Watched by crowds of tourists and Parisians alike, they would have walked up the boulevards with arms linked, kissed any girl they saw, snatched drinks from sidewalk tables, invaded restaurants and dance halls, even hotel rooms – all the while protected and authorised by police, who walked in front, behind or around a cohort, and were happy to do so.[85]

A ball has to have a theme. From its earliest days, the themes most favoured for the Bal des Quat'z'Arts were the ancient worlds of Greece and Rome. An artist's model was arrested for being quite naked at the second ball, in 1893, and this set something of a trend – the nudity, not the arrest. Participants were expected to dress according to the designated theme. Drink and dancing, music, noise and licentiousness in general could be expected, as could nudity. The invitations for 1924, which had a Phoenician theme, were two: one had a Phoenician soldier carrying off a naked maiden; the other featured a bearded Phoenician merman cavorting with five naked women. Both carried the usual warning: *Le comité se dégage des poursuites judiciaries qu'entrainerait l'exhibition du nu sur la voie publique.* ("The committee takes no responsibility for any legal proceedings that may result from the public display of nudity.") So, as was now traditional, everyone knew what to expect. Everyone painted Phoenician red over already exposed flesh, and – for those who thought they might need to give colour continuity as the night wore on – under flimsy garments as well.

Invitations to the Bal des Quart'z'Arts, 1924

Luna Park was a huge entertainment centre on the Thiers Wall at Porte Maillot, near the Bois de Boulogne. Its dance floor could house more than 2,000. Tickets were carefully allocated to arts students – cheaper for women than men – and they were not transferable. There was also a special category – "committee tickets" – which were invitations issued to distinguished artists or others, like movie stars, who might add lustre to the occasion. This created a small black market.

Entry was closely policed. On arrival, women were sent in one direction where their bona fides and their conformity with the dress code were checked by perhaps a couple of committee members. Men faced deeper scrutiny, with as many as eight such inspectors. Beefy bouncers stood by to deal with any problems. A ticket was required, but so too was knowledge of what faculty the student belonged to and the name and interests of the professor who was his or her supervisor. Interlopers were shunted off. Some unfortunates were sent to a door which led to a door, multiple corridors, corners, steps and so on – until they found themselves back on the street.

At the 1924 ball, a middle-aged American couple turned up at two in the morning when the event was in full swing. Because they had committee tickets, they were admitted without question. The Americans soon happily took to the dance floor. Everyone could see that they were improperly dressed: they were in evening dress, very fancy ensembles apparently, but not *Phoenician*, as was clearly marked "de rigueur" on the invitation. To "whoops of glee", the howling students swooped upon the stout couple; they disrobed them, item by item, until they were quite naked in the middle of the dance floor. The distressed couple fled to an exit, still naked, hailed a cab and retired to the Crillon – whence, cleaned up and dressed, they decamped to Ohio, leaving Paris forever.[86]

Each year prizes were awarded for the most elaborate and inventive headdresses and for costumes too, such as they were. There were two orchestras in 1924. As the night developed, streamers and confetti were thrown down to the dance floor from Luna Park's balconies, the most secluded of which were much favoured by lovers. Not that discretion was required.

Caresse and Harry Crosby moved to a grand new apartment at 119 rue de Lillle in late 1925; it was just around the corner from the Beaux-Arts, and Caresse befriended the students. The Crosbys were soon given committee tickets for the Quat'z'Arts balls, and for the next few years – until Harry's unfortunate demise – the Crosbys would put on a raucous pre-ball dinner party for their sponsors. Harry Crosby described a scene from the 1927 ball: "At one o'clock it was WILD...men and women stark naked, dancing people rushing to and fro." Caresse went topless, sat astride a baby elephant and led a parade down the Champs-Elysées; Harry, naked to the waist and with a string of dead pigeons around his neck, released ten snakes onto the dance floor (as you do):

> "...I remember two strong young men wrestling on the floor for the
> honour of dancing with a young girl...and I remember a mad stu-
> dent drinking champagne out of a skull...and in a corner I watched
> two savages making love... and beside me sitting on the floor a plump
> woman with bare breasts absorbed in the passion of giving milk to
> one of the snakes."[87]

The Ball would typically go on to about six or seven, when everyone would form a circle and close down the event with the cry "Vive le bal des Quat'z'Arts!" In 1924, the stragglers were roughed up by a posse of radical malcontents who apparently objected to the "privilege" represented by the ball and its participants; police moved them on. And everyone went off to the fountains at the Place de la Concorde for the traditional dip; but the red Phoenician dye did not wash off readily, and many students continued to wear it as a badge of honour for another ten days.

Cycling was among the most popular sports at the time, along with boxing and football (soccer). The top teams and the top sportsmen in each of these sports were professional. Cycling, boxing and football were all Olympic events – but, consistent with the amateur Olympic ethos of the time, professionals were banned from competing in the Games. Accordingly, few of the top performers in these three sports competed in the 1924 Paris Olympics.

High among the most popular events in France, every year, was – as it still is – the Tour de France.

In these early days of the Tour it was a purely endurance event. In 1924, it took a full month to complete, starting in Paris on 22 June (a Sunday) and ending back in the capital on Sunday, 20 July. There were fifteen "stages", one every second day, as the Tour moved counter-clockwise around the perimeter of France. No time trials, just pure road racing. Everyone started a stage at the same time – the so-called *départ* – and then the cyclists were off for a stage of between three and five hundred kilometres. A stage could be incredibly gruelling, starting and finishing in the dark and often lasting twenty or more hours. The winner of each stage got a time bonus of three minutes subtracted from his actual time, but otherwise a rider's standing was determined by the simple addition of his times recorded on each stage.

The overall winner was the rider with the least accumulated time.

One hundred and fifty-seven cyclists started the 1924 Tour, and sixty finished. It was the largest field since the first Tour in 1904. Past winners Henri Pélissier and Philippe Thys were among them, as were many *touriste-routiers*, private entrants who came along for the ride.

No help could be given for flat tyres; riders had to do any repairs themselves. (Hence those atmospheric old photos of tyres swung over a rider's shoulders.) Nor could a bicycle be replaced. Gears were banned and tyre rims had to be made from wood (for fear that the heat from braking would melt the glue that held tyres on metal rims). A further constraint was that teams had to start and finish a stage with the same equipment. This rule had been introduced some years before because Pélissier – in preparing for a sprint finish – had once discarded not just his spare tyres and the food he was carrying, but his pump and repair tools too. And, since contestants had taken to discarding excess jerseys when the weather warmed up, the ban extended to clothing; the same clothing had to be worn from the start of a stage to its finish.

Henri Pélissier was an all-round cycling star, and an endurance race like the Tour was not his forte. Even so, he had won the 1923 Tour. He rode because the race was prestigious, not because it suited his talents. Pélissier had argued for shorter stages, ones that might encourage better racing and exciting sprints. And thus, on Stage Three of the 1924 Tour, came high drama.

After the usual rest day, the riders prepared for the départ of a seemingly innocuous 405 km flat run from Cherbourg to Brest. On the starting line Pélissier was confronted by the manager of a rival team. The manager lifted the champion's jersey, wanting to see if Pélissier was wearing two jerseys, as he believed that Pélissier had discarded a jersey on the second stage. It was an inauspicious start to a day that was to become famous in the Tour's history.

When the peloton reached Granville, about 100 km from Cherbourg, there was no sign of Pélissier or of his brother, Francis. It was six am and the race had been running for perhaps three hours. When the touriste-routiers passed through and there was still no sign of the Pélissiers, the news came that the brothers had abandoned the race. With the race having only started a few days previously, this was big news. The press retraced the route and at the Café de la Gare in Coustances, less than thirty kilometres back, the Pélissiers were holding fort.

It transpired that after his interchange with the rival manager, Pélissier had sought out the founder and director of the Tour, Henri Desgrange. Desgrange was tough and authoritarian. Pélissier was tough too, and a star, and headstrong; according to his account they had this acrimonious conversation:[88]

> P: *I am not allowed to throw my jersey by the road, then?*
> D: *No. You must not throw away anything belonging to the team.*
> P: *It's not the team's, it's mine.*
> D: *I'm not discussing this on the road.*
> P: *If you won't discuss it on the road, I'll go back to bed.*
> D: *We'll sort it out in Brest.*
> P: *At Brest, everything will be sorted, because I will have thrown in my hand. The Pélissiers not only have legs, they have a head. And in that head they've got judgment.*

So the Pélissiers never made it to Brest, abandoning the Tour at Coustances. But there was more. The brothers and their colleague, Maurice Ville, who had been coming second and had also abandoned the race, let fly.

Journalist Albert Londres at left front, with Maurice Ville at the table
and the brothers Pélissiers opposite

They complained about the conditions the riders had to suffer. Not simply the clothing question, although they did mention that riders often moved during a stage from near freezing to heat suffocation. ("And if I so much as stick a newspaper under my jersey at the start, they check that it's still there at the finish.") They said they accepted the torment of the Pyrénées and the daily grind – the wind and rain, the sleet and mud. No, it was the petty rules to which they objected, like making sure that the riders themselves had drawn the water from the water pumps when they filled their water bottles. Then came the bombshell: "You want to see how we keep going?" Henri Pélissier asked rhetorically. "Here. This, that's cocaine for the eyes, that's chloroform for the gums…and the pills? Would you like to see the pills? Look, here are the pills." His brother added: "In short, we keep going on dynamite." And Henri concluded: "At night, in our rooms, we dance the jig, like St [Vitus], instead of sleeping."

Doping was not illegal. Everyone knew that something was going on, but the Pélissiers blew the whistle on the chemist shop of drugs that were taken regularly by riders – and did so at the start of the mythical Tour de France, no less.

As to the stage itself, notwithstanding the many flat tyres, it ended up with a bunch finish at the Brest velodrome, as expected. The stage winner drew level with the Italian Ottavio Bottecchia, who had held the yellow jersey from Stage One. By this time, Bottecchia was thirty. He came from the most humble of circumstances, and after brave service as a bicycle messenger and reconnaissance soldier in the Great War, he had moved to France for work. By 1920, however, he was back in Italy as a professional cyclist. Illiterate as a young man, he was taught to read by a fellow rider who shared his interest in sport and his anti-fascist politics. Bottecchia had come second to Pélissier in 1923, having worn the yellow jersey for much of the race, and he was widely thought to be the coming man.

In the event, Bottecchia led the 1924 Tour from start to finish. The race had started in Paris at the Parc des Princes, as usual, and finished there too – with Bottecchia winning the final stage and winning the overall race by thirty-five minutes. It was a comprehensive victory, and the first by an Italian. Bottecchia won again in 1925.

The next year he started to manufacture the Bottecchia racing bike, still a leader in the field. In June 1927, however, when he did not return from a training spin near his Italian home, he was found by the roadside with a deep headwound and a broken collar bone. Ottavio Bottecchia died twelve days later. All the evidence pointed to a Fascist assassination.

Track cycling is wonderfully exciting, and Parisians flocked to see it in the 1920s. The varieties were many: sprints, match races (where the opponents would hover for minutes on their bicycles, like gymnasts but barely moving, waiting for one to make the first move), one-hour distance events, motor-paced sprints and the enormously popular six-day races. There were three major venues: Vélodrome Buffalo, near Porte Maillot, which was set up in the American style with fast wooden boards and had a circuit of about 300 metres and a capacity of about 8,000; the Parc des Princes (officially the Stade Vélodrome du Parc des Princes) at Auteuil, with a much bigger cement track of 666 metres and a crowd capacity in 1924 of 20,000; and the indoor Vélodrome d'Hiver.

The Vél d'Hiv, as it was universally known, was something special. Centrally located on the corner of the boulevard de Grenelle and the rue Nélaton, it had started life in 1910. A banked cycle track measured exactly 250 metres at its circumference. Two tiers of seats rose around it like cliffs. Capacity was 20,000 – and it was the perfect venue for track cycling. Hemingway described the scene:

> *"…the smoky light of the afternoon and the high-banked wooden track and the whirring sound the tires made on the wood as the riders passed, the effort and the tactics as the riders climbed and plunged, each one part of his machine…the magic of the demi-fond, the noise of the motors with their rollers set out behind them that the entraîneurs rode, wearing their heavy crash helmets and leaning backward in their ponderous leather suits…the riders…bent low over their handlebars their legs turning the huge gear sprockets…the riders elbow to elbow and wheel to wheel up and down and around at deadly speed…"*[89]

Six-Day races were the most popular. Over six evenings, teams of two would compete in multiple events – sometimes an elimination race, sometimes a points race, sprints, time trials and motor-paced races – but the heart of any evening was the "madison", named after Madison Square Garden. Essentially the madison involved the two team riders trying to gain laps against their competitors. Both riders stayed on the velodrome throughout the event, one passing responsibility for the race to his teammate in a sort of team-tag; as his teammate raced off, the retiring teammate would continue to circle and rest until taking over the race from his colleague. The change from one rider to the other was usually effected by a highly technical slinging manoeuvre, which invariably thrilled the crowds.

And crowds there were. It was not unusual for police to be called in to control them. The king of the Six-Days was an Australian with a French name: Alfred Goullet. He had moved to New York in 1910 to race professionally. By 1912, aged only twenty-one, Goullet started breaking world records for distances up to a mile. Together with an American colleague, Joe Fogler, he won the inaugural Paris Six-Day at the Vél d'Hiv on 13 January 1913. It was an enormous success: gates had opened at 6 pm, and soon all twenty thousand seats were occupied. The Great War meant that no race occurred from 1915 to 1920.

Cycling at the Vélodrome d'Hiver, 1925

Alf Goullet returned to the track after war service; he won fifteen Six-Days in all, but he could not be induced back to Paris again. (He was earning too much in the USA, becoming one of the highest paid athletes in the world, and he retired in 1925.) The 1921 *Six Jours de Paris* did not need Goullet to bring back the crowds. Cycling was exciting, and track cycling in particular. The top riders were heroes and media stars. Inevitably people gambled on the results of the various events – some innocently, some not. Among the riders there was a temptation (and no doubt inducements) to influence the outcomes. It became clear to most that not all races were decided on the merits of the participants. Indeed, it was widely thought that an inner circle of riders in the *Six Jours de Paris* fixed races and split the proceeds. Not that it affected the crowds.

They were huge: the working class came with their families and brought along food and drink to consume in the balconies; sporting enthusiasts and toffs, meanwhile, patronised the fancy restaurants and bars that were set up on the lawn area in the centre of the track. The Vél d'Hiv's *Six Jours de Paris* became a total experience of showbiz, sporting competition and festivity for the full spectrum of social classes. More often than not mounted police were needed to patrol the streets outside, keeping people back behind the barriers, and turning away those without tickets. And that continued through the 1920s and 30s.

Since the Second World War, however, the Vél d'Hiv has had a more sinister reputation. In 1942, Parisian Jews were impounded there after the notorious "roundup" of 16 and 17 July. Thirteen thousand men, women and children were held in the velodrome for five days under the most appalling conditions, before they were sent off to Hitler's death camps.

Boxing was the other great attraction. Championships were held in at least four major locations – the Vél d'Hiv, the Cirque de Paris (also known as the Cirque Métropole), the Cirque d'Hiver and the Stade Anastasie.

The Vél d'Hiv was easily converted into a boxing arena. In 1924, it staged the French welterweight title fight between Raymond Porcher and Daniel Arnaud on 4 April; Porcher won on points over twenty rounds.

The Cirque de Paris, however, was probably the top venue. Immediately after the Great War, the YMCA had leased the Cirque for a series of boxing events for Allied soldiers, and boxing at the venue had become a fashionable night out for men about town. Located at 18 avenue de la Motte-Piquet, the Cirque de Paris had the usual seats set out around the boxing ring, but it also had smart boxes in a balcony, where enthusiasts and society leaders alike typically turned out in black tie. In 1924, it hosted three French title bouts: two on one night in January, when François Charles knocked out Georges Rouquet in the third round for the middleweight title, and when André Routis beat Charles Ledoux on points over twenty rounds for the bantamweight title. Then, the following month, Ledoux moved up a division – and, strangely perhaps, he beat Edouard Mascart on points over twenty rounds for the featherweight title.

The Cirque d'Hiver, at 10 rue Amelot, had served many purposes since being built in the 1850s. Its actual circuses, so evocatively preserved for history in Georges Seurat's *Le Cirque*, have always been its most famous performances. But it also hosted boxing matches. Hemingway remembered going there in the '20s on Friday nights for twenty rounders.

The most interesting venue, however, may have been the Stade Anastasie. It was a dance hall and restaurant up a hill to the north east, at 136 rue Pelleport, and also a boxing and PE school. In the summer, late spring and early autumn, the proprietor would set up a ring under the trees in the large courtyard. And after dinner, patrons from the restaurant and spectators who only turned up for the fights could together watch a series of contests.

The great French star of the era was Georges Carpentier. He came from Lens in northern France and, once his boxing talent had been identified, he moved to Paris. Carpentier's first professional bouts were said to have been when he was just fourteen, although there is some dispute as to his actual birthdate. As he grew he moved up the divisions. In 1909, as a fifteen year-old bantamweight, he beat the tiny Charles Ledoux on points over a full fifteen rounds. (Ledoux was two years older than Carpentier and barely five feet tall; he became a national champion, as noted above, and continued boxing until 1926.) By 1911, still said to be only seventeen, Carpentier was French middleweight champion.

Carpentier was also a boxing referee. On 28 June 1914, he refereed the world heavyweight championship between Jack Johnson and Frank Moran, at the Vél d'Hiver. It must have been an incredible evening. Not the fight; the crowd. Women were in abundance, led by the Baroness de Rothschild, the Duchess d'Uzès, the Countess de Noailles and the Duchess de Rohan. Seriously. The men were just as prominent: the Duke of Westminster and the Earl of Sefton, the Marquis de Lafayette and so on. The bout went for the full twenty rounds, and there were no knockdowns. Moran was outclassed. At fight's end and without hesitation, Carpentier declared Johnson the winner. No doubt he learnt some lessons that night simply by watching the great Jack Johnson. Whatever, Johnson was happy to announce that "Carpentier was a fine referee."

After the war, in which Carpentier had served as a pilot, he moved up to cruiserweight (light heavyweight). In 1919, he knocked out Battling Levinsky for the world championship. Now came the real bigtime.

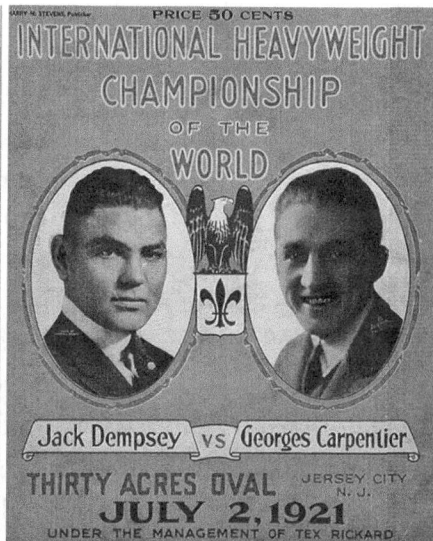

Georges Carpentier crossing the Atlantic for
"The Match of the Century"

Carpentier was very handsome. Known as the "Orchid Man" because of the flower he habitually wore with a smart suit, Carpentier was charming and universally liked. And he was a war veteran. Jack Dempsey had not gone to war, and much was made of this distinction when Carpentier moved up a division to challenge Dempsey for the world heavyweight championship.

On 2 July 1921, promoted by Tex Rickard as "The Match of the Century", it was boxing's first million dollar gate. By today's standards they were not big men. Carpentier stood at just under six feet (182 cm) and was probably eight or nine kilos lighter than the 6' 1" champion who weighed 87 kilos. Despite his great skill and style, Carpentier was knocked out in the fourth round.

The next year, moving back to his correct weight division, he lost his light heavyweight title to Ho Chi Minh's hero Battling Siki, when Siki didn't take the agreed dive. Carpentier had been coasting along and unwittingly hurt the Senegalese fighter; this riled Siki, and he knocked Carpentier out. This could have been the end of his career but, married since 1920 and with a daughter, Carpentier somewhat surprisingly regrouped, trained hard and boxed on successfully.

Although Jack Dempsey was still champion, by 1924 Gene Tunney was the coming man. Carpentier was matched with him. Having lost to Dempsey so convincingly, most expected Carpentier to lose again when, on 24 July 1924, Tunney and Carpentier met at New York's Polo Grounds. (The Olympic boxing tournament had taken place between 15 and 20 July, but keen followers of the sweet science were focused on this bout.) Only his strongest French supporters thought Carpentier was in with any real chance. The silky and stylish Tunney dominated at first, but then Carpentier landed some of his trademark savage rights. It was a terrific fight. Tunney was clearly ahead, however, when Carpentier went down in the fourteenth with what appeared to be a low blow. He could not continue, and Tunney was declared a winner by TKO in the fifteenth round. *Ring* magazine declared it the "Fight of the Year".

Georges Carpentier returned to France a hero, a status the Orchid Man enjoyed for the rest of his life.

CHARIOTS OF FIRE

In the morning the Prince of Wales had a practice game of polo with a few friends on soggy ground at the Bagatelle in the Bois de Boulogne.[90] Afterwards he hastened to the Élysée Palace where, together with his brother, Prince Henry, Duke of Gloucester, and members of the IOC, he had lunch as a guest of President Doumergue. It was Saturday, 5 July 1924, and the President would be opening the Olympic Games that afternoon.

Spectators arriving for the Opening Ceremony;
the warmup track is centre left

It seemed that all Paris was streaming to the Stade de Colombes on this dull, grey day – coming by bus, train, tram, bicycle and on foot. The stands were full by 2:30, although the outer was not. Bands played and choirs sang as South Africa ("Afrique du Sud") led the teams out into the arena in alphabetical order. Only the French and Belgians received greater applause than the huge American contingent. The Cameron Highlander pipe band made a memorable entrance as they pumped out a rousing set of Scottish tunes behind the large British contingent.

A flying boat made a dramatic turn in the sky over the Presidential stand, where Gaston Doumergue entertained the Prince of Wales on his right, Crown Prince Carol of Rumania to his left, the aforementioned Prince Henry (not the Navigator), Crown Prince Gustaf Adolf of Sweden, the Princess of Serbia, the Shah of Persia (who was on an extended tour of Europe in anticipation of his likely removal) and, from Ethiopia, thirty-one-year-old Ras Tafari[91], the exotic Regent Plenipotentiary and Crown Prince.

Géo André takes the Olympic Oath
while giving the Olympic Salute

French athlete Géo André, a four time Olympian and former national rugby representative, then took the Olympic Oath on behalf of all the competitors. (In taking the oath he gave the Olympic Salute, a salutation that was later discontinued with the advent of the almost identical Nazi greeting.) And, then, with great solemnity, the President declared the Games of the Eighth Olympiad open. Twenty aeroplanes flew low overhead and loud cannon fire suddenly erupted – this caught the crowd off-guard and caused a degree of panic – and 5,000 pigeons were released to the skies.[92] The Games would last for three weeks, until 27 July.

Eric Liddell was a twenty-two year-old Scots track athlete; he was in Paris to compete at the Games. His specialities were the 100 and 200 metres. On Sunday, 6 July the heats of the 100 metres would take place at 2:30 in the afternoon. But Liddell would not be racing. A devout Christian, he refused to compete on a Sunday. Instead, on this Sunday he read the lesson (from Isaiah 40) at the Scots Kirk, 17 rue Bayard, in the smartest corner of the 8th arrondissement.

Most national teams had arrived two weeks before the kick-off. For the first time, there was an Olympic Village – a series of portable wooden huts with pitched tile roofs and running water set up in an empty field within walking distance of the stadium. The rough warm-up track and a large swimming pool were adjacent to the stadium, so they too were conveniently nearby. Each hut had three bedrooms, and within the village there was a money changer, a post office with telephones and a restaurant. Accommodation was 30 FF a night, and board (which included three full meals and laundry) was another 25 FF. The Americans, except for the male swimmers, were accommodated elsewhere, at the grand and beautiful Chateau de Rocquencourt, 20 kilometres and a full hour's drive to the west. The Australians, who enjoyed a favourable exchange rate like the Americans, set themselves up in the centre of the city at the Hotel Normandie, near the Louvre; and the Finns rented four villas in Colombes, close to the Olympic stadium, where they constructed a special Nordic sauna in the grounds.

The Games had attracted forty-five nations, the largest ever, and 3,256 athletes. Only 156 of these were women. Women were allowed to compete in swimming, tennis, fencing and yachting – but there were no events for them in track and field. (English newspapers *The News of the World, Daily Mirror* and *Sporting Life* staged a one day "Women's Olympiad" in London on 4 August 1924. Representatives of eight nations competed in twelve track and field events.)

The 100 metre dash is a major event at every Olympics and, as every sports enthusiast knows, that of the 1924 Olympics was no exception. Indeed it is immortalised in the wonderful and largely accurate 1981 British movie "Chariots of Fire".

Charlie Paddock of the USA was the defending champion. Fair-headed, short and chunky, in 1919 Paddock had come to prominence when he won the 100 and 200 at the Inter-Allied Games. The next year, at the Antwerp Games, he won two gold medals, one for the 100 and a second as a member of the 4x100 relay team; he also finished second in the 200. By 1921, when he started breaking world records, Charlie Paddock had become known as "the fastest man alive". He was popular (except with the AAU) and flamboyant, not least for his trademark leaping finish – a dangerous manoeuvre requiring perfect timing if it were not to backfire. Having graduated from USC in 1923, Paddock would have been happy to rest on his laurels and not go to a second Olympics – he still held the world records for both 100 (10.2s) and 200 (21.0s) – and he had to be persuaded to compete in Paris.

The favourite, however, was Jackson Scholz. After graduating from the University of Missouri, he ran for the New York Athletic Club. He was twenty-three at Antwerp where he had come fourth in the 100 and earned a gold medal with Paddock in that US 4x100 relay team. Later that year, 1920, he equalled the world record for the 100 (then 10.6s).

Dark-haired, lean and light (61 kg versus Paddock's 76 kg), he was proving to be something of a late bloomer and by 1924 was known as "The New York Thunderbolt".

Eric Liddell and Harold Abrahams would have been the British hopes until Liddell found out about the Sunday scheduling of the 100 metre heats. Liddell settled on preparing himself for the 200 and 400, leaving Abrahams as the British standard-bearer. Abrahams had attended the English "public school" Repton where, because of his Jewish faith and despite his athletic prowess, he was treated as something of an outsider; this continued when he studied at Cambridge, where he graduated in 1923. (He was in fact a very secular Jew, marrying "out" and bringing his children up as Christians.) Abrahams was a natural athlete; he stood at six feet (183 cm) and weighed 75 kg, a physique well-suited for sprinting. By 1924 Abrahams was practising law as a barrister during the day and training as often as he could; he was determined to shine at the upcoming Olympics. To that end, and somewhat controversially, he hired the noted professional coach Sam Mussabini. Mussabini worked on Abrahams' start and his form; he adjusted Abrahams' stride and arm action. Often criticised for being somewhat arrogant, Harold Abrahams was certainly single-minded. He had great will power and, importantly, he had a great temperament – being able to stay relatively calm under pressure.

On the Sunday afternoon, the first day of the Olympic competition, there were seventeen heats, with the first two finishers going through to the quarter-finals later that afternoon. All the aspirants got through safely on a slippery, rain-soaked track. In the quarter-finals, of which there were six, the lanky Abrahams won his in 10.6s (equalling the Olympic record) and both Paddock and Scholz won theirs in 10.8s. All was going to plan for the two semi-finals and final which were scheduled for the following day.

At 2 pm that next day, Monday 7 July, Scholz won his semi-final in 10.8. Second, perhaps surprisingly, was the New Zealand Rhodes Scholar, Arthur Porritt. In the second semi-final, Abrahams won clearly from Charlie Paddock. Abrahams again ran 10.6s.

It would be nearly four hours before the final. Staying calm in such circumstances can be difficult, and even the equable Abrahams later confessed to feeling "like a condemned man feels before going to the scaffold".[93] The final was scheduled for 7 pm and it started five minutes late. Abrahams had missed the start in his semi-final; for the final, however, after a long silence, all six runners set off together. Sam Mussabini had told him: "Only think of two things – the report of the pistol and the tape". No-one stood out for half the race as the athletes kept between those strange low-slung ropes that separated lanes in those days. At mid-point, however, Abrahams started to prevail and move slightly ahead. He maintained his lead to the tape, winning by perhaps a metre from Jackson Scholz with Porritt third. Charlie Paddock, defending his title, was a disappointing fourth. The time was, once again, 10.6s, the Englishman equalling the Olympic record for the third time. Harold Abrahams had peaked perfectly, and he had run the perfect race.

Harold Abrahams wins the 100 metres

Not everyone was at the Games. Paris had other things going on that Monday evening. Ezra Pound and his wife, Dorothy Shakespear – "M. et Mme. Ezra Pound" – had invited a select list of their friends to a 9 pm "audition privée" at the (old) Salle Pleyel, 22 rue de Rochechouart.

Three days later than the Declaration of Independence, the concert was designed to celebrate that anniversary as new "Musique Américaine". The key performers were Olga Rudge and George Antheil, both Americans, plus the French tenor Yves Tinayre, and Ezra Pound himself. Everyone could expect the show to be pretty avant-garde, indeed challenging. And so it proved to be.

Olga Rudge was Pound's latest mistress. He had met her two years earlier year at one of Natalie Barney's Friday evenings, and he was entranced by the celebrated concert violinist. A pretty woman with dark hair, bobbed and fashionably parted in the middle, Rudge was nearing thirty. She had money, Ohio steel money, and lived comfortably on the Right Bank in Auteuil. Within a few months of this evening's private event, she would be pregnant with Pound's child.

"Musique Américaine " featured Olga Rudge,
Ezra Pound and George Antheil

Antheil was a musical wunderkind. Still only twenty-three, he had been brought up in working class Trenton, New Jersey. The ambitious American was short and slight with clipped blond hair that made him look even younger than his age: "[a] regular American high school boy."[94] He described himself as an ultra-modern "pianiste futuriste", and Ezra Pound championed him as America's answer to Stravinsky. (When Stravinsky heard that Antheil was putting it about that the Russian master "admired" the young American's work, Stravinsky immediately cut contact with him.) George Antheil composed and played harsh music. It was mechanical, hard-edged, brazen and abstract. In his new world, melody and harmony only existed to give strength to rhythm.

The programme started off with three strange short pieces by Pound, two derived from XVth century music and another based on a "Javanese fiddle" (sic), all played by Olga Rudge on her violin. An Antheil sonata for piano followed, and then there were another couple of pieces by Pound, a violin suite by Rudge and a song where she accompanied Yves Tinayre. Interval beckoned, probably not too soon for some of the audience, but not before Antheil's second sonata for violin and piano. It must have been exhausting.

James Joyce was among the small group of invitees, and he brought along his nineteen year-old son Giorgio – apparently in the hope that he could interest the boy in modern music. There was a brace of sapphic supporters – Djuna Barnes, Sylvia Beach and Adrienne Monnier. Cocteau, although a friend of Pound's, was an absentee; he was already in Villefranche for the summer, trying to wean himself of opium and his continued mourning of Radiguet.[95] We know that Hemingway wasn't there either – he was in Pamplona for the week, getting sloshed and jumping wildly in and out of bull rings – and, in any event, although he was a great pal of Pound's at the time, he was not an admirer of Antheil's work; rather unkindly Hemingway had written that he "preferred [his] Stravinsky straight."[96]

Ezra Pound had developed an interest in music composition through Rudge. He tried to play various instruments, although more than one acquaintance believed him to be tone deaf.[97] Antheil, for his part, was happy to have Pound as his de facto promotor and press agent. Olga Rudge was just happy to be with the goateed svengali. They were a bizarre threesome. Rudge had real talent, of course. Some saw genuine creativity in Antheil, although many did not. The self-identified bad boy of music believed in uncontrolled "modernity", with wild, unusual sounds and orchestrations in which "[he] refuses to recognise the piano as a musical instrument."[98] To most ears, it was not pleasant.

And so, after the interval, the attendees at this challenging event suffered the première of Antheil's dissonant "Quatuor à Cordes" – with Antheil at the piano, Rudge on first violin, a second violin, a viola and cello, and Ezra Pound turning the pages.

Douglas Fairbanks and Mary Pickford were in Paris for the Olympics. Fairbanks was a very strong man and a skilful fencer. He was famous for his athleticism in the movies, and it was known that he performed most of his own stunts. He was a keen supporter of many sports, particularly track and field; so much so that, in addition to the well-equipped gym and the famous kidney-shaped swimming pool at "Pickfair", the vast Fairbanks/Pickford estate in Beverly Hills, he also had a proper cinder running track. Invitations to Pickfair were a measure of social standing in Los Angeles at the time. And Fairbanks made sure that the local stars from USC, like Charlie Paddock, were welcome to come and work out at this grand set-up; they formed genuine friendships with the "King of Hollywood", who was happy to support them in their careers on and off the sporting field. Indeed it was Fairbanks who had persuaded Paddock to continue running and defend his Olympic 100 metre crown.

On the Tuesday, William DeHart Hubbard became the first African American to win an individual gold medal at the Olympics. A champion sprinter, he was twenty-two and a freshman at the University of Michigan. Although Hubbard would equal the world record for 100 yards in 1925, his best event was the long jump. He was the greatest jumper of his era, and the best ever until Jesse Owens appeared in the 1930s. Early on in the 1924 event, he had a few fouls, as is so often the case in long jumping, but eventually he got his run-up right and "[shooting] into the air like a frightened frog", he won easily with his last jump.

Among other events that afternoon, Doug Lowe of Great Britain won the 800 metres. (Paul Martin of Switzerland came second. By 1936 he was a five time Olympian and, although he never won another medal in those further Olympics, he was the beneficiary of the much-appreciated personal services provided for some athletes at the Berlin Olympic Village.[99]). And Paavo Nurmi won his 5,000 metre heat "as he pleased, without exerting himself".[100] The event attracting most interest, however, was the 200 metres preliminaries. Almost everyone had run to form except Charlie Paddock. To cheer Paddock up and to encourage him for the finals scheduled for the next day, Fairbanks and Pickford invited him to join them for dinner at the Hotel Crillon. The Hollywood stars included Maurice Chevalier in their party, and Chevalier amused them all with send-ups of various athletes and movie personalities. Paddock spent the night at the Crillon, and got a good sleep.

The next day Charlie Paddock returned to form, winning the second semi-final of the 200 in 21.8s, the same time as Scholz had achieved in winning the first. In the final itself, Paddock looked set to win. He was leading for most of the race when, approaching the finish, he turned to see where Scholz and the others were placed – and mistimed his famous leap, injuring his right leg. Paddock finished in 21.7s – faster than he'd run in Antwerp – but Scholz just beat him to the line, with Eric Liddell somewhat further back and third. Harold Abrahams blew up, finishing sixth and last.

One of the greatest feats in athletic history took place the next day, Thursday, 10 July 1924. Paavo Nurmi was the perpetrator, and he became the unquestioned star of the Games.

Paavo Nurmi, the star of the 1924 Olympics

Nurmi was a phenomenon. He was born in Turku, Finland in 1897. His father was a struggling carpenter. Nurmi left school at twelve when his father died, and the boy had to help provide for the family. To the delight of Finland, Hannes Kolehmainen had won the 5,000 and 10,000 metre events at the 1912 Stockholm Olympics, bringing pride to a nation that was still under Russian hegemony. Nurmi was fifteen, and always said that Kolehmainen's victories inspired him to emulate the Olympic hero. From this point, Nurmi trained hard and diligently; during military service he would be out running before reveille, and his athletic career flourished accordingly. On discharge, when the roads were covered with snow such that it was impossible to run, he would walk for hours to and from work in Helsinki. These efforts were handsomely rewarded in 1920, when he won three gold medals at the Antwerp Games.

A relatively tall man for a middle-distance runner, Nurmi was 5'9" (174 cm) and a trim 65 kg. He subjected himself to the most gruelling workouts, but they were scientific. How fast could he run? How long could he maintain a particular pace? ("There were no 'breathers' in Nurmi's races, no chances to store up energy for a final sprint…"[101]) Interval training – that discipline of alternating intense, hard running with periods of relaxation – became an essential part of his twice daily routine. He had a very slow heartbeat. Even so, Nurmi always argued that it was his mental attitude more than physical fitness that made the difference: "All that I am," he said, "I am because of my mind."[102] He was stoic and incredibly tough. Nurmi had an effortless stride, and appeared to run with his chest as much as legs; chest out, head held high and with his arms high and elbows out, he had a bounce to his movement and oozed determination and power. Nurmi's opponent was himself and time. Indeed he would usually run with a stopwatch in his left hand, not just in training but in races too.

Nurmi did not take to the press, nor to publicity in general. Ignoring the press only made sports journalists more interested in him than they might otherwise have been. He was intriguing. The press invented stories, not an unusual phenomenon in that milieu, such as making something of the tale that he lived exclusively on black bread and fish when his preferred dish was actually oatmeal.

Ritola was a genuine competitor for Nurmi. A year older than his fellow Finn, Ritola too came from humble circumstances. The fourteenth of nineteen children, no less, the family had migrated to New York when Ritola was seventeen. They lived in the Bronx; he always ran for Finland but never competed in the Finnish national championships. Nurmi and Ritola had not met before the Olympics and, denied the opportunity to defend his 10,000 title, Nurmi developed an intense dislike for his countryman, who he saw as a usurper. On the first day of competition, the Sunday, the same day as the 100 metre preliminaries, Ritola had won the 10,000 in fine style – winning by half a lap in a new world record. What Willy Ritola didn't know, but most everyone soon came to learn, was that – outside the stadium on the warm-up track – Nurmi had run 10,000 metres, starting at the same time as the official race, and that he ran even faster than Ritola in the stadium, "beating" the Olympic champion (and new world record holder) home.

And so to Thursday, 10 July. It was insufferably hot. Nurmi was to run in the finals of both the 1,500 and the 5,000 – with the second event scheduled to start at best fifty minutes after the first. Paavo Nurmi knew the challenge. Indeed he had tested himself on it three weeks earlier: he had undertaken a trial in Finland, running 3:52.6 for the 1,500 metres and then, an hour later, 14:28.2 for the 5,000. Both were world records! So he knew he could manage both events, one after the other. In his own mind, and that is the essential point, all Nurmi had to do was beat the opposition on the day.

Fresh from his victory in the 800, Doug Lowe tried to set the pace in the 1,500. Nurmi would have none of it. He matched Lowe, and passed the 400 metre mark in front in 58.0s. He had his stop watch in hand and he knew what time would burn the others off. Soon it became a race for second place, and that race was furious. But Nurmi just sailed ahead, winning easily and slowing down at the finish. He was a second outside his world record. With no discernible emotion, Nurmi ignored the cheers of the crowd, found the stopwatch he had discarded, picked up his tracksuit and went off to the changing room to rest up briefly.[103]

It was obvious that Nurmi would be tired for the 5,000. And it was still very hot. Ritola and the other contender, Sweden's Edvin Wide, sought to exploit the heat and Nurmi's inevitable fatigue. (Wide had been born and raised in Finland but had moved to Sweden in 1918, aged twenty-two.) Nurmi's two opponents set off at a torrid pace, and they were fifty metres ahead after 1,500 metres. At this point, Nurmi let himself out. Soon he was level with the two leaders and then, stopwatch in hand, he made his own pace. Wide dropped back. With a lap to go Nurmi threw his stopwatch onto the grass and picked up the tempo. Ritola stuck with him and clenched his teeth. For a moment he passed Nurmi:

"With 300 metres left in the race I was in front of Paavo and feeling very strong. Paavo tried to pass me but I held him off. For any other runner than Nurmi, that would have been the end of it. But on the final turn he made another surge. I could not believe that after running the 1500 earlier, he still had the strength. But he did."[104]

Nurmi won by two metres. No-one had ever seen anything like it.

Eric Liddell knew the Stade de Colombes well. He had represented Scotland there in 1922, playing against France during the Five Nations rugby tournament. It was the first of his seven appearances ("caps") for Scotland, and he had scored a try. (The match was a draw 3-3.) Liddell was a very fine wing three-quarter but only played two international seasons, asking to be excused from that of 1924 because he wished to prepare himself for the Olympics.

By 1924, as noted, he was twenty-two. The son of Scottish Christian missionaries to China, he had been educated at a London secondary school in Blackheath that had been established for the children of such missionaries, Eltham College; he then went up to the University of Edinburgh. Liddell and his family always thought of themselves as Scots, even though all of them – his parents, his siblings, even his future wife – lived and worked most of their lives in China as missionaries.

As we have seen, Liddell didn't compete in the 100 and had come third in the 200. The 400 was his chance, but the favourite was the American, Horatio Fitch. By the quarter-finals – held on the Thursday of Nurmi's incredible triumphs in the 1,500 and 5,000 – the Swiss Joseph Imbach had emerged as a challenger; he broke the world record with a 48.0s run. The semi-finals and final were scheduled for Friday, 11 July – and the heatwave continued. Fitch confirmed his favouritism by beating Guy Butler, a great English runner, in the first semi, in another new world record, 47.8s. "Suddenly pipers of the Cameron Highlanders, who had assembled in the middle of the stadium, began playing, and the crowd broke into cheers at the lively strains of a Scotch air."[105] An inspired Liddell beat Imbach in the second semi-final, winning in 48.2s. It was a personal best for the "Flying Scotsman", his previous best being a distant 49.0.

The Highlanders were outside the stadium for the final later that afternoon. Perhaps they'd been expelled. Whatever, they knew exactly when the final would start, and it is said they pumped out the bagpipes for a good hour before the gun. Liddell had been given the worst possible draw, the outside lane, and Fitch was behind him in lane five. Silence is essential for the start of every race, but observers report that this one was especially so.

Eric Liddell famously wins the 400 metres,
with American Horatio Fitch second

Eric Liddell ran like a man possessed. He ran the first 200 in 22.3s and, rather than fading, he kept going. Imbach caught his feet on the lane ropes and fell. Liddell was not a pretty runner. He would run with his head thrown back and his chest out, and he would throw his arms about in such a strange clawing motion that, in the early rounds, the Americans found it amusing. Not now. Fitch reported later: "I couldn't believe a man could set such a pace and finish. But Liddell pushed himself like a man possessed. He didn't weaken. With the tape only 20 yards away I again spurted closer but Liddell threw his head back, gathered himself together and shot forward."[106]

Eric Liddell won the race in the world record time of 47.6s, and he became a national hero.

There were two days left in the track and field competition, and Paavo Nurmi dominated both.

No-one in Paris could remember a hotter day than the Saturday. It was unbearably hot – at least 45° C (113°F) – and it was muggy, and the four stacks of the nearby coal-fired electricity plant seemed to be pumping out a special quota of noxious fumes. This was the second of the two decathlon days; all thirty-six men had worked their way through the first day, but only twenty-five managed to get through the second. Harold Osborn of the Illinois Athletic Club eventually won quite clearly from his US compatriot, Emerson Norton. It was a unique double for Osborne, as he had also won the high-jump earlier in the week, on 7 July, the same day as the 100 metres final.

But the real drama was to come in the 10,000 metres cross country. Such was the heat, wags suggested that the sauna the Finns had erected in their nearby housing complex might have prepared them for the day; that was meant as a joke, but it proved not to be. The course was incredibly difficult. It started near the warm-up track and cleared the stadium precincts after about 800 metres; that was the easy part. Soon the forty-two starters were running near the river through hollow and narrow paths bordered by brambles and thornbushes; a tough stone fence had to be traversed at 2,300 metres; some of the paths were made of stone and were unstable; and at 3,000 metres the runners were faced with a high sloping embankment thick with undergrowth. This circuit had to be traversed twice.

The race's progress was reported back to the stadium in vanilla form: "Nurmi is leading", etc. In truth, only a few were managing to progress with any self-control. Nurmi and Ritola were OK, but they were almost alone. Runners collapsed from sunstroke and fatigue. Many started vomiting from their exertions. It was a disaster. Nurmi came home first, "as cool and unruffled as an Eskimo"[107], nearly ninety seconds ahead of Ritola, and thereby claimed the individual gold; and the three-man Finnish team won the team gold.

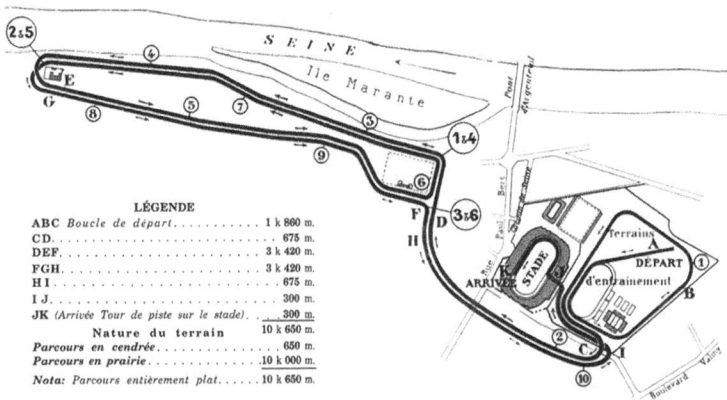

Only fifteen of the forty two starters finished the race; "[the] rest were picked up unconscious all along the course, and the ambulances were out for hours afterwards."[108] The event proved to be so traumatic that it disappeared from the Olympic calendar. An attempt was made by World Athletics to revive the event for 2024 Paris Olympics but the proposal did not find favour with the IOC.

On the Sunday, the US won the two sprint relays. Great Britain came second in the 4x100, just 0.2s behind the Americans. Britain came third in the 4x400, this time 1.2s behind the winning Americans. Eric Liddell was once again preaching at the Scots church. He had made his position clear – "I object to Sunday sport in toto" – and almost everyone was too polite to mention that, had he run, Britain might have won both relays.

During the afternoon, Nurmi led the three Finns to a clear victory in the 3,000 metres team race. Nurmi himself finished first, more than eight minutes ahead of Ritola who came second. The marathon saw out the track and field competition. The 3,000 metres team event had been Nurmi's fourth. It was also his fifth gold medal, and he would forever be remembered as the brightest star of the Paris Games.

And so came to an end the first and most important of the Games' three weeks. Swimming was next, for a week, and then the Games would tail off.

Manly is a beachside suburb north of Sydney. Because it is on the peninsular that forms the northern head of Sydney Harbour, it enjoys access to both the harbour itself and its famous white-sand beach on the Pacific Ocean. In 1924 Manly was something of an antipodean Brighton, albeit smaller and with consistently better weather than the English town; the suburb was widely and fairly advertised as "seven miles from Sydney and a thousand miles from care". Its population was just 18,000. And, in Paris, it produced three gold medallists.

Manly's *Welcome Home Committee* greets the seaside suburb's three
gold medallists: Nick Winter (holding his daughter's hand), Boy
Charlton (to Winter's left) and Dick Eve (front right); 4 October 1924

First up had been "Nick" Winter. Anthony William Winter, always
"Nick", was a twenty-nine-year-old fireman who also helped his father
out in the local snooker rooms. He was a veteran of the Great War, and
a superb all-round athlete. Tallish at 5'11", muscular, double-jointed
and ambidextrous, Winter played rugby league, tennis, cricket and golf;
he excelled in single tug-of-war, was a competitive wrestler and could
beat anyone cycling backwards. Anything that required speed, stamina,
strength and determination attracted him, but jumping events were
his forte.

Eventually Winter found his specialty in the triple jump. Perhaps
because of his age, he was the last athlete to have been chosen for the
Australian team. The triple jump competition took place on the pen-
ultimate day of the athletics, the Saturday of the horror 10,000 cross
country. As the surviving runners staggered into the stadium, the triple
jumpers sweltered away under the blazing sun in the centre of the field.

Winter was always a contender. He led his pool with a personal best, although the Argentinian, Luis Brunetto, had jumped further than Winter in winning the other pool. (It is irrelevant to the story, but almost everyone noticed that he was a doppelgänger for his famous countryman, the boxer Luis Firpo.[109]) When it came to the final, Brunetto, led until the final round. Winter was coming second. With his final jump, however, Winter achieved another personal best – indeed he broke the world record that had stood for fourteen years – and claimed the gold.

The one sport in which Nick Winter didn't excel was swimming. But Manly did.

Andrew "Boy" Charlton first came to prominence in 1923 when he defeated Frank Beaurepaire, the Australian swimming champion, over 440 yards; Charlton was only fifteen. The following year, Arne Borg, the "Swedish Sturgeon", made a tour of Australia in January. The twenty-two year old Borg already held several world records, but Charlton beat him by twenty yards in the local 440 yards championship, equalling the Swede's world record. The venue was the vast pool of water in the harbour near downtown Sydney known as the Domain Baths. It had wooden stands that could accommodate 2,000 spectators – and they were full for this contest – plus diverse pontoons and diving towers. The twenty-two year-old Borg, always a bit of a showman, was so impressed by the boy that he commandeered a small dinghy and rowed Charlton past the cheering crowds. Later in the week they met again, over 880 yards and 220 yards, with Boy Charlton prevailing on both occasions; in the 880, Charlton had broken the world record. (The Domain Baths were replaced in 1968 by the wonderful outdoor swimming complex known as the Andrew "Boy" Charlton Pool.)

In mid-May, the Australian team set off for the Paris Olympics by sea. It took five weeks to reach Marseille, and they arrived with two weeks to spare. Swimmers need to actually swim to keep their condition, and the three metre square canvas tank on the *RMS Ormonde* was little better than the "lukewarm bath" they found in Aden along the way.[110] Unfazed, in Paris the Australians set about regaining their form. Charlton could have been expected to be out of sorts, as his mentor and coach had suffered a breakdown on the voyage and had thrown himself overboard! The man was rescued, but it must have greatly upset the sixteen year-old. Charlton seems, however, to have been a resilient fellow. Certainly he was physically strong; barrel-chested, he stood a full 6'0" (1.83 cm). A self-effacing boy, his modesty hid a fiercely competitive spirit. Andrew Charlton must have known that he was a good chance for the 1500 metres and even the 400.

Paris built a special new swimming pool for the Olympics. It was at Tourelles, in the north east of the city. The main pool was 50 metres long and 33 metres wide. A diving tower stood to the side at the deep end, which was five metres in depth. The shallow end was just 1.2 metres, a perfect depth for fast races, and there were five lanes. An innovation was cork floats which separated the lanes for the first time. Starting blocks were yet to be introduced. The natatorium, now known as the Piscine Georges Vallerey, is still there. It has a new façade and a new see-through retractable roof, but otherwise it is unchanged – and it is still among the best swimming pools in Paris.

Swimming had the best gender balance of any discipline at the Games. Indeed it was the only sport that really gave women a go. There were 118 male swimmers and 51 women. The women had fewer events than the men – five not six – because the men competed over 1,500 metres and the women did not. The competition would run for a week, from Sunday, 13 July to the following Sunday.

Charlton didn't have to wait long for his showdown with Borg. The heats of the 1,500 were on the first day. Charlton won his with a world record. Then Borg bettered it. Charlton and Borg were drawn in the same semi-final on the Monday. Charlton won, but it was clear that neither was extending himself. The thirty-three year old Australian, Frank Beaurepaire won the other semi-final; it was his fourth Olympics – it could have been five, but he was temporarily banned over allegations of professionalism in 1912.

In the final, Borg was an early leader. He had very high flotation and a fast stroke. Charlton and Borg turned together at 300 metres but thereafter Charlton drew steadily ahead. Charlton's stroke was a modified trudgeon, which meant that his stronger right arm could have him drift a little to the right; the new lane ropes gave him guidance and helped him swim right in the middle of his lane. By 1,200 metres Charlton was more than a lap ahead of everyone except Arne Borg. He won by twenty metres in a new world record – 21 minutes 6.6s – a good minute faster than Borg's two-day-old standard.

The crowd went wild. Borg proclaimed him "the world's wonder", and the American coach Bill Bachrach described the sixteen-year old boy "an escaped torpedo".[111]. (Beaurepaire came third. He never won a gold medal at the Olympics but medalled in all four Games in which he was allowed to compete: 1908, 1916, 1920 and 1924.)

But there was more for Manly that afternoon. Dick Eve was Australia's top diver. He had won the national championships since 1921 but, without the intense competition the Americans enjoyed in their collegiate tournaments, he was not expected to be able to match them in Paris. Short, like most divers, Dick Eve was just 5'4" (163 cm) with a good strong body and solid legs. He was a specialist in springboard events, but in Paris it was the high tower that proved to be his triumph. Eve's grace and crispness captured the judges' eyes, and a perfect swan dive was the coup de grace. He won the gold medal. (He took over the management of the Manly Baths in 1926 and was deemed a professional – thereby thwarting any ambition to defend his Olympic title at the 1928 Amsterdam Games.)

During that afternoon the female swimmers had their first final, immediately after Boy Charlton's 1,500 metres race. It was the 400 metres and Gertrude Ederle of New York was the favourite. Only eighteen, she came to the Games holding the world records for both the 100 metres freestyle and the 400 metres. A pocket rocket standing just 5'5" (1.65 cm) and weighing 64 kg, "Trudy" Ederle was a great stylist who had perfected the new "American crawl" with an eight-beat kick. In the 400 preliminaries, she sailed through her heat and semi-final. In the final, however, she was well beaten into third place by two fellow Americans, Martha Norelius, just fifteen years old and a growing champion, and Helen Wainwright. It was not a good start for New York's favourite.

Wednesday, 16 July brought the much-anticipated first appearance of Johnny Weissmuller. He was twenty, a magnificent physical specimen – 6'3" (191 cm) and 190 lbs (86 kg), tall and rangy, broad-shouldered with a narrow waist – and widely thought to be the best swimmer alive. He hadn't lost a race since 1921.

Many members of the press reported Weissmuller to be nineteen. This was because he had used his younger brother's birth details to obtain an American passport for the Games. Janos Peter Weißmüller was born on 2 June 1904 of ethnic German parents in the town of Friedhof in what is now Romania. Together with his parents, Johnny emigrated to the USA where his younger brother Peter was born on 3 September 1905. After Peter's birth in Pennsylvania, the family moved to Chicago where there was a Friedhof colony.

It didn't take the Illinois Athletic Club long to identify the talent the teenage Weissmuller enjoyed, and they quickly adopted the boy. In 1921, just seventeen, he broke Duke Kahanamoku's long-standing 100 metre world record with a time of 60.4s. By the following year he had lowered it to 58.6s, and coming into the Olympics his world record was 57.4s. Johnny was the all-American boy. With a somewhat high-pitched voice and always dressing well, he came across as a squeaky-clean good Catholic lad.

Johnny Weissmuller in Illinois Athletic Club swimsuit, 1922

The 400 metres freestyle would be Weissmuller's first test. (Integrating themselves with the locals, the family had dropped the umlaut soon after their arrival in the USA and Janos had become Johnny.) Borg and Charlton were his competition. It took two days of preliminaries to get to the final on the Friday. Weissmuller won his semi-final in 5:13.6, well ahead of Charlton; Arne Borg won the other semi in 5:21.0. The final was the best swimming race of the Olympics. For three hundred metres little separated Borg and Weissmuller, one was ahead and then the other;

there was never more than 1.5 metres between them, with Weissmuller uncharacteristically missing his turns. Charlton trailed. Eventually Weissmuller drew away on the second half of the last lap, as Charlton – who probably mistimed his race – rapidly closed the gap with a furious finish. It was Weissmuller first, Borg second and Charlton third.

Johnny Weissmuller looked wonderful in the water. Some called it "hydroplaning" – head and shoulders out of the water, his back arched and his feet trailing with a deep flutter kick. His coach, Bill Bachrach, was an enthusiast:

"[Johnny] brought to a new platform of style the American crawl stroke. He became the stylist of champions, getting more speed than any rival with a comparable amount of effort. His stroke reduced water resistance to a minimum, facilitated breathing, put the body in a position to make unimpeded use of all its strength and leverage, and got the propulsion for the effort expended."[112]

He swam with his head high, which is perfect for the movie shots featured in his later career and for water polo. Today's coaches would probably suggest that he lower his head into the water, thereby bringing his tail up and further improving flotation.

The fresh-faced twenty year-old had aroused great in interest in Paris. Not as much as Paavo Nurmi but, in contrast to Nurmi, he made himself available to the press and the public. One manifestation of this was his comedy diving routines with Harold "Stubby" Kruger in the Olympic pool. The Games had a more relaxed environment in those days, partly because there were none of today's security concerns. Kruger originally came from Honolulu. He was a backstroker in Bachrach's Chicago squad and had finished fifth in Antwerp. By 1924, he had become the "Improbable Water Comedian" and he played comedian to Johnny's straight man. They would put on a show to amuse the crowd between events. Spectators demanded encores, and the performances became so popular that the authorities, fearing the actual racing might be marginalised, banned such activity from future Olympics.

The final day of the competition, 20 July – a Sunday – would feature the blue-riband 100 metre sprints – for men and for women. Weissmuller had a particularly busy day. He swam the final leg in the victorious 4x200 metre relay team, finishing well ahead of the Australians. And he would play centre-forward for the US water polo team late in the day, when they won the bronze medal.

For the women's 100, Trudy Ederle held the world record of 72.8s – but she was not producing her best. While she swam a credible 72.6s in the heats on the Friday, her fellow American Mariechen Wehselau had already created a new world record in an earlier heat. The third American, Ethel Lackie, a seventeen year-old from Bill Bachrach's Illinois Athletic Club stable, had swum well too; she won her heat in 72.8s. All three had adopted what they could of Weissmuller's technique, and swam with six- or eight-beat kicks. On the Sunday morning Wehselau and Ederle easily won their respective semi-finals. In the final Wehselau led by two metres at the turn, with Ederle running second and Lackie third. Lackie then turned it on; she swam away in the last 25 metres to win in 72.4s from Wehselau in 72.8s. Gertrude Ederle was back in third, recording a disappointing 74.2s. It had not been a good Olympics for Gertrude Ederle – she had expected to win three gold medals but finished with one, in the relay. Her redemption came two years later when she was the first woman to swim the English Channel, bringing more fame to the New Yorker than any number of Olympic medals could have achieved.

Johnny Weissmuller convincingly won the men's 100 metres, as expected. He had recorded the fastest times in the heats and semis, and swam an Olympic record of 59.0s in the final. The immensely popular Duke Kahanamoku from Hawaii, gold medallist in 1912 and again in 1920, came second; he was now thirty-four and swam 61.4s – faster than in 1912 and equal to his winning time in Antwerp. Duke's much younger brother, Sam, who at twenty was Weissmuller's age, came third. Arne Borg came fourth and the Japanese swimmer, Katsuo Takaishi, in a sign of things to come, finished fifth and last among the finalists in 63.0s.

Trudy Ederle at Cap Gris-Nez, 26 August 1926

The US team had dominated the swimming. Their men won five out of the six events (Charlton's win in the 1,500 being the exception) and their women four out of five; Lucy Morton of Great Britain had won the women's breaststroke. Americans finished 1-2-3 in both 100 metres events. (Australian representatives equalled this feat in 1956, when they won all three medals for men and women. Thereafter, FINA limited entrants to two per nation.)

And the world had found its first swimming superstar in Johnny Weissmuller.

With the completion of the athletics events and the swimming, the Games wound down.

The rowing had taken place in the Argenteuil basin near the Colombes stadium. Britain's Jack Beresford had won the single skulls. For the USA, Grace Kelly's father repeated his double skulls victory of 1920, and Yale (with the future Dr Benjamin Spock in the engine room) had won the eights.

Out in the Saint-Cloud Country Club field, it was no surprise that the Argentinians had won the polo. Crowds were sparse, but the chukkas did attract a better sort of person. The host country had done well in fencing, which would have pleased gentlemen amateurs such as Pierre de Coubertin. The tennis had been something of a disappointment with none of the Four Musketeers taking gold and the incomparable Suzanne Lenglen injured; and the French team won the water polo.

Cycling events would be a feature of the final week, with French riders winning four golds – albeit that Olympic cycling, like boxing, was for amateurs and therefore the competitors were young or those athletes who could afford to stay amateur. Crowds for both the boxing (at the Vél d'Hiv) and the cycling were small, many boxing aficionados being more interested in the week's upcoming Tunney/Carpentier fight over in New York.

Once again, the USA had been the most successful team overall. The Olympics had come of age. Much larger in scope and numbers than ever before, with some wonderful performances, the Paris Games of 1924 were a success on all counts. They were the first truly successful Games since the 1896 revival.

Parisians had taken to the Olympics. Most stayed in Paris for the duration, either attending events or soaking up the atmosphere. On 20 July, once the swimming was over, Picasso and his wife with young Paulo left Paris for Antibes, where the master created some of his most famous works in what proved to be a very productive summer.[113] Gerald and Sara Murphy and their three children travelled with them. At first, both families stayed at the Hôtel du Cap; when the Picassos set themselves up in a nearby villa in Juan-les-Pins, the Murphys stayed on at the hotel while they remodelled and enhanced Villa America. The Beaumonts joined them all soon afterwards, basing themselves in chic Cannes. La

Garoupe beach was the centre of joint get-togethers – which Zelda and Scott Fitzgerald, who had been in Saint-Raphael all summer, would crash and ruin. Cocteau too was on the Riviera, already in Villefranche, having missed the Olympics entirely.

And, over in Spain, during the last week of the Olympics, Hemingway and his companions continued their recovery from the indulgences of Pamplona – fly fishing in the waters around Burguete and taking in the fresh air of the Pyrénées.

A SURREAL DANCE

One of the most influential, popular and ubiquitous artistic movements of the twentieth century was "Surrealism". It had an official launch in 1924. Surrealism meant different things to different people, and it held the attention of art and culture for about twenty years.

André Breton 1924

Actually, there were two launches. Two competing arms of the movement published separate manifestos in October 1924. By dint of superior tactics and his having more followers than the competitor, André Breton's *Manifeste du Surréalsime* prevailed. Beautifully written, even poetic, it hardly cleared things up.

Breton defined Surrealism as: *"Psychic automatism in its pure state, by which one proposes to express – verbally, by means of the written word, or any other manner – the actual functioning of thought. Dictated by thought, in the absence of any control exercised by reason, exempt from any aesthetic or moral concern."*

This takes some explaining. Perhaps it is best to go back to its predecessor, Dada.

According to Janet Flanner, "Surrealism…was a bastard descendent of Dada"[114]. Dada was born out of a heartfelt disgust for the causes of the First World War. Many artists were saying, "If this is what the world is about, I want none of it." These artists rejected the past and gave up on the bourgeois and capitalist order – rejecting reason and logic, prizing nonsense, relying upon intuition, and happy with irrationality. Dada had no specific purpose or focus; indeed, if anything, that was its purpose. Dada meant nothing, and its adherents had no intention of it meaning anything.

Elements of what was to become Dada were emerging during and after the Great War, in Germany, Spain and the Netherlands, even in New York. To the extent that there was a Dada birthplace, however, it was in Zurich. There, in 1916, a dark-haired charismatic poet emerged from the pack; he was only nineteen, a Rumanian who called himself Tristan Tzara.

He was born Samuel Rosenstock. "Tristan Tzara" was said to mean "sad in country" in Romanian, and Tzara soon became the leader of a group of avant-garde artists. This cohort centred themselves in the Cabaret Voltaire, at 1 Spiegelgasse, a small nightclub and performance space, where they exchanged anti-establishment and absurdist views, published polemic tracts, read poetry and enjoyed Tzara's amusing stage performances. Tzara himself took to shooting off letters which promoted their ideas to like-minded artists throughout Europe. Soon an art and literary journal, *Dada*, was born there in Zurich. (As to the term Dada itself, there are several theories concerning its origin; perhaps the most credible is that "da-da" is the double affirmative "yes-yes" in Romanian.)

Over the next few years *Dada* would have seven editions, the final two published in Paris – to which city most of the movement's adherents moved. In 1918, Tzara had published a Dada manifesto. By 1920, Francis Picabia, André Breton, Louis Aragon, George Grosz, Max Ernst and Jean Arp all identified themselves as Dadaists. Marcel Duchamp never took up the mantle, but his 1917 anti-art piece "Fountain", a urinal, had already shocked New York and has since become a Dada icon.

Tristan Tzara by Robert Delaunay, 1923

The term "sur-realism" was first used in 1917, when Guillaume Apollinaire – the most respected and popular art critic of the era – used it in private correspondence, and then again (*"une sorte de surréalisme"*) in the program notes for the ballet *Parade*. Somewhere along the line the terms Surrealism and Dada started to be interchanged. Many can still not identify a difference.

Pudgy-faced, of medium height and with fashionable long dark hair, André Breton was ambitious and self-important. He was a good writer, a better politician, and an outstanding self-promoter. Soon, Breton came to see Surrealism as a revolutionary movement, and he wanted it to assume a more political stance. And, if it suited his purpose, he could be nasty. In 1922, Tzara was the most prominent of their cohort; Breton publicly attacked him – "the leader of a foreign movement from Zurich"– arguing that Tzara's work and leadership lacked focus and were unnecessarily frivolous. This was partly true, and intentionally so. After all, these were the distinguishing features of Dada versus Surrealism: Dada was geographically decentralised, albeit that many of its famous adherents were now living in Paris; there was no explicit leader; and it encouraged non-conformity and nonsense. Surrealism, in contrast, was definitively Paris-centred and, while encouraging creativity per se, its leadership had started to accept, to seek out, and ultimately to require, a degree of collective action. For Breton, Surrealism was a movement, a faith – and he was its self-appointed leader.

To return to practicalities, in interpreting Breton's definition of Surrealism (as set out in his 1924 *Manifesto*), today's audience might understand it to mean something like:

"Letting the creative spirit free to express itself, in all forms (that is, written or otherwise) without social or moral constraints or influences."

To that end, these early Surrealists were inspired by Freud's mining of dreams and the exploration of the subconscious. The Surrealist painters created incongruous juxtapositions of found objects and explored non-sequiturs, they used new and unsettling materials and presentations, and they explored "automatism". Automatism encouraged the creation of work that flowed spontaneously, in literature and the plastic arts – ostensibly without interference from established norms or constraints. It was a sort of artistic Ouija board.

In 1922, when he was breaking with Tzara, Breton and his first wife had moved into an apartment at 42 rue Fontaine (where he would live until his death in 1966). It soon became a Surrealist salon and showcase. Breton's supporters had already usurped the Café Certa in the Passage de l'Opéra from the Dadaists, and now claimed it as their clubhouse. By 1923, these Surrealists were organizing theatre riots to break up performances of which they did not approve, and Breton himself was given to physical violence with opponents of his views. More gently, the public were invited to visit and record their opinions and experiences at the Bureau of Surrealist Research, at 15 rue de Grenelle on the Left Bank. Soon after the publication of the *Manifesto* in 1924, Breton and colleagues started an occasional publication *La révolution surrealiste*. By the following year they had mounted an exhibition of Surrealist paintings at the Galerie Pierre; artists represented included Miro, Klee, Man Ray and Picasso (who was claimed by the movement even though he maintained a distance).

André Breton was in his element. For the next ten years or so, Surrealism was at the centre of Western artistic developments in painting and sculpture and film. From Paris, Breton was its conductor. (Not of music, though; Breton never took an interest in music.) The painters split into two themes: hyper-realist, like Salvador Dalí, Yves Tanguy and Magritte; and exemplars of automatism, such as Miro and Max Ernst. Man Ray's photography was definitively surreal (which might not be the same as Surrealist), René Clair and Louis Bruñuel were signed-up cinematic adherents of the movement, and sculptors Arp, Brancusi and Giacometti were all claimed as part of Surrealism.

Insofar as he could, Breton kept everyone in check. He was autocratic, doctrinaire, homophobic, ruthless and dogmatic. He took to making public expulsions and excommunications of those who displeased him. One such was Giorgio de Chirico, the undisputed founder of the surrealist aesthetic, who – well into his sixties – was expelled for non-sanctioned work in 1932. Salvador Dalí fared no better; Breton expelled him in 1934, despite Dalí's painting *The Persistence of Memory* – with its limp, seemingly soft plastic watches – being perhaps Surrealism's most well-known work. Not that de Chirico and Dalí cared.

Haussmann had done such a comprehensive job on the built environment of Paris that for many years there was no room for anything else. Architecture and design concentrated on ornamentation and interior design. In 1924, however, a radical plan was proposed by Le Corbusier that, if implemented, would have transformed the Right Bank.

Charles-Edouard Jeanneret, a Swiss national, was yet another foreign artist attracted to the allure of Paris and its creative spirit. He arrived in Paris in 1917, aged thirty. A brief apprenticeship in the Berlin atelier of architect Peter Behrens had brought him into contact with his future fellow giants, Mies van der Rohe and Walter Gropius; after finishing secondary school, he had studied art, environmental design, urban and industrial design – but he had no formal tertiary qualifications. He and his cousin Pierre Jeanneret soon set up an architectural practice.

For seventeen years from 1917, Le Corbusier lived on the Left Bank at 20 rue Jacob – first in the attic and then in what he described as the "splendid" rooms on the first floor. This was a three-story building that ran along one side of a courtyard that led to Natalie Clifford Barney's famous abode. Her two-story pavilion at the end of the courtyard shared that rue Jacob address. For reasons unknown, Le Corbusier was never invited to Barney's Friday night soirées. (According to Barney's housekeeper, "We couldn't invite the whole neighbourhood.") He was an imposing figure of medium height, a sharp dresser with something of a swagger, and was readily identifiable in his signature spectacles – black and bold with circular lenses. Like many architects, he was economical in his praise for others, although he did express a liking for the work of Adolf Loos. (Tristan Tzara shared Le Corbusier's taste in architects: in 1925, when Tzara married the daughter of a rich Swedish industrialist, he commissioned Loos to design a grand new house on the Butte Montmartre at 15 avenue Junot.)

Le Corbusier was self-righteous and dogmatic and, in later life, his politics turned decidedly authoritarian – and ultimately fascist. He also loved fast cars, and he drove an exotic 14-cylinder Voisin manufactured by his patron, the aircraft entrepreneur Gabriel Voisin. From 1922, his companion was the Monegasque model Yvonne Gallis; they married in 1930. It seems Le Corbusier was something of a womaniser: we know he enjoyed a famous brief affair with Josephine Baker in 1929, when La Bakaire posed for him naked. Perhaps the womanising didn't endear him to his neighbour.

Together with Amédée Ozenfant, Jeanneret developed a painting school of pure, elementary geometric forms devoid of detail, which they called "Purism". They led a circle that has been somewhat neglected by history; Purists had moved on from Cubism, finding Cubism irrational, unnecessarily romantic and complicated. Still life studies were a common subject for them, and Fernand Léger would be considered an adherent at this time; his *Le Siphon* (1924) is an example of the genre.

Meanwhile, Charles-Edouard Jeanneret became active and prominent in debates about modernism and contemporary architecture, and in 1920 he took to using the pseudonym *Le Corbusier* in his architectural advocacy and works. It is derived from his maternal grandfather's family name, Lecorbésier.

In 1924, his architecture practice moved to a new atelier at 35 rue de Sèvres, opposite the Au Bon Marché department store. For the next forty years this workshop produced some of the most important architectural designs of the twentieth century. Many projects were not built and some, like the Plan Voisin for Paris, were outrageous.

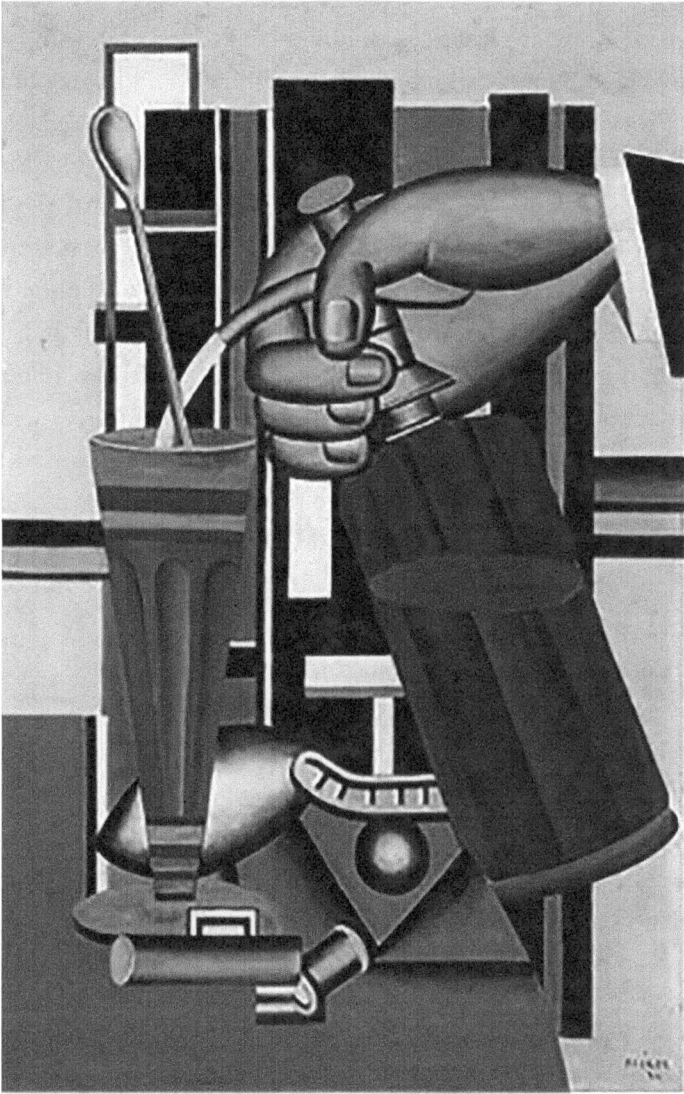

Le Siphon by Fernand Léger, 1924

Le Corbusier would typically spend the morning in his apartment, painting and drawing and making notes. The soon-to-be-famous atelier was on the second floor of an abandoned Jesuit monastery, reached via the monastery courtyard and up a dark staircase. In its immediately previous incarnation, the space had been a grocer's stockroom. The Atelier Le Corbusier, as it would soon be called, was a narrow high-ceilinged room that housed a row of perhaps a dozen drafting tables, each with its own adjustable black lamp – all orderly and uniform – and at each table sat a keen associate. The space was less than four metres wide; the light was excellent – it looked over the courtyard – and it was a hive of activity. By 1924, Le Corbusier was lecturing at the Sorbonne, in Prague and in Geneva, and Mies van der Rohe had invited him to participate in a major Stuttgart colloquium on the modern home.[115] In addition to the two principals, the architecture firm had twelve employees and would soon have thirty; Le Corbusier wrote to a friend that it was "impossible to think of such a thing as rest".[116]

It would take Le Corbusier less than fifteen minutes to walk from 20 rue Jacob to the workshop. He would invariably arrive at 2 in the afternoon. The associates were then quickly brought up to date with his latest plans and ideas. Soon the walls and desks would be full of new plans and papers, and new work.

Le Corbusier had well-developed ideas that he promoted forcefully. There were five points or principles of good architecture that he had espoused in his 1923 book *Towards a New Architecture*, each picking up elements of a "purist" philosophy that he believed would create better living spaces for an increasingly urban life. His work on domestic design was successful and enduring. Although his five points embraced principles that were intended to be universal and work across small and large buildings alike, the commissions Le Corbusier won at this time were almost always houses for rich patrons.

In 1923-25, he built the Villa La Roche at 8-10 square du Docteur Blanche in the 16th arrondissement for Swiss banker Raoul La Roche; it is now the headquarters of the Corbusier Foundation. At this same time, Gertrude Stein's brother Michael and his wife Sara, together with their friend Gabrielle de Monzie, commissioned the multi-occupant Villa Stein-de-Monzie in Garches on the outskirts of Paris. And in 1929, one of Le Corbusier's masterpieces, the Villa Savoye, was built in the fashionable Paris suburb of Poissy overlooking the Seine.

Le Corbusier's influential atelier was established in 1924

Each of these buildings embraced his five points for modern architecture. First, Le Corbusier called for the replacement of supporting walls by a grid of reinforced concrete load-bearing columns, which he called "pilotis"; among other things this freed up space under the building for various functions, including parking. His next three points flowed from the first:

- by removing the constraints of internal supporting walls, floor plans were opened up and free to be utilized or carved-up as desired;
- by separating the exterior of the building from its structural function that external design became free as well (not that Le Corbusier encouraged any fancy decoration; and
- with that freedom, horizontal ribbon windows could extend

across the facade of a dwelling, allowing all rooms to be lit
equally or provide a selective view of the surrounding environment; this helped blur the boundaries between the inside and the
outside of a building.

Le Corbusier proposed flat roofs, advocating their use as a garden, veg-
etable or otherwise, or for recreation.

Although, as noted, these principles were intended to be applied to
buildings of all sizes, they were clearly more successful with domestic
projects than with his larger buildings.

Le Corbusier was more interested in planning cities than designing
individual houses. For cities, he proposed symmetry and standardization,
vast green open spaces, integrated transportation solutions and an abundance of good light. "Space and light and order" was one of his mantras.
It needs to be said, however, that notwithstanding his concern for these
matters, his designs did not always fulfil his aspirations. His proposals
were invariably controversial and many remained unbuilt. (Years later
than these early days, Le Corbusier's master plan for Chandigarth, in
north west India, was an exception; designed and built in the 1950s,
it was a triumph and is widely applauded as an exemplar of successful
urban planning and design. Brasilia – albeit created by others – is certainly inspired by Le Corbusier's ideas; whether it is a success, however,
is a moot point.)

Le Corbusier's interest in urban projects was consistent and persis-
tent. He was keen on proper zoning – by segregating offices and large-
scale commercial activities, for example, from housing and entertainment. In 1922, he had set out his theoretical "Ville Contemporaine", a
city for three million inhabitants. He promoted these ideas in the journal
L'Esprit Nouveau, and many of them are now the established standard
for urban development. (The journal also served as a solicitation vehicle
for commissions.)

Throughout 1924, Le Corbusier and his colleagues were working on
an exhibit for a major international exhibition of modern decorative arts,
L'Exposition des Arts Décoratifs et Industriels. The Exhibition had been

deferred several times and finally took place in 1925. Its site was extensive: one axis ran along both sides of the Seine from the Place de la Concorde to the Grand Palais, while another ran over the Pont Alexandre III and along the Esplanade des Invalides. Extensive, if temporary, pavilions lined both these axes and the Pont Alexandre III linked the two, dressed up with fancy shops somewhat like Florence's Ponte Vecchio. Given his dislike for any form of decoration, the organisers were bold (or reckless) to have invited Le Corbusier to participate.

He was assigned a remote plot of land behind the Grand Palais in a grove of trees. No trees were to be removed, so Le Corbusier built the "Pavillon de L'Esprit Nouveau" around one, with the tree emerging through a hole in the roof. The pavilion itself was a stark white box. Le Corbusier saw it as an urban housing module, a standardised modular unit capable of being multiplied to form a block of flats. The prospective exhibit so upset the conservative organisers that, while it was still under construction, they built an eighteen foot fence around it, and only the most vigorous submissions from a government minister removed the obstruction.

Inside were a number of purist paintings – by Juan Gris, Le Corbusier (as C-E Jeanneret) and others – sometimes placed on violently coloured walls. There was a sprinkling of mass-produced furniture, these providing a stark contrast and offence to the elaborate one-of-a-kind pieces featured in other pavilions. Only a white Jacques Lipschitz sculpture and the paintings could be described as decorative. With all this, Le Corbusier had succeeded in his intention "to deny decorative art, and to affirm that architecture extends to the most humble piece of furniture [etc]…". The international jury selected the exhibit for its first prize, a decision vetoed by the organisers. That was but part of the controversy.

Because, inside the pavilion were two huge 100 square metre dioramas. One was a mock-up of Le Corbusier's theoretical Ville Contemporaine of 1922, and the other was Le Corbusier's actual plan for Paris – the Plan Voisin. (Gabriel Voisin paid for the printing and exhibition costs of the Plan.) It caused a storm of protest.

The outrageous Le Corbusier plan for Paris's Right Bank,
Le Plan Voisin

Le Corbusier proposed a "business city" and a "residential city", in total comprising nearly 600 hectares or two square miles north of the rue de Rivoli. It was radical in the extreme, proposing a complete transformation of Paris central. This was his tabula rasa. The business city would cover 240 hectares from the Place de la République to the rue du Louvre, from the Gare de l'Est to the rue de Rivoli. The residential city would be to its west, running from rue des Pyramides to the Rond-Point on the Champs-Elysées, from the Gare Saint-Lazare to the rue de Rivoli.

Eighteen identical cruciform office towers of 200m would be built in a symmetrical fashion on either side of the boulevard du Sébastopol; each tower would accommodate between 5,000 and 8,000 office workers. To understand the enormity of this proposal, it needs to be understood that the towers would each comprise about 60 stories and they would rise to be just short of the Tour Montparnasse's 210m.

Le Corbusier enthusiastically noted that the Plan would "eliminate a particularly run-down and unsanitary part of Paris". The residential apartment blocks would be more grounded, they being only 50m in height. Symmetrically placed on open spaces, as with the office towers, these apartments would have amenities such as a shopping street, restaurants, a kindergarten, parking and rooftop pools – and each block would be capable of accommodating up to 2700 residents.

There was to be a vast square in the middle of this new development, with a transport terminus on a subterranean level below the square. An elevated road would run east-west through the area, twenty kilometres in length and 120 metres wide, allowing traffic to flow right across the city without any intersections; there would be a similar road running north-south. Les Halles, the Marais and the Temple districts would all go. The Palais Royal, the Place des Voges and the Place Vendôme would survive; some important buildings would also be spared, and their immediate environs opened up. And the atheist architect of it all graciously confirmed that "the old churches [would] be preserved".

The Plan Voisin did not go down well, and its implementation was never seriously considered.

When Louis Honoré Charles Antoine Grimaldi ascended to the throne of the Principality of Monaco in 1922, as Louis II, it was a godsend for the Ballets Russes. The company had always sailed close to the wind, and now it found a quasi-permanent sponsor. The link was Winnaretta Singer.

It's a bit complicated. Winnaretta Singer was American by birth, one of more than twenty children of the sewing machine magnate, Isaac Singer; she had been brought up in Paris, in considerable comfort, and spoke French fluently. By 1924 she was fifty-nine and in a romantic relationship with Violet Trefusis. Although a confirmed lesbian, she had been married twice. Her second marriage, to Prince Edmond de Polignac, a rich aristocrat, was unconsummated (as was her first, which had been annulled). The Polignacs shared a love of music, however, and – on their own terms – the marriage was a success.

After her husband's death in 1901, the widowed Princesse Edmond de Polignac used her considerable fortune to support an extensive array of causes in the arts and sciences. The Ballets Russes was one such. Among the many musical works she commissioned over the years – from Fauré, Satie, Milhaud and Poulenc, for example – was a symphonic piece by Stravinsky that became the music for the Ballets Russes' 1922 ballet *Renard*.

In 1920, Winnaretta's nephew, Count Pierre Melchior de Polignac, had married Prince Louis' only child, Charlotte. (Prince Rainier III was their son, and the present monarch, Albert II, is their grandson.) Like Winnaretta, the young couple loved the arts and they were determined to become important patrons. When her father took the throne in 1922, Charlotte, now the Hereditary Princess of Monaco, wasted no time; that year the Ballets Russes and the *Société des bains de mer de Monaco*, the Monte Carlo casino operator, agreed to terms whereby the Ballets Russes would move to the Principality and become Monte Carlo's resident ballet corps.

Diaghilev's Ballets Russes had not only been under financial pressure. For some years, the Paris-based Ballets Suédois had been pushing them to the sidelines of the avant-garde. In 1920, Rolf de Maré, a rich and aristocratic young Swede, established the Ballets Suédois in Paris. This scion of a Swedish forestry fortune was known as a knowledgeable collector of contemporary art when he met Jean Börlin, a beefy fair-haired Swedish ballet dancer; the Ballets Suédois had been created as a vehicle for Börlin's talent. In their first season the Ballets Suédois staged fifty performances, as compared to fewer than a dozen by the Ballets Russes that year.

Superficially, de Maré's troupe was a Ballets Russes knock-off: the company's name was clearly a derivation and de Maré employed many of the same composers and collaborators as Diaghilev. Both companies performed in the Théâtre des Champs-Elysées. (It had been closed since before the War when, in 1920, de Maré revived the venue by taking out a head lease.) The company was aggressive in its marketing – "only the

Ballets Suédois can please an international public" – and de Maré started a journal, *La Danse*, which favoured his own productions. Diaghilev and the Ballets Russes were always on the verge of bankruptcy and as such were constrained by their audience's established tastes. With his considerable wealth, however, de Maré had no such inhibitions and was happy to take the risk in developing and staging more experimental works.

The Ballets Suédois embraced modernism in a way Diaghilev did not. The Ballets Russes was "Right Bank" and seemingly elitist, whereas the Ballets Suédois looked more democratic. (That said, the Ballets Suédois' dress rehearsals were grand events which attracted Parisian high society, its fashion designers and artists – much the same crowd as would attend a Ballets Russes gala.) Although a hands-on director, de Maré gave his collaborators more licence than did Diaghilev. Fernand Léger was a beneficiary in this regard, and visual design sometimes overpowered the company's dancing. De Maré was more radical and daring; Börlin often appeared on stage near naked. There was a greater emphasis on abstraction. De Maré was adventurous, and took on work that had been rejected by Diaghilev, such as Milhaud and Paul Claudel's *L'homme et son désir*; this piece, for example, required a four-tiered stage set! *Skating*, a 1922 production, with its feverish action was equally avant-garde. In 1923, *La création du monde* featured African themes. De Maré hired emerging artists too; Cole Porter was one when, in 1923, de Maré hired him and Gerald Murphy to create an "American" ballet for the troupe's US tour.

And in the summer of 1924, there would emerge a further competitor for the Ballets Russes. The Comte de Beaumont had decided to enter the arena and become a ballet entrepreneur.

These aristocrats had terrific names. Beaumont was Etienne Jacques Alexandre Marie Bonnin Joseph de Bonnière de Beaumont. He was forty-one in 1924, and he and his wife (Edith) were famous for putting on extravagant gala balls. Etienne de Beaumont was a Proustian figure: tall, elegant, fussy and long-faced, with a piping voice and bulging blue eyes. He was also manipulative: he seemed to get as much pleasure from leaving people off the list of invitees to their annual galas as including them. More often than not, these events were held at the Beaumont's grand townhouse, 11 rue Masseran, in the 7th arrondissement, and they rarely started before midnight. (When Misia learnt that Chanel had been excluded from the 1920 edition, she and her husband cancelled their acceptances and, together with Chanel and Picasso, ostentatiously stood in the street as the guests arrived.[117]) Each ball was choreographed and curated; the Beaumonts even planned full dress rehearsals. They encouraged exhibitionism and cross-dressing – so that their balls became something of a mélange of the *ancién regime* and contemporary Montparnasse. Cocteau invariably came dressed as the god Mercury.

Proust made one of his last public appearances at the Beaumonts' 1921 New Year's Eve number, which did start before midnight. Proust was not really an admirer of Beaumont: "He amuses me, but he is one of those men who borrow what little wit they have from those around them."[118] Pale, powdered and puffy, and reeking of the fumigations he used to hold off his severe asthma, Proust arrived at midnight, dressed circa 1910. He had sent two requests: a cup of scalding herb tea on arrival (for which he had sent the recipe in advance), and "not to be introduced to too many wearisome intellectual ladies"[119]. A rare public appearance by the famous writer could only add lustre to their gala, and the Beaumonts were happy to oblige.

It needs to be said that Etienne de Beaumont, unlike so many of his aristocratic cohort, was keenly and genuinely involved in the arts; he was knowledgeable, discerning and open to the new ideas. Since the Revolution – yes, 1789 – most of the French nobility had withdrawn to their country estates; there they hunted, supported horse racing and the local town. They hated Paris and the Third Republic, they withdrew from public life – thereby ceding politics to the bourgeoisie – and, typically, they would only come to the capital to entertain and enjoy their own. (In the 1970s, when the author was employed by what is now JP Morgan, he worked with a charming and well-born French woman who – it was said – was the first member of her family, male or female, to have been engaged in any paid employment since the Revolution.)

Beaumont was a great admirer of Erik Satie. For their 1923 ball, staged on 30 May, the Beaumonts engaged him to put together a series of musical tableaux vivants, the finale being a short divertissement for organ and trumpet, *La statue retrouvée*. Cocteau inveigled himself into writing the scenario, Satie brought in Picasso to do the costumes and Massine to help the amateur performers with the choreography. It was, therefore, an ad hoc reunion of the great 1917 *Parade* team. Olga Picasso was a performer. Satie's score survives but nothing else. In any event, it was such a success that Beaumont decided to put on a public set of performances – *Soireé de Paris*– in 1924, from 17 May to 30 June. (The rubric is a play on Guillaume Apollinaire's pre-War journal, *Les Soirées de Paris*.)

Advertised as being in aid of war widows and Russian refugees, Beaumont chose an unusual venue for his six week endeavour: La Cigale, the somewhat run-down theatre at 120 boulevard de Rochechouart, in Montmartre. The theatre could house an audience of about 1000. An art exhibition– "art in the music hall", with contributions from Picasso, Derain, Braque and Jean-Victor Hugo – would be on continuous display in La Cigale's foyer.

Beaumont was much taken by Léonide Massine. Massine had fallen out with Diaghilev, and Beaumont hoped the season would be an opportunity to relaunch Massine as a choreographer and dancer. Satie's influence was all-pervasive throughout the several weeks, of course, and the public announcements also gave prominence to Loïe Fuller, whose innovative lighting techniques would be employed.

A typical evening would comprise a number of events. Opening night, Saturday 17 May, included two one-act ballets by Massine, *Salade* (with music by Milhaud and sets by Braque) and *Le Beau Danube* (to Strauss' music) – which later became a staple of the Ballets Russes de Monte-Carlo – plus a "spectacle dramatique" by Tristan Tzara, *Mouchoir de Nuages*, a Dada number which is impossible to describe. Later in the season, in another "spectacle dramatique", Cocteau would rejig a version of *Roméo et Juliette* which he had written some years earlier; Cocteau played Mercutio, presumably as a continuation of his identification with the god Mercury, in a rather fey interpretation of Shakespeare's mercurial character. Daily advertisements would promote forthcoming offerings from the *Soirée de Paris*, together with variations and cancellations. (It was like that.)

The highlight of the season was the première of a new ballet, *Mercure*, on 15 June. This coincided with the publication of Raymond Radiguet's posthumous novel, *Le Bal du Comte d'Orgel*, in which he sent-up and ridiculed a pretentious noble couple who everyone identified as Etienne and Edith de Beaumont. (Edith had made the mistake of nodding off at a reading of Radiguet's first novel.) It didn't seem to put the Beaumonts off their stride; perhaps they enjoyed the added notoriety.

Rideau for *Mercure* by Picasso, 1924

Mercure reunited three of the four who had worked on *Parade* in 1917: Satie, Picasso and Massine. Absent was Cocteau. Satie and Picasso had taken offence at Cocteau's claims as to the importance of his contribution to *Parade*. So he was out. Worse for Cocteau, they vested in the character of Mercury a series of digs at Cocteau, which the incestuous arts crowd well understood. The original concept was Beaumont's: he wanted a series of theatrical vignettes, a plotless montage derived from ancient mythology. Satie was central to the work but he deferred to Picasso, asking him to create the themes around which he would compose the music: "[though] it has a subject, this ballet has no plot. It is a purely decorative spectacle and you can imagine the marvellous contribution of Picasso which I have attempted to translate musically."[120] Picasso took the opportunity to move on from his post-war neo-classism and re-establish his avant-garde credentials.

Satie's music was that of the music hall: ragtime, polkas and waltzes – perfect for the light and frivolous vignettes danced by Massine and staged by Picasso. Picasso's rideau or drop curtain – with a guitar-playing Harlequin, a Pierrot with violin and a stand-alone lyre, set in a landscape of muted earth colours – is an acknowledged masterwork. (The 1924 original is preserved in the Musée National d'Art Moderne, and an authorised tapestry copy was made in the 1960s for the Exxon Building in New York.) Picasso's costumes were bold monochromes, visually calligraphic and inventively constructed. Some props became part of the ballet itself as they became characters which moved about the stage, seemingly without any assistance.

There was just one act and three scenes, in all lasting no more than twenty minutes. Mercury, Venus, Pluto and Apollo all had roles in the show, as did an unflattering transvestite group of Three Graces – who the in-crowd readily identified as send-ups of Poulenc, Auric and the art critic Louis Laloy[121]. On Massine's entrance, Étienne de Beaumont let out an ostentatious and overly enthusiastic "Bravo", and applauded wildly. Misia was in the audience, just returned from a trip to New York for her husband's 1924 exhibition at the Wildenstein gallery (and with a new passport that had cut ten years off her age). A rusted-on supporter of the Ballets Russes, she hesitated to join the applause.[122] Gertrude Stein was there too, and Diaghilev also, looking "pale, agitated, nervous."[123]

The dreadful André Breton truly hated Satie, and he and his claque caused a ruckus. Aragon and Auric were part of it. They knew Picasso was untouchable, so they contrasted him with Satie. "En bas Erik Satie et vive Picasso", they cried. "En bas de Beaumont…et toutes soirées de Paris!"[124] Picasso's drop curtain was lowered temporarily and the Surrealists were removed. Satie left early; it was a Sunday night, and he had to catch a train.

The ballet was performed on five nights. Its reviews varied. The *Soirée de Paris* had run its course, however, and the Comte de Beaumont's ballet adventure seems to have closed early, on or about 22 June. The season did not make money, and there is no reason to believe that the war widows or Russian refugees received any benefaction. But Massine had returned triumphant. And Picasso's reputation soared further: *Vogue* magazine's July 1924 edition ran a glamourous feature on the ballet and Picasso's contributions to it. And in what he must surely have considered the ultimate accolade, the magazine dubbed Etienne de Beaumont the "Maecenas of Paris". Diaghilev allegedly said of the *Soirée de Paris* that it was simply "a soirée of the Ballets Russes in which the only thing missing is my name." Yet, two years later, in what surely is the greatest accolade, the Ballets Russes acquired all the rights to *Mercure.*

The Ballets Russes was fighting back. Their Paris season would run from 26 May to 30 June with twelve performances. With the agreement of the French Olympic Committee, the Ballet Russes de Monte Carlo (as it was now known) promoted their season as part of the "Grande Saison d'Art de la VIII*e* Olympiade"; Her Serene Highness the Hereditary Princess of Monaco and Prince Pierre were the patrons. The venue was the now traditional and very chic Théâtre des Champs-Elysées.

First up, on 26 May, was Poulenc's *Les Biches*; it had been premiered in Monte Carlo in January, and its four performances were well received by the capital's critical audience. Across town, Etienne de Beaumont's rival *Soirée de Paris* was already well in its stride. *Mercure* had been its major contribution to these ballet wars, and balletomanes were now wondering what to expect in response from the Ballets Russes in its upcoming première, *Le Train Bleu.*

Le Train Bleu was the glamourous express train that ran overnight from Paris to the Côte d'Azur. Opening night for the ballet was Friday 20 June, and many of the patrons had been present at *Mercure's* première the previous Sunday. The flimsy plot by Cocteau revolved around the trip to the south and the leisure activities there of the beau monde. Cocteau had suggested the idea to Diaghilev as a vehicle for Anton Dolin, with whom the impresario had recently become romantically involved. Born Patrick Healy-Kay, Dolin was Irish and not yet twenty; to this point he had not developed great technique, apparently, but he was very handsome and had an athletic build, which could be put to good effect in the beach scenes.

G.DE SAISON D'ART de la VIII.E OLYMPIADE

avec le concours du Comité Olympique Français et de l'Association Française d'Expansion et d'Échanges Artistiques

THÉATRE DES CHAMPS-ÉLYSÉES

Du 26 Mai au 30 Juin 1924

XVII.E SAISON de SERGE de DIAGHILEW

Sous le Haut Patronage de LL. AA. SS. la Princesse Héréditaire et le Prince Pierre de Monaco

BALLETS RUSSES

de MONTE-CARLO

— Créations —

LE TRAIN BLEU

LES BICHES

LES FACHEUX

LES TENTATIONS DE LA BERGÈRE

UNE EDUCATION MANQUÉE

— Au Répertoire —

NOCES - LE SACRE DU PRINTEMPS - PULCINELLA et PETROUCHKA
de STRAVINSKY

PARADE de ERIK SATIE - CIMAROSIANA

Chorégraphie LA NIJINSKA — Régisseur Général SERGE GRIGORIEFF
Chefs d'Orchestre: MM. IGOR STRAVINSKY, ANDRE MESSAGER, PIERRE MONTEUX
HENRI CASADESUS, EDOUARD FLAMENT

CALENDRIER DES SPECTACLES

MERCREDI 11 JUIN, Noces — Les Biches — Danses du Prince Igor
VENDREDI 13 — Une Education manquée - Les Fâcheux - Le Sacre du Printemps
VENDREDI 20 — GRAND GALA DE CHARITE
Une Education manquée — Le Train Bleu — Petrouchka
DIMANCHE 22 — SOIREE DE MUSIQUE FRANCAISE
Parade — Les Fâcheux — Le Train Bleu — Les Biches
MERCREDI 25 — Pulcinella — Les Biches — Noces
VENDREDI 27 — Cimarosiana-Parade-Le Train Bleu - Les Tentations de la Bergère
SAMEDI 28 — SOIREE STRAVINSKY
Le Sacre du Printemps — Pulcinella — Noces
DIMANCHE 29 — Une Education manquée-Les Fâcheux-Cimarosiana- Petrouchka
LUNDI 30 — Les Tentations de la Bergère — Le Train Bleu — Noces

PRIX DES PLACES:

LOCATION sans augmentation de prix AU THEATRE DES CHAMPS-ELYSEES

This was the Ballets Russes' first realistic ballet in a recognisable setting. It said nothing, it was frivolous and it was trendy. Everything is set on the beach, with beachgoers flirting with each other, celebrating the cult of youth and otherwise going about their business. In one act, taking perhaps twenty-five minutes, *la vie sportive* is extensively celebrated, with swimming moves, golf swings, tennis and even weightlifting. Despite the obvious opportunity, there is no blue train; and an aeroplane flies overhead and is heard but does not appear.

Rideau for *Le Train Bleu* by Picasso, 1924

Diaghilev put together an all-star creative team. He persuaded Milhaud to do the music. Fortunately, the composer was a quick worker; he had to move directly from finishing the Comte de Beaumont's *Salade* to whipping up *Le Train Bleu*. It took him but three weeks to create a featherweight score with a fair-like air that was perfect for what Diaghilev had in mind. Bronislava Nijinska did the choreography, Chanel the costumes and Picasso designed a memorable stage curtain.

Picasso's drop curtain came to be a Ballets Russes icon. The canvas, a new version of a painting from Picasso's neo-classic period, depicts two rather large women gambolling across a beach in white tunics, and it was so well received that Diaghilev came to use it as a sort of signature backdrop in future productions.

The Ballets Russes rehearsals for *Le Train Bleu* became a talking point too, when Chanel started to bring along her new lover, "Bendor", the Duke of Westminster. Her costumes were glamorous, and although the men found some of the fabrics difficult to grip, that was their worry:

Chanel's tennis outfits evoked Suzanne Lenglen's (even though Lenglen favoured Jean Patou), and the golfing plus-fours reminded everyone of the Prince of Wales's fashionable ensembles. A bathing beauty wore a flashy pink georgette costume, men wore brief swimsuits – not least Anton Dolin, as Beau Gosse ("handsome lad") – and flapper dresses prevailed throughout.

For some, *Le Train Bleu* was not serious enough. For others, it represented the spirit of the age. When the ballet reached London later in the year, *The Observer* declared it "one of the most simple and delightful works imaginable".[125]

The ballet wars of May and June 1924 had been a boon to the city's already fervent cultural life. The Ballets Russes was back in form. The troupe would soon be strengthened and given something of a new life by the administrative and entrepreneurial skills of René Blum, the younger brother of the heroic Léon Blum, when Blum became artistic director of the Théâtre de Monte-Carlo in late 1924. And Etienne de Beaumont was being widely lauded for his *Soirée de Paris* endeavour. For its part, the Ballets Suédois had not entered the mid-year contest. Rolf de Maré's troupe was gearing up for one last challenge, however, for November and December – when they would emerge with a new programme. Their key piece was "the first and last Dada ballet", the incredible two-act happening, *Relâche*, by Francis Picabia.

Picabia was a peripatetic figure. A painter and a poet, he was – like Picasso – somewhat older than many in the contemporary scene. Born into a bourgeois Parisian family in 1879, and financially independent, he had met up with Man Ray and Duchamp in pre-war New York. He had settled briefly in Barcelona, was in Zurich to participate in the birth of Dada, and had moved back to Paris; there, in 1921, he signed up with Breton and his Surrealists, and denounced Dada. As a painter, he created and coordinated *L'Oeil cacodylic* which was so prominent in Le Boeuf sur le Toit's bar. And now, having fallen out with Breton, he was relapsing to Dada – and collaborating with Breton's nemesis, Satie.

The advertisement said it all. *Relâche* was to be a two-act ballet *instantanéiste* – which embraced "instantaneism", whatever that might mean. (Picabia defined it in a pamphlet but it is incomprehensible.) Huge posters and an extensive media campaign promoted the new work. Advertisements identified Picabia as the creator of the ballet, with a cinematic entr'acte and *la queue du chien* ("the dog's tail"), music by Erik Satie and choreography by Jean Börlin. Attendees were advised to bring dark glasses and earplugs. Ex-Dadaists were explicitly asked to come, demonstrate and shout: A bas Satie! A bas Picabia!

It was clearly intended to be something of a revolutionary happening. The entr'acte, ingeniously named *Entr'acte*, was an essential part of the design. Picabia had explained to René Clair that he wanted a film to be projected between the two acts, something that had been a regular feature of the intermissions at café-concerts before the World War.

LES BALLETS SUÉDOIS DONNERONT
LE 27 NOVEMBRE
AU THÉÂTRE DES CHAMPS ÉLYSÉES
" R E L Â C H E "
BALLET
INSTANTANÉISTE
EN DEUX ACTES, UN ENTR'ACTE CINÉMATOGRAPHIQUE
ET LA QUEUE DU CHIEN
PAR
FRANCIS PICABIA
MUSIQUE
D'
ERIK SATIE
CHORÉGRAPHIE DE **JEAN BÖRLIN**
Apportez des lunettes noires et de quoi vous boucher les oreilles.
RETENEZ VOS PLACES
Messieurs les ex-Dadas sont priés de venir manifester et surtout de crier : « A BAS SATIE ! A BAS PICABIA ! VIVE LA NOUVELLE REVUE FRANCAISE ! »
" **391** "
N° 10   PRIX : 2 Frs
Dépositaire " AU SANS PAREIL "
37, Avenue Kléber, PARIS
Le Gérant. PIERRE DE MASSOT

The Théâtre des Champs-Elysées was the venue for the opening night, Thursday 27 November. "Relâche" means closed or cancelled. Patrons arriving for the 9 pm performance found the theatre's lights out. The show was not on. Variously amused and annoyed, the crowd assumed it had all been a joke, that the show was always going to be cancelled. Picabia may indeed have intended the title to mean a closing of doors to convention or tradition, but the Ballets Suédois did not intend to abandon the show. It was simply that the star, Börlin, was indisposed. In the event, *Relâche* opened a week later, on 4 December.

Together with many artists, Picasso was there, he being a great pal of Satie's. Everyone was anxious to see how Satie would fare with the unpredictable Dadaists.[126] No sooner had the curtain been raised when, upstage behind the actors, hundreds of klieg lights were set ablaze – momentarily blinding the audience.[127] (Well, they had been warned to wear dark glasses.) A man dressed as a fireman walked about, smoking and pouring water from one bucket to another. A woman in evening dress came from the audience and was joined by eight men similarly attired. Satie's music was simple and subversive: a couple of tunes were recognisable to almost everyone as variations on risqué army songs, "Cadet Rouselle" and "Le Père Dupanloup". The lights dimmed and brightened in time with the music. The dancers played jumping jacks; the woman stripped down to a pink bodystocking until one of the men carried her off stage. She returned to her seat in the audience. It was all rather perplexing, as no doubt was the intention. The crowd had been invited to join in, and they did, as they had been provided with penny whistles.

Although René Clair alone is credited with the film *Entr'acte* these days, on opening night he and Francis Picabia were jointly identified as its creators. It lasted for something more than twenty minutes, and has become an iconic piece of cinematography. The film opens with a cannon trained at the audience, and a giant bang. Well known members of the avant-garde appeared in recognisable Paris settings; Man Ray and Marcel Duchamp, for example, were shown playing chess on the theatre's roof top. In a breakthrough for cinema, Satie's music follows the film's rhythms as the film varies speeds and sometimes goes into reverse. A crowd of mourners follow a camel-drawn hearse, in slow motion, then faster and faster; the hearse escapes the camel and the streets fill with racing cars; the coffin spills into a field, the corpse steps out as a magician, who makes the mourners disappear one by one.

Relâche's second act was no more understandable than the first. The scenery was a series of provocative slogans, such as "There are some – poor imbeciles – who prefer the ballets at the Opéra". The men in evening dress returned to the stage, as did the woman, she still in her bodystocking; she started to get dressed while the men stripped down to white unitards. The woman piled their clothes into a wheelbarrow and dumped them in a corner. The fireman reappeared; there was a dance with a crown, revolving doors, and so on. The woman then returned to her place in the audience. And finally, Satie and Picabia drove around the stage in Börlin's motor scooter, waving and cheering.

Relâche and its klieg lights

Picabia and Satie had a flair for the irreverent and for controversy. Their creation was meaningless and nonsensical, although Satie's music did hold it all together in a strange way. Certainly, it was as iconoclastic as *Mercure* had been for the *Soirée de Paris* back in June. René Clair said

"…it was never known precisely why this ballet was 'instantanéiste'. As for *The Dogs Tail*, no one ever saw hide or hair of it."[128] The reviews were not good. It was as if that was always the intention.

Relâche had twelve performances. No doubt Picabia and his colleagues enjoyed the exquisite irony of seeing fresh "relâche" banners splashed over the posters for *Relâche* that were still widely on display in the weeks flowing its closure. De Maré's troupe was exhausted, like its audience, and these performances of *Relâche* were the Ballets Suédois last hurrah. Dada had run its course too, and *Relâche* – fun as it was – proved to be pretty much Dada's death rattle.

OF BREAD AND BOARD

If the carrefour Vavin at Montparnasse was the centre of activity in the 1920s, the 6th arrondissement – down the road – was a more attractive place to live. At its heart were three restaurants near the Abbaye de Saint-Germain-de-Prés: Les Deux Magots, opposite the church; Café de Flore, beside Deux Magots and along the boulevard Saint Germain; and opposite the Flore, the Brasserie Lipp. Each of these now famous restaurants had its own character and style – and each was run by a "Bougnat".

Bougnats are immigrants to Paris from the Auvergne region. Theirs is a strange and uplifting story. Those who arrived in the 1800s were typically humble water-carriers; they expanded this activity to supplying coal and firewood. ("Bougnat" is a neologism derived from the Auvergne word meaning coal seller.) To these products was added wine, and the Bougnats soon started to establish rudimentary cafés from which they could sell or transport each of these. The term "bougnat" came to mean both the people themselves (upper case) and their shops (lower case). By the first half of the 1900s, every local community in Paris had one bougnat or more; they were ubiquitous. The wife served a bite to eat, a glass of wine; the husband delivered the coal or firewood. The local bougnat was a social institution at which you could leave a message or just drop in for a chat or a glass of wine. By the Second World War most cafés in the city were run by Bougnats.

Marcellin Cazes, the proprietor of Lipp, became the most famous and accomplished restaurateur – and Bougnat – in Paris. Born in Laguiole in 1888, he came to Paris as a fourteen year-old boy and worked as a commis waiter; he soon owned his own bougnats in the 11th and then in Les Halles. After war service, he and his wife managed a small Alsatian brasserie – Brasserie des Bords du Rhin – on the boulevard Saint Germain; in 1920, they bought it, abandoned the German-sounding name, adopted the moniker of the previous owner, M. Lipp, and kept the Alsatian menu. Actors from the nearby Vieux-Colombier soon frequented it, adding lustre, while Clémence Cazes worked up a storm on the stoves and Marcellin Cazes managed carefully-selected staff.

By 1925 the Cazes had bought the adjacent courtyard, expanded into it, built a first floor over the site and decorated the place in the warm and glowing fashion we know it in today: Belle Epoque ceramics, mosaic panels with huge wood-framed mirrors perfectly tilted so that a diner facing the mirror can take in what is behind him, brown leather ("moleskin") banquettes, white table cloths, black-dressed waiters with white aprons, a painted ceiling and subtle hanging lights. Cazes had increased the seating from ten tables to eighty, upstairs and down and outside under the street awning. Prime Minister Edouard Herriot was a patron, the Bismark herring being his favourite; it is still on the menu. Léon Blum too; he preferred the choucroute, also still there. (It was said that governments of the Third Republic were formed at Lipp – and dissolved in the Parliament.) The vespasienne outside the front door disappeared and the bus stop was moved, thereby opening a vista of the Saint Germain church. Lipp has always been kept as a brasserie, serving draft Alsatian beer with good food and wine (the cheese selection and house riesling both being excellent), with a clientele from the arts, the nearby Sciences Po and all sides of politics. Bookings are still not taken – you can wait for a table in the chairs under the canopy; it's even acceptable to simply have a drink there – and there is a strict pecking order once you enter through the revolving door: best tables to the right, purgatory at the back and tourists upstairs.

Across the road at the Flore, the café was yet to be taken under the wing of another great Bougnat, Paul Boubel. It looked marvellous with its long white marquee and outside chairs. The food and wine were apparently fine, but the Flore took itself rather seriously. Downstairs, it always looked somewhat melancholy with its red leather interior; upstairs was downright uninviting. Perhaps this had to do with the presence of an entirely different clientele from Lipp and Deux Magots. Café de Flore came to be identified with the extreme right in the 1920s and 30s and, in particular, with the talented but odious Charles Maurras of Action Française. In 1933, he even called his polemic memoire *Au Signe de Flore*. But it was fashionable with a certain element. The smart set did not sit outside, despite its obvious attractions, nor did they stay downstairs; upstairs was their place.

The most prominent site of the three was surely, then as now, Les Deux Magots. Sitting opposite the church, it commands the corner of the rue Bonaparte and the boulevard Saint Germain. Its green marquee with gilt lettering wraps around the corner and establishes a presence, where outside tables allow patrons to take in the whole scene. Auguste Boulay, a Bougnat, had bought the site in 1914 when it was a struggling café and bar, and he transformed it into what we see today. In the 1920s, it was adopted by the Surrealists – Breton, Prévert, Aragon, Gide, Léger and the like – and it soon came to be the place to be seen. James Joyce was a regular. It also took on a decidedly left wing aura, in contrast to its neighbour. Now run very professionally by Boulay's great-great-granddaughter, it has become something of a tourist trap.

Bougnats also ran the great establishments up on the boulevard de Montparnasse: La Coupole, Le Dôme, La Rotonde and Le Select. Today, the Dôme has gone way up-market, serving some of the best seafood in the city, and the Rotonde has had much of its 1920s glory carved away to create a cinema. La Coupole has been completely refurbished and glitzed, and has lost much of its allure. In contrast, the Select has kept its original stamp. It looks much the same (albeit with none of the "air of picturesque squalor" that some saw in the 20s); it has much of the old menu, and it is reasonably-priced.

Although each of these places was successful and gave enjoyment to a wide audience in the 1920s, none was recognised as being a representative of top French cuisine – nor did they seek such accolades. The *Michelin Guide* of 1924 rated the top restaurants as Voisin, Larue, Lucas and Marguery; all but Lucas, now Lucas Carton, are gone.

Voisin had occupied various sites over its many years of life, and by 1924 it was located on the ground floor of a building on the corner of the rue Saint-Honoré and rue Cambon. The head chef at Voisin was Alexandre Choron, famous for two things: choron sauce (essentially sauce béarnaise plus tomato purée), and the meal he created out of animals from the Paris zoo (elephant, giraffe, etc) on Christmas day 1870, during the Commune siege. (As a young man, not yet twenty, César Ritz worked as a waiter at Voisin for a couple of years leading up to the siege.) Choron died in 1924, aged eighty-seven. Voisin attracted "the best type of the English and Americans…and the more elderly amongst the statesmen…":[129] it specialised in soups, filet de sole, Poularde Voisin, terrines, foie gras, of course and it had a great cellar. The restaurant closed in 1930.

Larue was the chicest place in town. Located at 3 place de la Madeleine, opposite and taking in a view of the church, Larue always had a few small tables and chairs outside its entrance. Inside, the restaurant was a symphony of pink and mirrors, which was perfect for Cocteau to dance on tables – as he did. Its specialty was cold dishes – fish, and cold eggs in jelly being favourites. Frogs legs too.[130] French speakers were seated to the right of the front door, English to the left; it had something to do with the waiters' tongues. When Larue closed in 1954, the fabulous cellar sold for a fortune and they were still publishing the recipe for the cold eggs in jelly:

Cut six hard-cooked eggs in half crosswise. Remove yolks, mash, season to taste and add a teaspoon of mayonnaise. Stuff into whites and chill. Soften an envelope of gelatin in one-quarter cup of cold water and dissolve over boiling water. Add to one and three-fourths cups well-seasoned consommé. Pour one-eighth-inch layer of consommé into a loaf pan and chill until firm. Chill remainder of gelatin until syrupy.   Stand stuffed eggs in pan and pour syrupy consommé over them. Chill until firm. Cut into strips allowing two halves a serving. Place on lettuce and serve with mayonnaise. Six servings.

It's a commentary of some sort on urban development that the sites of both Voisin and Larue are now occupied by fashion houses, Roberto Cavalli taking up all Voisin's old corner on rue Saint-Honoré and Cerruti occupying Larue's at the Madeleine.

Lucas became Lucas Carton when Louis Carton acquired the famous restaurant in 1924. With Alain Senderens now retired, it continues afresh at the old site – 9 place de la Madeleine – still with its stylish Majorelle woodwork, and a Michelin star. In the old days, "a number of the better-class visitors from the provinces [made] it their headquarters at mealtimes",[131] and one imagines this is still the case. Upstairs, there is a modern new space, Le Marché du Lucas, which shares the kitchen.

In addition to Lucas Carton, a number of high-class restaurants that were favoured by Michelin and others in 1924 are still in existence and at their original sites: Bofinger, Drouant, Lapérouse and Prunier.

Bofinger is an institution. Located in a back street on the western side of the place de la Bastille, it was a tiny Alsatian brasserie when first established in 1864. It still uses the original address – 5 rue de la Bastille – even though it now occupies the whole street, as the long red awning attests.

Inside, it's like a movie set for the 1920s: polished wood panelling and banquettes, ceramics, a wrought-iron staircase, high ceilings with art-nouveau lights and polished brass. But Bofinger is no theme park. The clientele is still predominantly Parisian. It is unpretentious and democratic; politicians and academics are still habitués just as they were in 1924. Maurice Chevalier and Mistinguett were clients then, just as Johnny Halliday became one in his era. Bofinger lives on. Seafood is a feature, with several varieties of oyster on display; as a tribute to the restaurant's Alsatian roots, there is sauerkraut ("choucroute") in several varieties; there are meats of all sorts, of course, salt cod, boudin noir, pigeon, daily specials, a great lobster salad, all the usual French desserts – and draft beer. Everything is done with flair. The critics say food quality has been maintained and that the friendly service sometimes lacks crispness. Everyone wants to sit in the back room under the stained-glass dome, preferably with one's back to the wall on one of the dark leather banquettes.

Drouant has hosted France's most prestigious literary prize – the Prix Goncourt – every year since 1914. Although renowned for its oysters and seafood, by 1924 Drouant needed a spruce up from what looked like a bistro. It wanted to look like the gourmet restaurant that it had become. Emile-Jacques Ruhlmann was engaged for the task; he was France's most famous exponent of Art Deco, and everything was redone by Ruhlmann – chairs, tables, wall coverings, the lot. The spanking new décor now justified the attention that came with the Prix. The restaurant had expanded into the adjacent building, its address now being 16-18 place Gaillon. As happens, however, over the coming decades the establishment fell into a period of benign neglect. No longer. Recently refurbished and updated, and with top class chefs, Drouant is once again one of Paris' chicer destinations: the original woodwork has been polished up and some Ruhlmann designs restored, with the Prix Goncourt announced, as it should be, from the much-celebrated Ruhlmann staircase.

There has been a restaurant and bar at 51 quai des Grands Augustins since the 1700s. In 1866 it was acquired by Jules Lapérouse, who named it after the famous navigator with whom he shared a family name but no known kinship. Downstairs was a bar and upstairs a dining salon, and a rabbit warren of small rooms. A portrait of the Comte de Lapérouse soon appeared upstairs, a sketch of the *l'Astrolabe* started to grace the carte du jour, and the restaurant soon came to be known colloquially as "le navigateur". In the Belle Epoque, the small rooms were converted into private "boîtes" where the rich and privileged could entertain their co-cottes; a waiter always coughed discretely before entering. Escoffier was the original chef, and sole, bouillabaisse and tripe were specialties.[132] This is how the restaurant presented itself in 1924 when Michelin awarded it two stars. (It is often said that the Guide Michelin did not award stars, technically rosettes, until 1931. The author's copy of the 1924 edition shows stars, actual five pointed stars – ranked from one to three – against each of the few restaurants it rated.)

By 1933, Lapérouse was one of Michelin's first explicit three star restaurants. Self-satisfaction followed over the next decades and, living on its past glories, Lapérouse became somewhat dowdy and tired. Here too, no longer. Lapérouse has recently been completely refurbished and largely rebuilt; partly backed by a scion of Bernard Arnault (the richest man in France) at great expense and with considerable taste, it is once again at the forefront of Paris's culinary establishments. The "boîtes" have been made into sumptuous small redoubts, more suitable than ever for their earlier purpose and, during the rebuild, a secret passageway that leads to the Senate was discovered – giving credit to the salacious stories of yesteryear.

In the 1920s, Prunier stretched almost half way along rue Duphot in the fashionable first arrondissement. Its proprietor was Emile Prunier, the son of the founder. What had been started by his father, Alfred, as a small oyster shop was now a major enterprise. Outside the restaurant was a long counter displaying every kind of oyster imaginable; French, of course, but also English Burnhams, Colchesters and Whitstables; Emile even imported Blue Points from Long Island. Men shucked the oysters for service inside, and boys also delivered them to households throughout the fashionable parts of the city. A delivery boy from Prunier, basket on his head, was a common sight *en ville*; on arrival at a bourgeois apartment, the boy would shuck the fresh oysters and place them for consumption that evening. Emile Prunier had introduced the idea of a "tasting bar" at 9 rue Duphot in 1915, and he also adopted the bistro practice of selling wine by the glass. It took off, and soon the tasting bar commandeered the whole ground floor. A glamorous full-service restaurant was set up on the first floor serving oysters (of course), American lobsters, lobster bisque, what was called Sole Prunier and the full range of *fruits de mer*.

The new Lapérouse

Restaurant Prunier took up much of
rue Duphot through the 1920s

In 1918, presumably as a result of the Revolution, Emile obtained the global monopoly for Russian caviar. Soon after, he became aware of an alternate source: sturgeon fish were living in the Gironde. Caviar became a house specialty. Then, in 1924, Emile Prunier identified a site in the increasingly fashionable 16th that would be suitable for a new venture; Prunier-Traktir opened the following year at 16 avenue Victor Hugo, on the corner of rue Traktir. A bold, indeed garish, art deco exterior of turquoise tiles led to a series of small rooms that were decked out in onyx and black marble with touches of gold. People loved it or hated it, but everyone loved the caviar. Then Emile dropped dead. His daughter Simone took over, opening a very successful branch in London and a caviar business that is famous to this day. The original Prunier on the rue Duphot now trades as Restaurant Goumard, with continued success under new ownership. The old Prunier-Traktir, now known as Café Prunier, is as successful as ever; it has a branch at 15 place de la Madeleine, where there is a shop downstairs (with a champagne bar and light meals), and a well-regarded restaurant on the first floor.

Omitted from the 1924 Michelin, but not from other sources, was La Tour d'Argent. It was not, however, what it is today. Everyone who has had the pleasure of dining at the Tour d'Argent remembers the panoramic view over the Seine to Notre-Dame cathedral. The restaurant did not have this view until 1936, when two floors were added to the building that housed the restaurant and it moved up into them. Up until then the restaurant was on the ground and lower floors, and there was no view of Notre-Dame. Indeed the entrance was not on the corner, at number 17, as it is now; the entrance was on the quai at 15 quai de la Tournelle until 1925. But some things never change.

In 1911, André Terrail, the grandfather of the present *maître d'hôtel*, married the daughter of Claudius Burdel; Burdel owned the discrete Café Anglais over the river on the boulevard des Italians.[133] Terrail bought the Tour d'Argent from the legendary Frédéric Delair in 1912; Burdel closed the Café Anglais in 1913, and Terrail acquired that establishment's great cellar. All Delair's recipes were kept. Terrail became a celebrated host, and La Tour d'Argent went on from strength to strength. It enjoyed three stars in the 1930s, slipped to two in 1996 and one ten years later.

Today the Tour d'Argent is a Paris icon: brilliant, smart and expensive. The new generation has subtly revitalised and rejuvenated the place. It can afford to employ the best chefs, and it still has a fabulous cellar. Service is impeccable. Classic dishes are done to new-found perfection. Frédéric Delair's "Sole Cardinal" is still one of the specialities. Duck from the house's own farms is offered with two options. One is Delair's original recipe, where he perfected the extraction of the last blood from the duck before it was whipped up into the traditional sauce. The alternative is lighter and addressed to today's preferences. Both dishes come in two servings, and a ceremonial duck pressing is an essential part of the service. Today's one star may soon be three.

If an army lives on its belly, in the 1920s Paris lived *for* its belly. The wholesale market of Les Halles was its digestive system. (The pronunciation is "lay-ull"; the "s" is not pronounced.)

Occupying seventy hectares in the centre of the city, this had been the site of the city's open-air food market for centuries. Under the auspices of Emperor Napoleon III, Haussmann had the area raised, redesigned and rebuilt. Victor Baltard was the architect. Inspired by London's Crystal Palace, Baltard designed twelve enormous pavilions of steel and glass – Les Halles. It was the major architectural project of the Second Empire, and Les Halles' pavilions became the model for covered markets throughout France and around the world.

Les Halles in its full glory

Every day, early in the morning, trains brought tonnes of food from the provinces to Paris. This was transferred to carts and wagons at the main terminals, almost everything being bound for Les Halles. As these convoys approached the market, they were joined by streams of horse-drawn farm carts that had weaved their way from the outskirts of the city, driven by the farmers who had "raised the produce and picked it that very morning before daylight...from the market gardens that en-circled Paris – white beans from Noyon, asparagus from Argenteuil, peas from Clamart, string beans from Bagnolet, cauliflowers from Arpajon, carrots from Crécy."[134] Hordes of porters awaited the carts and wagons and, with crates and sacks strapped to their backs, these famously strong men ("les forts") took over the last leg of the daily logistical exercise.

Les Halles was incredibly busy in the hours before dawn. Everyone went about their business – shopkeepers and tradesmen, butchers and porters, thieves and whores. Bistros populated the market's fringes, and they did a good early morning trade serving onion soup to the fur-coated socialites and their companions, still out for the night, checking out the hoi polloi. It was noisy and exciting; people shouted instructions, horses whinnied and neighed, motorised trucks backfired, and bells and whistles sounded out everywhere. The smell of horses was all-pervading. Not that anyone cared, it simply confirmed the importance and vitality of the market. And in the halls themselves, there were the sweet fragrances of fresh flowers and vegetables, and meat.

The pavilions of Les Halles opened about 5 am. First customers tended to be small restaurateurs and buyers from the military barracks, religious institutions and colleges. Top restaurants and hotels would arrive about some time later, and ostentatiously park their delivery vans in front of the old church of Saint-Eustache. By 10 am most produce was sold, and by midday the scene was being cleaned up for the next day's deliveries.

Top merchants occupied the vast pavilions. With their huge glass vaulted ceilings, all metal struts and arches and innards cleared of any supporting structures, the pavilions provided efficient and continuous space for the tenants; and they looked magnificent. Small farmers rented space on the sidewalks outside. Beneath the pavilions themselves, subterranean stockrooms housed live animals waiting to be slaughtered or sold. Pavilion No 3 was for meat; by opening hour, beef, lamb and pork was all properly carved and beautifully set out on marble counters. Pavilion No 4 had a special ventilation system because it sold live animals – duck, chicken, rabbit, lamb, poultry of every variety – and was not only noisy but potentially pungent.

On the periphery of Les Halles, circa 1924

Cheese, eggs and butter were sold in their own designated pavilion. Huge packages of eggs – thousands to a box – were delivered to it. A team of inspectors subjected the butter and milk to strict verification as to quality. The cheese market was of such indulgence and variety that it caused Emile Zola to give it a two-page rhapsody in *Le Ventre de Paris* ("The Belly of Paris"), thus:

> *"All around her, cheeses were stinking, Brittany butter was overflowing from its basket. Normandy butters, wrapped in canvas, looked like models of stomachs into which some sculptor had thrown wet cloths to keep them from drying out…a Romantour, wrapped in silver paper, was reminiscent of a nougat bar, a sugary cheese that had strayed into the land of sour fermentation."*[35]

In his "cheese symphony", Zola went on to celebrate a cornucopia of Bries "on round boards as sad as waning moons", Cantal on leaves of white beet "as though split by blows from an axe", golden Cheshire cheeses, Gruyere, Dutch cheeses "in dried blood and as hard as skulls", Parmesan adding an "aromatic tang", strong-smelling Livarots, Camemberts and so on. This was back in 1873, but almost nothing had changed in the ensuing fifty years.

One pavilion specialised in fresh flowers. Another sold vegetables. Outside these two, in a large outdoor market along the rue Rambuteau, small traders set out their own flowers and their vegetables; there were vegetables of every conceivable variety: "masterpieces of edible architecture – red pyramids (radishes), green cubes (cabbages), purple parallelepipeds (eggplants)."[136] Fresh seafood would arrive a little later than the other produce – between six and seven in the morning – from Normandy and Brittany (and England and Belgium); this was delivered to its own special seafood pavilion. As soon as the fish arrived it was cleaned and sold out.

Oysters had their own section in the separate multi-purpose Pavilion No 12. (Major retailers like Prunier took delivery direct from the train stations.) No 12 largely housed bakers and fruit sellers. It also sold a special category of produce – *rogations* – which were leftovers from the grand hotels, the best restaurants and government receptions. Food was sorted and plated, and many of the workers took their meals here; bones for stock and bread crusts for breadcrumbs were sold separately.

Les Halles is no more. Traffic for the market came to overwhelm the city, and for years after the Second World War there was agitation to move it elsewhere. A new site was found at Rungis on the outskirts of Paris and, in 1971, the whole grand complex was torn down. (One pavilion – now designated the Pavillon Baltard – has been preserved as a National Monument. In 1974, it was re-erected in the eastern suburbs of Paris at Nogent-sur-Marne, where it is a popular venue for pop concerts and the like.) The Eglise Saint-Eustache still stands to the north of the site, and Au Pied de Cochon and adjacent restaurants along the rue Coquillière give some feel for the many bistros and bars that once surrounded the old complex. And it is no accident that Paris' great kitchenware shop, E. Dehillerin, a veritable mecca of pots and pans and every conceivable kitchen utensil, has been located at 18 and 20 rue Coquillière since 1890.

A massive underground transport interchange was dug out where Les Halles once stood: Châtelet-Les Halles, Paris' largest interchange. This works very well, but successive redevelopments of the site above have struggled to be embraced by anyone, Parisians and visitors alike.

The difference between a bistro and a restaurant is supposed to be that bistros never close – welcoming walk-ins at any time for a drink or a meal – whereas restaurants close between lunch and dinner. It's all a bit confusing, because what we think of today as Paris' best bistros all close just like restaurants.

In 1924, there was no confusion. Bistros typically did close, but few would have noticed. This is because the licence fee would double if you stayed open for the full twenty-four hours. So the husband and wife who ran the show would close the doors for an hour in the dead of night. It was a hard life. The proprietors would live on the premises, as might a young relative or two who had joined them from the country to learn the trade. A zinc bar was a necessity; it was the neighbourhood meeting point, a place to have a stiffener in the morning or a settler at night. The kitchen was inevitably tiny, out the back somewhere, and it would be dominated by "the piano" – a large metal stove – which did run twenty-four hours; where the bistro was a bougnat, the piano would run on the proprietors' coal or wood. There would be a dog and perhaps a cat. If you didn't give credit, you had no business. Great ceremony accompanied the payment of outstanding bills, typically acknowledged by a small glass of house *gentiane* from the Auvergne.

Not all bistros were humble bougnats. In 1912, a young butcher from Burgundy – Benoît Matray – bought a simple restaurant at 20 rue Saint-Martin, not far from Les Halles and near today's Pompidou Centre. He turned it into a Lyonnais bistro with authentic Lyonnais food, and excellent service. Benoît cooked the food and greeted his clients at the door. Traders from Les Halles quickly adopted "Benoît", as the restaurant soon came to be known, and it has gone on from there – first under Benoît

Matray's descendants, the Petit family, and now as part of the Ducasse stable. If it wasn't the best bistro in town in 1924, Benoît is certainly a candidate now.

Benoît today

A distinctive red canopy circles the corner site and "Benoît" is announced in gold script. Once through the double doors, the ideal bistro appears. It is the perfect size, with a capacity of perhaps sixty. The tablecloths are spotlessly white, the chairs are bentwood and the banquettes red velvet; the brass sparkles and the woodwork looks freshly polished, as do the etched-glass mirrors. This is a cosy, comfortable and warm place. It has been said that Lyons' favourite son, Paul Bocuse, named it his favourite restaurant in Paris. Certainly the food stands up: traditional Lyonnais dishes – terrines, brawn salad, duck with turnips, gigot d'agneau and so on – are complemented by Benoît's special smoked salmon and seasonal dishes like coquilles and asparagus. The cheese is perfect, desserts are classic and a reasonable bottle or two of Beaujolais will be at hand. Benoît has beautiful floral china, and it has the most attractive menus in Paris, the originals having been designed by the pyrographer Lasage. It is now part of the Ducasse stable, and the only "bistro" in Paris to hold a Michelin star.

The most famous and expensive bistro in Paris, L'Ami Louis, was established in 1924. Inside and out, it looks as though nothing has changed in its near one hundred years of life. Except the prices, which are astronomical. This is a restaurant for big eaters. Meat prevails. There is a choice among the duck, veal, chicken, lamb, pigeon and beef – of course – but most patrons go for the roast chicken, an ancient Breton breed, or the gigot d'agneau; shoestring potatoes or a garlicky potato cake ("galette") is the preferred accompaniment. That's it. If the diner has chosen the slab of foie gras to start his meal, there will be little room for the outstanding tarte Tatin.

"Chez L'Ami Louis" proclaims the sign over the door at 32 rue du Vertbois in a not very fashionable corner of the 3rd arrondissement. From the outside it looks like any good local bistro in a provincial town: dark polished wood and two large windows with a central wooden door in between, and a red-checked half-curtain running across the windows to provide privacy for those inside. The words *foie gras* and *gibiers*, which appear high up on the shopfront, might give a clue to the seriousness within. There are but twelve tables in a long narrow dining room. It looks dilapidated, with the aged wood panelling being the worse for wear; a huge stainless steel stove pipe incongruously bisects the room as it reaches up one wall and runs across the ceiling. Only the salmon pink table cloths show an effort towards style and class. Old stoves heat the restaurant in winter and overheat it in summer. Finding access to the bathrooms is a challenge. The wine list now includes some wines with prices that do not deter, but the cost of the food itself is like the cost of running JP Morgan's yacht: if you need to ask how much, you cannot afford it. It is nearly impossible to secure a table.

In the 1920s, a gentleman still had his club. He could go there for lunch or dinner, to gamble and gossip or just to get away from his spouse (or mistress). If things weren't going well at home, he could stay the night. Just as the Great War caused havoc to the established order in Europe, so it brought other small changes in society, such as the consolidation of the Parisian clubs; and like the Paris Peace Conference, it established a new order which, in the case of these clubs, has remained valid to this day. By 1924, there was keen debate as to which of the surviving clubs was the most prestigious – the Jockey Club or the Cercle de l'Union Interalliée.

The Jockey Club had a long association with thoroughbred horseracing – "the sport of kings" – and its membership had always been largely drawn from the aristocracy. Proust called it "the most exclusive club in the world" and he cast his character Charles Swann as a member (indeed, the only one with Jewish heritage). All through the Second Empire and the Belle Epoque, the club had been located near the Opéra, on the first floor of a prominent corner, that of the rue Scribe and boulevard des Capucines. The story that the young bucks from the Jockey Club insisted that every opera include a ballet mid-performance (and that this was used to inspect the members of the corps de ballet) is not apocryphal. By the 20s, though, such behaviour was more subdued. In 1923, the Jockey Club moved what Proust called this "sanctuary of the elite" into splendid new premises at 2 rue Rabelais – barely a five minute walk from the official residence of the French President, the Palais de l'Élysées.

Proust's Charles Swann was also a member of the Cercle de la Rue Royale. It merged with the equally prestigious Cercle de l'Union in 1916, and together they formed the basis for an entirely new entity – the Cercle de l'Union Interalliée. It was in a spirit of *fraternité* that the good and the great put together this new club at the same time as the USA entered the Great War. US officers and diplomats were particularly welcome. In 1920, the Interalliée bought the grand mansion and grounds of Henri de Rothschild at 33 rue du Faubourg-Sant-Honoré, and Maréchal Ferdinand Foch became its President. Next to the British Embassy and in the same block as the Élysées, it could not have enjoyed a more advantageous address. The nobility populated its board together with successful businessmen such as André Citroën.

Not that the other great gentlemen's club, The Traveller's, was anything but first rate. It had been created in 1903 out of the Second Empire mansion built for Thérèse Lachman, Marquise Païva, one of the great nineteenth-century courtesans. When the Hôtel de la Païva was constructed for the Marquise, the Champs-Elysées was lined with such buildings; today, largely hidden behind a high wall, 25 avenue des Champs-Élysées is the last *hôtel particulier* still standing. The staircase and furnishings are brilliant, ornate and famous, and – with much accommodation upstairs – it took little adjustment to create the necessary bar, billiards room and the like that would turn it into a grand club.

None of these establishments admitted women, of course. That would have defeated much of their purpose.

Ladies were entertained in restaurants and the grand hotels. Each of the other grand hotels recognised in the *Michelin Rouge* of 1924 had stylish public rooms, professional staff and a first-class dining room; they were Claridge's, the Crillon, the Grand, the Lutetia (alone on the Left Bank), the Majestic, the Meurice, the Moderne, the Palais d'Orsay, and the Plaza Athénée. The Bristol did not open until 1925. But there was nothing like the Ritz.

By 1924, the Ritz had been in business for more than a quarter century. On opening night, 1 June 1898, *le tout Paris* was in attendance: French aristocrats were joined by a loyal ducal contingent from Britain, bankers from both sides of the Atlantic, and a 37-year old Marcel Proust, "small, dark and nervous looking, effacing himself behind some person considered to be more important."[137] The British were there, not just out of loyalty; they had come to see if César Ritz could repeat his London triumph where, throughout the 1890s, he and Auguste Escoffier had made the Savoy Hotel the social heart of that city. He could.

Ritz had put together a syndicate to buy the 18th century Paris mansion of the Duc de Gramont, at 15 place Vendôme. He had come from humble beginnings in Switzerland, but Ritz now knew the world's elite; and they – Alfred Beit, Calouste Gulbenkian, Jacques de Gunzburg et al – knew him, and had backed him. He employed architect Charles Mewès to reconceive the building into a grand hotel that had the "atmosphere of a gentlemen's townhouse". To that end, the Ritz really had no lobby (thereby avoiding any undesirable loitering); so, from the entrance one quickly moved into a room where Persian carpets covered the floors and tapestries hung on the walls, and a grand white marble staircase stood to the right near a discretely-placed elevator. The restaurant was ahead, with the garden to the left.

Upstairs, in the suites and guest rooms, Ritz introduced his signature touches. Every room had its own bathroom; every room had a telephone. The ceilings were high, carpets were fitted wall-to-wall, each room had a small Swiss clock, and the light-fittings were gold-plated. Wherever possible he had built-in cupboards and wardrobes. Cleanliness and good hygiene were important to César Ritz; since plush fabrics like velvet and brocades were difficult to keep clean, Ritz eschewed them, substituting light fabrics such as muslin and silks, and he painted the walls in flat pastels and white. The restaurant, which could be opened to the garden, was grand and ornate; it had indirect lighting and apricot pink lanterns which Ritz believed enhanced and flattered a lady's complexion. The internal walls had latticed mirrors, reaching to the ceilings, which created the impression of being large windows. The garden abutted adjacent buildings, so it had trellises of greenery set among the architraves along the walls; wicker furniture was placed among planter boxes, and there was a small fountain, together with classic urns and statuary.

In 1912, the hotel was greatly expanded when the buildings at 17 place Vendôme were leased; there were two new buildings, with the block running from place Vendôme back to the rue Cambon. An ingenious solution was found to link all three buildings – the now famous Ritz corridor. Running from the back entrance at rue Cambon, where a small reception area was created, a corridor was built to run nearly 80 metres towards the place Vendôme, where it jinked into the original hotel; the genius was to build a row of glass vitrines on both sides of the narrow corridor, mirror everything around them (thereby creating a greater sense of space), and induce the local jewellers and boutiques to display their wares in the glass cases – and pay for the privilege. Grand hotels have copied the concept ever since.

César Ritz was the greatest hotelier of his day. He was forty-eight when the Ritz was opened, and at the height of his powers. Dynamic and industrious, he was a detail man. Ritz never said "the customer is always right". No, he told staff *le client n'a jamais tort* ("the customer is never wrong"); it is a subtle difference. Ritz remembered names and faces. He worked the room, looked after his people and made sure they were impeccably trained. He insisted upon everything being done correctly, something he passed on to his staff. This is just as well because, in 1902, César Ritz had a breakdown from which he never recovered.

Henry Ellès, who had been with Ritz since his Savoy days and had been managing the restaurant, became the General Manager. He would serve in that capacity, with insight and courtesy, until 1925. Of Swiss and English parentage, Ellès emulated César Ritz. He dressed like him – that is, like an English gentleman – he acted like him and adopted and inherited all Ritz's good traits and qualities. Olivier Dabescat replaced

Ellès as the *maître d'hôtel* of the restaurant. He would hold that position for nearly forty years, during which time he would become the face of the Ritz. But Henry Ellès really ran the show, albeit largely behind the scenes. He was located behind the discreet "Private" sign at the reception desk, up to the right after you came through the Vendôme main entrance. That's where everyone had to comply with the French law that all overnight guests must present full identity papers; even at the Ritz. And at the Ritz, if the papers did not confirm that a couple was married to each other they would be required to take separate rooms.

Marie-Louise Ritz joined the board when her husband fell ill. Madame Ritz came from a family of hoteliers; she was but thirty-four and still had charge of two young boys. The family lived together in a set of rooms on the top floor under the mansard overlooking the garden. (Today's Appartement Ritz has the same space.) Ritz rallied from time to time but then he would revert to melancholy and lassitude. He was hospitalised in Switzerland in 1913, and died a few weeks before the 1918 armistice. Madame Ritz lived on in the hotel for the rest of her life. Early in her husband's illness she had assumed responsibilities for decoration and housekeeping; chic and small, she soon patrolled the hotel's corridors largely unrecognised by the clientele and newly-respected by the staff.

The life of the show, however, was Olivier Dabescat. A Basque by background, he had worked in hotels since the age of twelve. Elegant with an aquiline nose, César Ritz had spotted the twenty-something Dabescat at the restaurant Paillard and he came to work at the Ritz soon after its opening. Utterly professional and unobtrusive, Dabescat moved around a room with grace and a "quick, cat-like tread".[138] By 1924 he was fifty-five. He was a model of courtesy, tact and etiquette; an intimate of the high and mighty, he spoke fluent English as a result of an early stint in London. Olivier Dabescat was a snob yet he knew his place, "blending with a masterly precision the servile and the protective, the deferential and condescending."[139]

He was "Monsieur Olivier" to most guests, although stablished patrons felt free to call him "Olivier" if they were in good standing with the undoubted master of ceremonies. Dabescat had a particularly close relationship with Marcel Proust. Proust would repay his social debts with dinner parties at the Ritz and, as his health declined, he would dine very late in the restaurant or in a first floor private room overlooking the garden – and Dabescat would always be in attendance. (That private room is now the Salon Proust.) Over the years the two talked for hours, and there is no doubt that Dabescat was the source of much of the material about high society that Proust used in his opus. Proust hoovered up everything he heard. Yet Dabescat was discreet; society ladies shared their confidences with him, and he quietly introduced Proust to young waiters that had taken the author's eye. Ladies regaled each other with their latest Olivier anecdote. Exchanging gossip without losing the sources of your material requires a special talent, and Olivier Dabescat obviously had that.

He was a master maître d'hôtel. When US officers were expected to stay teetotal during the Great War, Dabescat would serve them alcohol in teapots. When a famous client came for a late dinner and Olivier had remembered that the gentleman liked an omelette but could not recall whether he liked it with kidneys or without, he prepared both. In his final years, Proust would request special orders from the Ritz, which Dabescat would arrange to have delivered to the author's apartment. Indeed, he organised an iced beer for Proust on the very morning in 1922 that he died.

A Ritz advertisement circa 1900
Olivier Dabescat, 1934

The Ritz was always as much a place to eat and be seen as it was an hotel providing accommodation. *Le five o'clock* tea, the fashion at the time, could be taken in the passage beyond the lobby or, in fine weather, out in the garden. Sunday night gala dinners were spectacular. The garden might be tented for special events, and the restaurant was always the centre of genteel attention. Music could be played until midnight but never beyond. Indeed, that is why the Proust/Joyce dinner in 1922 was held at the Majestic; the hosts' first choice had been the Ritz. By the mid-20s, Madame Ritz was given to making an entrance at dinner:

"She came into the dining-room hatted, gloved and parasoled, although she was in her own home. Every male form rose from its chair a little as she passed. The gentlemen bowed; Madame bowed. The more important waiters pushed minor waiters behind them... She acknowledged the bows regally, yet one knew her eye was taking in everything everywhere."[140]

Of course everything was not always sweetness and light. The chef de cuisine was Georges Gimon; he famously once averred that English dishes could be quite good – if cooked by Frenchman. A disciple of Escoffier, by 1924 Gimon had run the Ritz restaurant for more than twenty years; he always thought himself to be in charge, superior to the maître d'hôtel (as chefs do). Henry Ellès and Madame Ritz would settle things down, and no client would be any the wiser. And Olivier Dabescat would continue to be a celebrity among the celebrities.

Much is made these days of the Hemingway Bar at the Ritz Hotel. There was never such a bar in the 1920s, of course. Originally, the Ritz had no bar at all. Its first bar was created on the Cambon side in 1921, as "Le Café Parisien". To the left, as you came in that back lobby, behind a screen, a men-only redoubt had been created. A massive mahogany bar in the "English style" was at one end, with foot railings and spittoons. It was a place for serious drinking and the occasional snack. The spittoons quickly disappeared – Ritz patrons were not spitters – but the bar was not reconfigured until 1936, when women were first admitted. On the other side of the lobby was a small writing room, available to ladies. In 1926, the newly-married Mrs Charles Ritz improperly entered the men's bar and it caused an uproar. As a result, the writing room was converted into a space explicitly available to ladies. This was known as Le Petit Bar; gentlemen could join their wives there, but they could not go in alone. This is the site of today's Hemingway Bar.

Back across the lobby, Le Café Parisien quickly came to be known as the Ritz Bar. It was the domain of the incomparable Frank Meier. Designated simply as "head bartender", Austrian-born Meier had learnt his trade in New York, the home of the cocktail. A somewhat austere looking man, with dark black hair parted exactly in the middle, his looks belied a gentle manner. (In later years, his presentation softened with age, as he grew a moustache and took to wearing distinctive pince-nez spectacles.) He ran the Ritz Bar from its inception in 1921 until a year or so before his death in 1947.

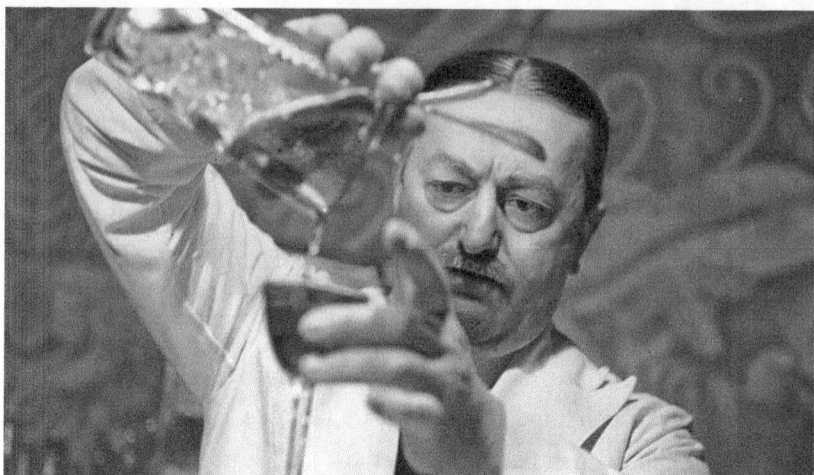

Frank Meier, 1938

Meier became the master of the barman *as host*: moving around the tables and at the bar, he listened and advised; he was witty and wise. As he circulated, he was happy to pick up a glass, clear an ashtray, or take drink orders. Once the Great War was over and America and things American became fashionable, cocktails were the go. Meier knew his martinis and Manhattans better than anyone, and he created an extraordinary array of exotic cocktail recipes over the years, more often than not in honour of a celebrity client. These are documented in his 1934 opus, *The Artistry of Mixing Drinks*. Favourites included:

- the *Bees Knees* (the juice of one-quarter of a lemon, a teaspoon of honey, one ounce of gin; shake well; it's the honey that makes the difference);
- *Frank's Special* (peach brandy, sweet vermouth and gin);
- the astringent *Seapea Fizz* ("CP", as in Cole Porter: sugar, lemon and absinthe); and
- his original pick-me-up – orange juice, Cointreau, brandy and champagne.

Hemingway once wrote to a friend: "When I dream of an afterlife in heaven, the action always takes place in the Paris Ritz."[141] He is said to have taken over Le Petit Bar on Saturdays and Sundays in the '20s during the racing season; the story goes that he would put a couple of tables together and spread the form guide out, before setting off to Auteuil for the afternoon, where he would place bets from Frank Meier and the other bartenders. That narrative may suit promotors of the new small bar, but it doesn't ring true. Hemingway could only have gone into that space to join a wife, and neither of them had been a Ritz person. Nor does the chronology hold up: he and his second wife left Paris for Key West in early 1928; with Le Petit Bar created in 1926, that leaves just one racing season before the writer left Paris permanently.

Any such routine would surely have taken place before this, in the clubby and masculine – and larger – Ritz Bar, somewhere among the immaculately-cleaned ashtrays and the backgammon sets. And the Ritz Bar is the one Hemingway and David Bruce liberated on 25 August 1944. Frank Meier would not have had it any other way.

QUO VADIS?

Whither goest thou? Coco Chanel knew exactly where she was going.

She had spent much of the year in England and Scotland with her new lover, Bendor, the Duke of Westminster. They came to Paris a few times in 1924, notably when they were spotted at *Le Train Bleu*'s rehearsals. It was during this time that she had struck a deal with the Wertheimer brothers to market the perfume line she had created in 1921. The first advertisement for Parfums Chanel appeared in the *New York Times* of 16 December 1924, a very discreet announcement for Bonwit Teller. The perfumes, now properly packaged and promoted, were an enormous success, in particular the light and clean Chanel No. 5. Chanel soon came to believe she was short-changed, and spent the next twenty years trying to better or unwind the Wertheimer deal.

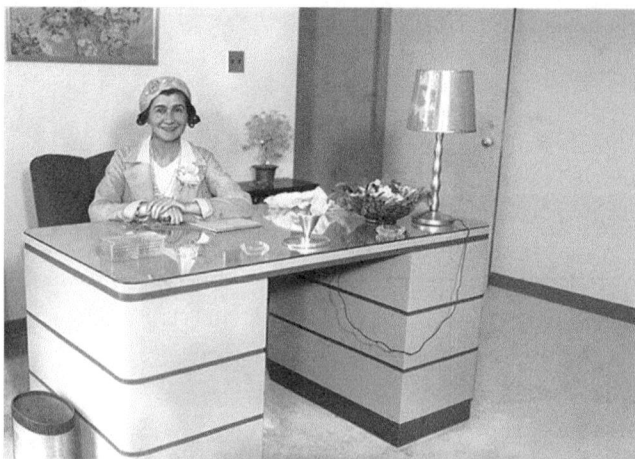

Coco in Los Angeles, 1931

THE MOST TREASURED NAME IN PERFUME

CHANEL

Chanel's business – her boutiques and perfumes– made her rich. She set herself up in a grand townhouse at 29 rue du Faubourg Saint-Honoré, in the same precinct as the British Embassy and the Cercle Interalliée. Her rivalry with Jean Patou intensified, not least when Suzanne Lenglen hired Patou to design her tennis outfits. Chanel's interest in the arts, in particular the Ballets Russes, was genuine. Brilliant and driven, she loved her business and backed her taste, and she loved rich aristocratic men. Bendor bought her a townhouse in London, showered her with jewellery and, in 1929, gave her the five acres at Roquebrune-Cap-Martin where she built her classic "La Pausa" estate. By the mid-'30s, she was competing with Schiaparelli and her romance with Westminster had faded.

Come the Second World War, she took up with a German military intelligence officer, Baron Hans Günther von Dincklage. They lived at the Ritz which the Germans had taken over. Her collaboration was not simply horizontal, however, and only the intervention of powerful friends saved her from post-war retribution. Chanel had closed her fashion house at the start of the war and in 1946, after an interrogation, she fled to Switzerland. By 1954, however, she was back. The Wertheimers, with whom she'd settled her perfume dispute in 1947, bought all the rights to the Chanel name and Gabrielle "Coco" Chanel started the fashion house anew. Dior, Balenciaga and Balmain were on notice. And soon the House of Chanel was once again a leader in women's fashion, while Parfums Chanel made the Wertheimers a further fortune and Coco one too.

Coco Chanel died in 1971 at the age of eighty-nine. She had transformed the sartorial tastes of women, led an active love life and died very rich. Her wartime collaboration prevented the grand public funeral she might have expected. She had kept a room at the Ritz for a number of years after the Great War and, once she moved out of the rue du Faubourg Saint-Honoré in about 1931, she went back. During the Second World War she was probably von Dincklage's guest; then, when she restarted her fashion house, it opened at the old address in rue Cambon, opposite the back entrance of the Ritz. From then on the Ritz was her home.

A grand hotel is a living organism. It needs to maintain its distinctive features yet change with fashion. One year a restaurant or bar or garden might be popular and the next year not so. The Ritz is no exception.

One of the ways to success is to have long-serving staff. In that respect, the Ritz has been exceptional. There have been just six chief executives: when Henry Ellès died in 1925, he was succeeded as General Manager by Victor Rey; Claude Auzello succeeded him in 1937; next came Janus Zembruski and Bernard Penché. Frank Klein has been President since 1979. In effect, each has been a "lifer". This has been true of the other senior personnel too: each of Olivier Dabescat as maître d'hôtel, Georges Gimon as head chef, and head bartender Frank Meier, held those roles throughout the '20s and '30s.

When Paris fell, "Mme Ritz gave stability to the whole establishment. There were many people who did not believe in her existence – that there could be a Madame Ritz – or they thought that if there had been she must be dead."[142] She quietly went about her business, a chic little woman checking out the rooms with her two small dogs at her feet, giving support to the staff, and ignoring the occupants as best she could. The Occupation was difficult for everyone working at the Ritz, not least because the German officers who took up residence there varied from courtly to decidedly uncivil (as did their colleagues from Italy, Japan and ostensibly neutral Spain).

Madame Ritz died in 1961; she had lived at the Ritz through two world wars. Although she became very much the grande dame, it had not been an easy life. Her husband, the vigorous and driven genius, the hotelier's hotelier, had become a basket case whom she had protected for more than fifteen years before he died. She had kept his dream alive and balanced that with working out a relationship with his successor managers. Her second son, perhaps her favourite, had died of spinal meningitis in 1918 a few months before César. Her elder son, Charles, took some time to settle down. After Swiss military service and some work at the Ritz under Ellès, he emigrated to the United States in 1916. He was twenty-six. By 1918, he was serving in the US Army in France. As a veteran, he was entitled to US citizenship. This he took up, thereby becoming a dual

Swiss and American. The next few years were spent in the US working in the entertainment industry and exploring his passion for fly-fishing. By 1928, his mother had prevailed upon him to return to the Ritz. Charles Ritz never served there in any executive capacity, although he ultimately became chairman of the board from 1953 until 1976.

Things have been spruced up and changed over the years. Whenever a renovation or refurbishment was contemplated, great care seems to have been taken to maintain the essence of the original hotel's style and comfort. Some changes have been substantial: in 1960, to great controversy, at the initiative of Charles Ritz, the very comfortable grill room on the Cambon side was transformed into a fish restaurant, L'Espadon ("swordfish"). It proved to be a masterstroke, ultimately winning two Michelin stars. Soon after, in order to provide a bar for the main restaurant, a very correct "cocktail lounge" or "garden bar" was created to the left of the entrance on the Vendôme side at the end of the garden. It had a faded gentility to it, being decorated with chintz, light tan leather chairs (but no antimacassars, that would not have worked in Paris), aspidistras and the like. The Ritz Bar, having first been reworked in 1936 when women were admitted to it, was redone again in 1962. Then, when the hotel was acquired by Mohamed Al-Fayed in 1979, it underwent an eight-year renovation; it never closed, not even while a substantial swimming pool and spa were created in the basement.

In 1997, the Ritz made the headlines on two occasions. In February, the US Ambassador to France, Pamela Harriman (aka "La Grande Horizontale"), suffered a cerebral haemorrhage while taking her daily swim in the pool, and died soon after. Proust had observed that, at the Ritz, "nobody jostles you", yet in August this sadly proved not to be the case. Princess Diana, together with her companion Dodi Al-Fayed, the proprietor's son, were being hounded by photographers gathered outside the Vendôme main entrance and abandoned their plan to dine at the restaurant Benoît; they elected to try an escape via rue Cambon, where those last photographs of them were snapped in the chaos that erupted around that small egress. (Their driver had been drinking in the Vendôme bar.)

The Ritz's most recent renovation cost hundreds of millions of dollars, and closed the hotel for five years until 2016. The old restaurant has been transformed into Les Jardins de L'Espadon, and the L'Espadon site is now a private dining room. The cocktail lounge on the Vendôme side is now the very chic Vendôme Bar; it opens out onto a completely revamped garden capable of being protected from the elements with the switch of a button. The Ritz Bar is still the best in town. Inevitably, something is made of famous patrons, so there are now suites named after Maria Callas, Hemingway, Scott Fitzgerald, Charlie Chaplin, the Windsors and Proust.

The Ritz today

The Ritz is more expensive than ever. Royals are few, and nobility is a concept that has seen its day. But the Ritz has moved with the times. The latest renovation proves that the French do luxury better than anyone. The Ritz is once again the grandest hotel in Paris, and César Ritz would almost certainly be happy with it.

Johnny Weissmuller returned to Chicago a hero. In 1925, one poll ranked him second among the world's best ever athletes. (Jack Dempsey was rated the greatest, with nine of the top positions being filled by Americans; Paavo Nurmi was ranked sixth.) He continued to swim and break records, and won two more gold medals in the 1928 Amsterdam Olympics. Weissmuller retired in 1929 – still only twenty-five. There is no record of his ever losing a race, over any distance, from 1921 until his retirement.

Weissmuller had a quirky and unpredictable charm, as evidenced by his comedy diving act in 1924. He was also physically beautiful. Underwear manufacturer BVD hired him to promote their new swimwear, and in 1929 he returned to Paris for the summer to open and serve as a life-guard at the new Piscine Molitor. He made a cameo movie appearance as "Adonis" before he was signed as Tarzan by MGM. Between 1932 and 1948 he made twelve Tarzan movies, usually with Maureen O'Sullivan as "Jane"; O'Sullivan as the innocent ingenue and Weissmuller's heroic physicality resonated with a wide audience. His most famous line was "Me Tarzan. You Jane." Then, for six years, Johnny switched to the role of Jungle Jim in another thirteen movies. With the advent of television, he made two Jungle Jim series between 1956 and 1958.

Weissmuller married five times, the most notable and tempestuous marriage being that with the "Mexican Spitfire", Lupe Velez (1933-1939). The callow youth of 1924 turned into something of a pants man, albeit that he was given to whipping his own off without invitation. Esther Williams, herself a champion swimmer and only nineteen, starred with Johnny in Billy Rose's 1940 *Aquacade*:

> *"He thought he was God's gift to women...He had remarkable genitalia that he loved to exhibit and he was constantly stripping his clothes to his swimsuit and beyond so that everyone could appreciate his extraordinary male attributes."*[143]

Johnny Weissmuller was the greatest swimmer of his era. One of his world records stood for no less than seventeen years and, in 1965, he was installed as the inaugural chairman of the International Swimming Hall of Fame. He died in 1984.

Paavo Nurmi made an exhausting tour of the USA in 1925, competing in fifty-five events. He lost only once. In 1928, at the Amsterdam Olympics, he won the 10,000 metres title that he had been denied defending in Paris. Indeed, over a fifteen year career he was never defeated over that distance. After Amsterdam, he turned to longer distances including the one hour race and the marathon.

For years Nurmi was plagued with accusations of professionalism. There is little doubt that he did take appearance money – although some of the accusations, like his having claimed the same travel expense twenty four times, were surely believed by no-one. It was said that Nurmi had "the lowest heart beat and the highest price of any athlete in the world" and, following his 1925 and 1929 tours of the USA, "[he] found America like a cash register and broke records and banks with equal ease."[144]

The president of the International Amateur Athletic Federation (IAAF) was Sigfrid Edström. A prominent and flamboyant Swedish industrialist, he had been president of the IAAF since its establishment in 1912. Sweden has always thought of itself as the senior Nordic country; too often it has patronised the smaller Finland, which has about half the population of the bigger country. Envy and nationalism came into play between Nurmi and Edström. It's fair to say that a Flying Finn who flew in the face of amateurism did not gain Edström's favour. Edström ran a campaign against Nurmi for years. And so, in 1932, just days before the LA Games opening ceremony, with the connivance of Avery Brundage of the American Athletic Union and Ritter von Holt, a German athletic official (and Nazi), Edstrom struck: the IAAF suspended Nurmi from international competition, and thereby banned him from the Games.

He could neither defend his 10,000 title nor compete in the marathon, as planned. Nurmi continued to compete as a "national amateur" for another two years, and retired in 1934. Naturally enough, the "Nurmi Affair" poisoned relations between Sweden and Finland; athletic competitions between the two countries were suspended, and the companies of which Edström was chairman, such as the huge ASEA, were widely boycotted.

But Nurmi was not the retiring type. He had been studying business administration and commerce. He established a clothing store which soon became a tourist attraction. Next he started building apartments, ultimately becoming one of Finland's most successful property developers and financiers, and he became a very rich man.

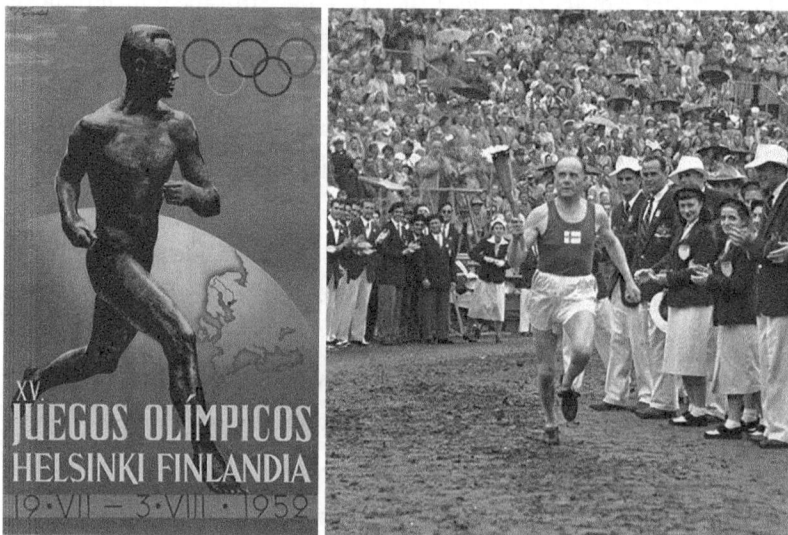

1952: Paavo Nurmi carries the Olympic torch into the
Helsinki Olympic Stadium

Paavo Nurmi married and had a son. The marriage did not last. He became an inspiring coach, including as a coach for his talented son, and was a noted advocate of clean living and exercise. Sigfrid Edström became president of the IOC in 1946. And, after twenty years, Nurmi got his revenge: at the Helsinki Games of 1952, he carried the Olympic torch into the stadium at the opening ceremony – to a standing ovation.

It was a provocative and deliberate slap in the face for the eighty-two year old Swede. He retired from the IOC after the Olympics in favour of his fanatical ally Avery Brundage.

When Nurmi died in 1973, he was given a state funeral. The President of Finland was Urho Kekkonen, who had represented Finland in the high jump at the 1924 Paris Olympics. His valedictory was undoubtedly heartfelt:

> *"People explore horizons for a successor. But none comes, and none will, for his class is extinguished with him."*[145]

Leaving aside the visitors for the Olympics and some expatriates, the protagonists in this story all stayed on in Paris after 1924. Hemingway left in March 1928 to settle in Key West and then Cuba. By this time he had moved on from Hadley to his next wife, Pauline Pfeiffer. Late in life he wrote the popular memoir *A Moveable Feast* (Scribner's, 1964) which chronicled his stay in Paris through the 1920s, sometimes unreliably.

Cocteau became even more central to French cultural developments in the decades after 1924. André Breton continued to hate Cocteau, and continued to disturb for the sake of disturbing. Misia lost her man, although she briefly established a threesome with her successor. Chanel stood by her best friend through thick and thin, as they continued to share their common addiction to morphine; Misia died in 1950, probably aged seventy-eight. Etienne de Beaumont tried to stay relevant. He, together with Chanel and Cocteau (and a number of other cultural leaders) sadly compromised themselves under Vichy.

Picasso went from strength to strength, becoming more famous with the years and richer too. His marriage to Olga lasted *de facto* until about 1928; he had many affairs, and she eventually filed for divorce in 1935.

In early 1937 he moved from the rue La Boétie back to the Left Bank, and it was in his new attic studio at 7 rue des Grands-Augustins that he soon created his masterpiece *Guernica*. Picasso was a Leftist but he was also a Spaniard, and as such he lived and worked in his studio relatively undisturbed throughout the Second World War. When he was evicted from the premises in 1955, Picasso moved permanently to the French Riviera together with Jacqueline Roque, his second wife and final muse. The master died in Mougins aged ninety-one, in 1973.

Josephine Baker and Sidney Bechet would not arrive in Paris until 1925, but the city had already found jazz and black artists. The year 1924 had established the platform for Les Années Folles, those five crazy years in Paris before the Wall Street Crash, and there was soon an intriguing contemporaneous overlap between Les Années Folles in Paris and the brief explosion of black artistic and intellectual life in New York (and elsewhere) known as the Harlem Renaissance.

Langston Hughes spent just four months in Paris in 1924. He was back in the USA by late November that year. Soon, with "the negro vogue of the 1920s"[146], Hughes became a leading light of the Harlem Renaissance. By 1930, however, it was all over: "We were no longer in vogue…we Negroes", wrote Hughes. "Sophisticated New Yorkers turned to Noel Coward."[147] Langston Hughes made only one more substantive trip to Paris, in 1937, when he was promoting the Spanish Republican cause. For rest of his life, however, he was the poet of his generation – a philosopher, civil rights advocate and urban lyricist. He died in 1967.

By 1924, France had found an accommodation with Germany, and the spirit of Locarno beckoned. The Olympics had come of age. Paris was at peace with itself. It was fun and vital. Paris was enjoying its role as the centre of European culture and Western civilisation. Ideas and creativity flourished. The city was tolerant and inclusive. This extended beyond tolerance of lifestyle and race, to religion. (The wonderful Grande Mosquée de Paris was built between 1922 and 1926 as a celebration and expression of national gratitude for the Muslim soldiers who had served in the Great War.) There were still elements of the Proustian life about, of course, after all Proust had died at fifty-one and his contemporaries lived on; but the world around them had moved on.

Christmas Day 1924 had perfect mild weather, and Christmas Eve was the "gayest the French capital has seen since the World War."[148] The bourgeoisie typically had dinner at home, went to the theatre until perhaps 11:30, then attended midnight mass, and finished the evening with a celebratory supper at a smart restaurant; such restaurants took advantage of their clientele, charging as much as the market could bear. Workers in the outer suburbs took to the bistros and bal musettes too, albeit where proprietors were more sensitive to their proletarian budgets. President Doumergue gave a Christmas party for children at the Elysées Palace, and the annual swimming race across the Seine took place in a water temperature of just 2°. Seventeen foolhardy contestants swam the diagonal course near the Pont Alexandre III, the winner taking a little under three minutes.

Finally, Rolf de Maré decided to organise a gala to end the year. On New Year's Eve he staged a spectacular show at the Théâtre des Champs-Elysées. Picabia was charged with putting together *Cinésketch*, a theatrical farce starring Jean Börlin and the entire Ballets Suédois team. Erik Satie and René Clair were co-copted to assist. All de Maré's friends were invited – Cocteau, Léger, Milhaud, Paul Guillaume – and acquaintances too. No-one could really follow the narrative, except that it seemed to involve a love affair and a police chase. The New Georgians, a great new jazz band from New York, who were white not black, put on a set.

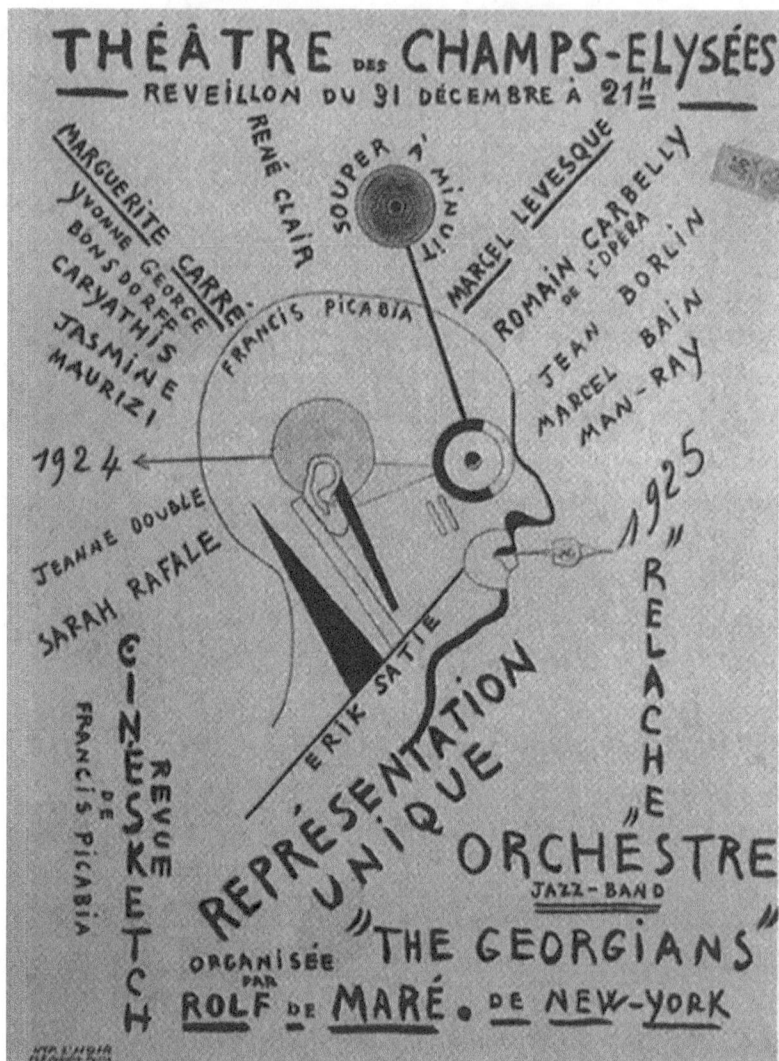

Marcel Duchamp and Bronia Perlmutter, Radiguet's last love and the future Mme René Clair, appeared naked in a *tableau vivant*. (Man Ray's photo confirms the story that Duchamp wore a fig leaf and that Ms Perlmutter did not.) And to finish, as was appropriate to see out this eventful year, the Ballets Suédois put on a final performance of the bizarre *Relâche*.

Then everyone went off to a party at Le Boeuf sur le Toit, where they heralded in the New Year.

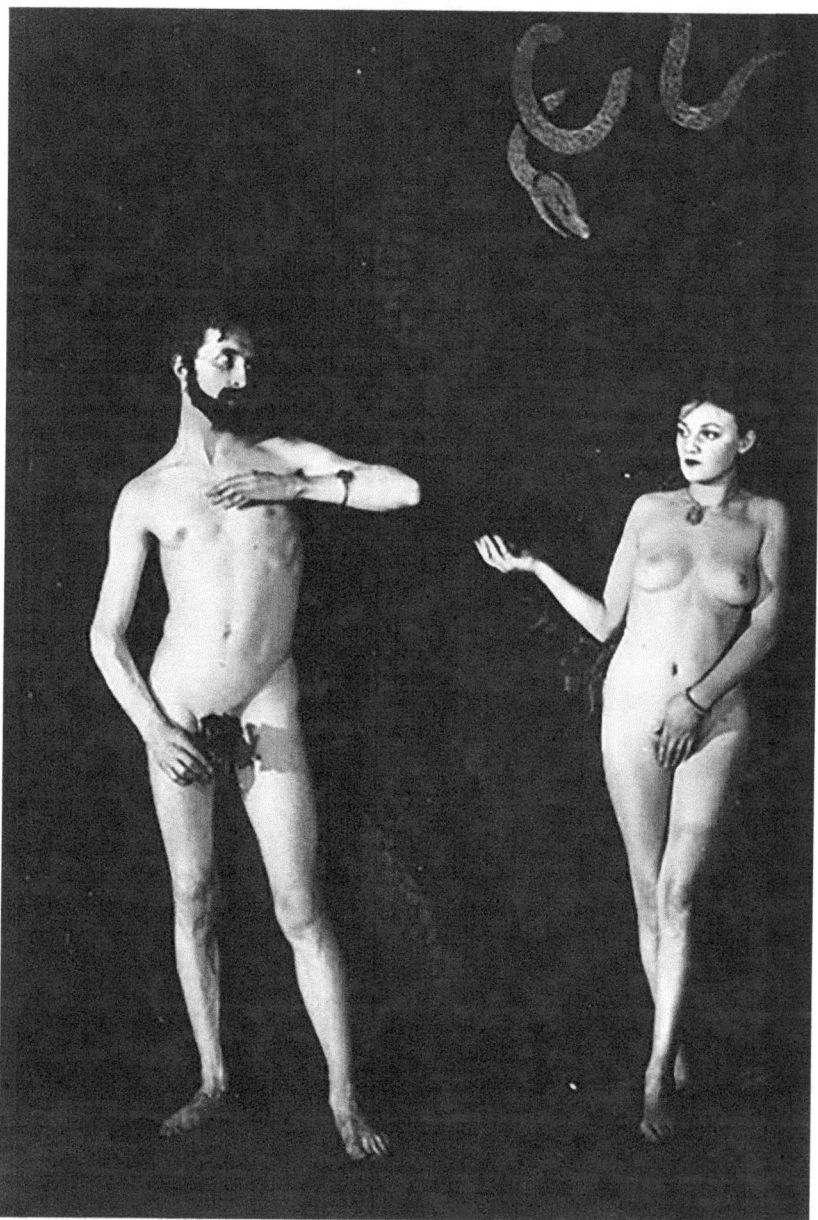

Adam and Eve by Man Ray, 1924 (Marcel Duchamp and Bronia
Perlmutter) in Francis Picabia's *Cinésketch*

KEY TO SOURCES

AATOG Harry Gordon, *Australia at the Olympic Games*
(University of Queensland Press, 1994)

ADF Philip Greene, *A Drinkable Feast; A Cocktail Companion to
1920s Paris* (TarcherPerigee Books, 2018)

ALOP John Richardson, *A Life of Picasso; Volume III, The
Triumphant Years 1917-1932* (Jonathan Cape, 2007)

AMF Ernest Hemingway, *A Moveable Feast*
(Charles Scribner's Sons, 1964)

ANATM Richard Davenport-Hines, *A Night At The Majestic*
(Faber and Faber, 2006)

CT *The Chicago Tribune*, Paris Edition

D Sjeng Scheijen, *Diaghilev, A Life* (Profile Books, 2010)

EBB Lesley MM Blume, *Everybody Behaves Badly*
(First Mariner Books, 2017)

EP Arlen J Hansen, *Expatriate Paris, A Cultural and Literary
Guide to Paris of the 1920s* (Arcade Publishing, 2012)

EWSY Amanda Vaill, *Everybody Was So Young*
(Broadway Books, 1999)

HTPY Michael Reynolds, *Hemingway: The Paris Years*
(WW Norton & Company, 1999)

JC Claude Arnaud, *Jean Cocteau, A Life* (Yale University Press,
2016); translated by Lauren Elkin and Charlotte Mandell

LWITBR Calvin Tomkins, *Living Well Is The Best Revenge*
(The Museum of Modern Art, New York, 2018)

M Arthur Gold and Robert Fizdale, *Misia* (Macmillan, 1980)

NYT *The New York Times*

PBOAC Colin Jones, *Paris: Biography of a* City (Penguin, 2006)

TBS   Langston Hughes, *The Big Sea* (Hill & Wang, 1993)
TCP   Marie-José Gransard, *Twentieth Century Paris* (Tauris Parke, 2020)
TGGTE Lieut.-Col. Newnham Davis, *The Gourmet's Guide to Europe* (Brentano's, 1908)
TMBTP Jimmie "The Barman" Charters, *This Must Be The Place* (Collier Books, 1989)
TPE   Waverley Root, *The Paris Edition* (North Point Press, 1989)
TR   Stephen Watts, *The Ritz* (The Bodley Head, 1963)
WPS   Mary McAuliffe, *When Paris Sizzled* (Rowan & Littlefield, 2016)

Endnotes

1   TBS 144
2   *Te Aroha News*, 19 February 1924
3   TBS 146
4   Martin du Gard, *Mémorables, I,* 265
5   Ford Madox Ford, ANATM, 315
6   Gerard Hopkins trans, *Letters of Marcel Proust to Antoine Bibesco* (1953), 16
7   Bill Bryson, *The Body* (Doubleday, 2019), 217
8   John Russell, *Paris* (Harry N Abrams, 1983), 37
9   5 Place du 18-Juin-1940, formerly place de Rennes.
10 Clive James, *Cultural Amnesia* (Picador, 2012), 171
11 Cyril Beaumont, *The Diaghilev Ballet in London* (1951), 231-2
12 D, 388
13 Francesco Rapazzini, *Un soir chez l'Amazone* (Fayard, 2004)
14 ALOP 297-299
15 Clive James, *Cultural Amnesia* (Picador 2012), 131
16 JC 1
17 JC 238
18 *Avec Stravinsky* (Monaco: Du Rocher, 1958), 46
19 CT, 8 January 1924
20 TPE, 105
21 It is also celebrated as the site of General von Choltitz's surrender to General Leclerc on 25 August 1944.
22 Market gardens populated the site when Citroën bought it and, in a delightful serendipity, the site has now been returned to open space as the Parc André Citroën.
23 WPS 178
24 *In Search of Lost Time; The Germantes Way*
25 CT, 19 May 1924, 3
26 CT, 19 May 1924, 1; NYT, 19 May 1924, 1
27 John E Finling and Kimberly D Pelle, eds, *Encyclopedia of the Modern Olympic Movement* (Greenwood, 2004), 84
28 Robert O Paxton, *Vichy France* (Columbia University Press, 2001), 39
29 Janet Flanner, *Paris Was Yesterday* (Angus and Robertson, 1973), 82
30 JC 289
31 William C Carter, *Marcel Proust* (Yale University Press, 2013), 785
32 JC 303
33 M 216
34 NYT, 15 July 1981
35 ALOP 299
36 TBS 145

37   EP 268

38   TBS 160

39   TBS 161

40   TBS 177-178

41   Robert McAlmon, *Being Geniuses Together* (Doubleday, 1968), 316-317

42   Sylvain Bonmariage, *Gagneuese!* (Clé d'Or, 1951)

43   Together with some soldiers and other young men and a number of fellow older gentlemen, Proust was arrested   at the Hotel Marigny on the evening of 11-12 January 1918.Proust was drinking champagne with Cuizat and two soldiers. Cuizat was sentenced to four months in prisonand fined 200 francs for inciting minors to debauchery and serving drinks after the statutory time. For "Proust Marcel, 46, annuitant, 102 Boulevard Haussmann" nothing came of it. [Laure Murat, *La revue littéraire*, 2e année, no.14, mai 2005, 82-92]

44   Lucy Hughes-Hallett, *The Pike* (Fourth Estate, 2013) 542

45   Dominique Kirchner Reill, *The Fiume Crisis* (Harvard University Press, 2020) 72

46   "Voilà un homme admirable, courageux, qui a toujours des couilles au cul. Dommage ce ne sont pas toujours les siennes."

47   Michael Goebel, *Anti-Imperial Metropolis* (Cambridge University Press, 2015) 25

48   Norman Lewis, *A Dragan Apparent* (Eland, 2003), 47

49   Robert Gerwarth, *November 1918: The German Revolution* (Oxford University Press, 2020), 221

50   Peter Ross Range, *1924: The Year That Made Hitler* (Little Brown, 2016) 2, 73, 247 There is dispute as to the number of brownshirts Hitler had supporting him; Hitler himself told the 3,000 terrified captives in the beer hall that the "building is surrounded by six hundred heavily armed men"; independent observers settle on about half that number.

51   Peter Ross Range, *1924: The Year That Made Hitler* (Little Brown, 2016) 101, 112, 185-187

52   www.balblomet.fr

53   HTPY 163, quoting the Paris *Herald Tribune*.

54   HTPY 24

55   Ernest Hemingway, *The Sun Also Rises* (Scribner, 1926), 49

56   TPE 182

57   Le Nègre de Toulouse was at 159 boulevard du Montparnasse.

58   Sue Roe, *Inside Montparnasse* (Penguin, 2018), 153

59   TCP 46

60   TMBTP 11. Much of this section is sourced from Charters' book.

61   TMBTP 202

62   TMBTP 27

63   EBB 275

64   EBB 86

65   Emily Barge in *London Review of Books*, 1 July 2021, 14

66   TMBTP 74

67   HTPY 228-9

68   TMBTP 51; ADF 126

69   ANATM 226

70   EWSY 96

71   AMF 17
72   AMF 16
73   AMF 20
74   WPS 134
75   Lynn Haney, *Naked at the Feast* (Robson Books, 1995), 44
76   LWITBR 35
77   EBB 80
78   EWSY 163
79   TPE 116
80   HTPY 191
81   TMBTP 29
82   ADF 253
83   PBOAC 462
84   Andre Antoine: "La leçon des Quat'z'Arts", *Le Journal*, 23 June 1923
85   TMBTP 109-110
86   TMBTP 112
87   Quoted from Crosby's diary in David Milner, *A Cultural History of the American Novel, 1890-1940* (Cambridge UP, 1966) 74
88   This story and the quotations come from the article "Les forçats ['forced labourers'] de la route" by Albert Londres in *Le Petit Parisien*, 27 June 1924
89   AMF 64-65
90   *The Observer*, 6 July 1924, 13; *The Brooklyn Daily Eagle*, 6 July 1924, 37
91   Ras is an Ethiopian noble title meaning Prince. Ras Tafari became Emperor Haile Selassie in 1930. The Emperor's pre-coronation name was appropriated by the Rastafarian cult in Jamaica in the 1930s.
92   AATOG 108
93   David Wallechinsky, *The Complete Book of the Olympics* (Hardie Grant Books, 2000), Track and Field, Men, 4-5
94   TCP 39
95   JC 366
96   HTPY 225, EBB 64-65
97   EP 273
98   CT, 19 May 1926
99   Nicholas Whitlam, *Four Weeks One Summer* (Australian Scholarly, 2017), 90
100 *Manchester Guardian*, 9 July 1924
101 *Manchester Guardian*, 7 May 1930
102 KP Silberg, *The Athletic Finns* (Suomi Publishing Co, 1927), 141-142
103 *Manchester Guardian*, 11 July 1924; David Wallechinsky, *The Complete Book of the Olympics* (Hardie Grant Books, 2000), Track and Field, Men, 42
104 Bud Greenspan, *100 Greatest Moments in Olympic History* (General Publishing Group, 1993), 63
105 *Press Association*, 12 July 1924
106 Quoted by Simon Burton in *The Guardian*, 4 January 2012
107 CT, 13 July 1924
108 *Manchester Guardian*, 13 July 1924
109 CT, 13 July 1924
110 AATOG 111

111   AATOG 111-112
112   David A Fury, *Johnny Weissmuller; Twice the Hero* (Artist's Press, 2000), 108
113   ALOP 265-273
114   Janet Flanner, *Paris Was Yesterday* (Angus and Robertson, 1973), xiii
115   WPS 181
116   WPS 165
117   ALOP 174
118   ANATM 241
119   Misia 239-241, ANATM 241
120   A rough translation of an interview with Pierre de Massot in *Paris Journal*, 30 May 1924.
121   ALOP 259
122   M 238
123   ALOP 260
124   Lydia Lopokova, Maynard Keynes' wife, as quoted in the *Journal of the Royal Musical Association*, 123 (1998); ALOP 260
125   *The Observer*, 23 November 1924
126   ALOP 275
127   Erik Näslund, *Rolf de Maré* (Dance Books, 2009), translated by Roger Tanner, 356-368
128   Quoted in Bruce Elder, *Dada, Surrealism, and the Cinematic Effect* (Wilfrid Lanier University Press, 2013) 191
129   TGGTE 9-11
130   TGGTE 16-17; NYT 5 July 1954
131   TGGTE 29
132   TGGTE 28
133   TGGTE 6
134   TPE 104
135   Emile Zola, *The Belly of Paris* translated by Mark Kurlansky (Modern Library, 2009)
136   TPE 104
137   TR 60
138   Pyra Wise in *Proustonomics.com*, "Olivier Dabescat: du Ritz à l'autre de côté de chez Swann", 17 April 2021
139   Harold Nicolson, *Some People* (Houghton Mifflin, 1927), 176
140   TR 87
141   Letter to EA Hotcher; Nancy W Sindelar, *Influencing Hemingway* (Rowman & Littlefield, 2014), 102
142   Louis Bromfield, *What Became of Anna Bolton* (Harper and Brothers, 1944)
143   Esther Williams and Digby Diel, *The Million Dollar Mermaid* (Simon & Schuster, 1999)
144   www.isoh.org
145   Bud Greenspan, *100 Greatest Moments in Olympic History* (General Publishing Group, 1993), 62
146   TBS 224
147   TBS 334
148   NYT, 26 December 1924

INDEX

ABOUT THE AUTHOR

A keen Francophile, Nicholas Whitlam is a company director and former banker. *Paris 1924* is his fourth book, his previous publications being *Nest of Traitors* (The Jacaranda Press, 1974 co-author John Stubbs), the memoir *Still Standing* (Lothian Books, 2004) and *Four Weeks One Summer* (Australian Scholarly, 2016). He lives in a coastal village south of Sydney with his wife of nearly fifty years, the redoubtable Sandra Judith Whitlam.